Performance Requirements and Investment Incentives Under International Economic Law

ELGAR INTERNATIONAL INVESTMENT LAW

Series Editors: Andrea K. Bjorklund, *University of California, Davis, USA* and August Reinisch, *University of Vienna, Austria*

This monograph series provides a point of convergence for authoritative, original works focused specifically on international investment law in all its forms. Works will be single or co-authored, theoretically rigorous and analytically precise, often considering the intersection of investment law with other fields of law such as trade, intellectual property, environment or public international law. The series will comprise works from established authors as well as from younger scholars whose work is genuinely innovative and challenging. Proposals are encouraged that primarily engage with new and previously under-developed themes in the field, draw on other disciplines in order to further thinking in the field, or alternatively attempt to offer a definitive statement on areas of uncertainty in the existing law.

The development of original thinking in international investment law and research of the highest quality is the main emphasis of the series. Both international and comparative in its approach, it aims to include some of the best theoretical and empirical work from both well-established researchers and the next generation of scholars.

Titles in this series include:

International Investment Law and the Environment
Saverio Di Benedetto

Intellectual Property Rights as Foreign Direct Investments
From Collision to Collaboration
Lukas Vanhonnaeker

Performance Requirements and Investment Incentives Under International Economic Law
David Collins

Performance Requirements and Investment Incentives Under International Economic Law

David Collins

The City Law School, City University London, UK

ELGAR INTERNATIONAL INVESTMENT LAW

Edward Elgar PUBLISHING

Cheltenham, UK • Northampton, MA, USA

Published by
Edward Elgar Publishing Limited
The Lypiatts
15 Lansdown Road
Cheltenham
Glos GL50 2JA
UK

Edward Elgar Publishing, Inc.
William Pratt House
9 Dewey Court
Northampton
Massachusetts 01060
USA

A catalogue record for this book
is available from the British Library

Library of Congress Control Number: 2015945470

This book is available electronically in the **Elgar**online
Law subject collection
DOI 10.4337/9781784712044

MIX
Paper from responsible sources
FSC® C013056

ISBN 978 1 78471 203 7 (cased)
ISBN 978 1 78471 204 4 (eBook)

Typeset by Columns Design XML Ltd, Reading
Printed and bound in Great Britain by TJ International Ltd, Padstow

Contents

Abbreviations

AOA	Agreement on Agriculture
AIT	Agreement on Internal Trade
ASEAN	Association of Southeast Asian Nations
BIT	bilateral investment treaty
CETA	Comprehensive Economic and Trade Agreement
CJEU	Court of Justice of the European Union
COMESA	Common Market for Eastern and Southern Africa
ECT	Energy Charter Treaty
FDI	foreign direct investment
FET	fair and equitable treatment
FTZ	free trade zone
FTA	free trade agreement
GATS	General Agreement on Trade in Services
GATT	General Agreement on Tariffs and Trade
GPA	Government Procurement Agreement
ICSID	International Centre for the Settlement of Investment Disputes
IFC	International Finance Corporation
IIA	international investment agreement
IICA	Interstate Investment Cooperation Agreement
IMF	International Monetary Fund
MIGA	Multilateral Investment Guarantee Agency
MNE	multinational enterprise
MAI	Multilateral Agreement on Investment
NAFTA	North American Free Trade Agreement
OECD	Organisation for Economic Co-operation and Development
OPIC	Overseas Private Investment Corporation
PSNR	permanent sovereignty over natural resources
RCT	randomized controlled trial
RTA	regional trade agreement
SCM	Agreement on Subsidies and Countervailing Measures
TBT	Technical Barriers to Trade Agreement
TFEU	Treaty on the Functioning of the European Union

TPP	Trans Pacific Partnership Agreement
TRIMs	Trade Related Investment Measures Agreement
TRIPs	Trade-Related Aspects of Intellectual Property Rights agreement
TTIP	Transatlantic Trade and Investment Partnership
UNCITRAL	United Nations Commission on International Trade Law
UNCTAD	United Nations Conference on Trade and Development
WTO	World Trade Organization

Table of cases

GATT/WTO

INVESTOR–STATE ARBITRATION

OTHER INTERNATIONAL

EUROPEAN UNION

UNITED STATES

Treaties and statutory instruments

WTO

BILATERAL INVESTMENT TREATIES

FREE TRADE AGREEMENTS AND REGIONAL ECONOMIC INTEGRATION AGREEMENTS

OTHER TREATIES

DOMESTIC LEGISLATION

Introduction

Foreign direct investment (FDI) is widely seen as a major contributor to the economic development and continued growth of numerous developed and developing states around the world. FDI can play a vital role in the development process of host- as well as home-states. In addition to providing capital inflows and tax revenue, FDI can be a vehicle for increasing employment and upgrading the skills of the local work force. It can contribute to the establishment and expansion of infrastructure and in some cases lead to advances in technology. However, neither inflows of FDI nor the benefits associated with them should be viewed as the automatic consequence of the activities of internationally mobile firms taking place in foreign countries. It is far from clear that the aggressive pursuit of international investment agreements or World Trade Organization (WTO) membership will lead to an increase in FDI that is beneficial to host states. This is precisely why there is increased awareness of the need for policies that can not only incentivize the acquisition of FDI, but that can augment the developmental benefits associated with it through the application of conditions crafted according to the requirements of the host state. Performance requirements dictating the nature and extent of inward FDI have the potential to operate as market distortions, causing firms to behave otherwise than how they would choose to behave of their own accord. Likewise, investment incentives aimed at encouraging the inward flow of FDI may create costs that are difficult for both host states and firms to predict and manage effectively. It can be problematic for governments issuing incentives to identify the precise conditions, (for example, type of incentive, industry, and duration) under which incentives will operate to fulfil their economic goals.

In many ways, the debate surrounding the use of tools such as performance requirements and investment incentives to manipulate FDI flows can be framed as an issue linked to the rise of emerging markets as key participants in economic globalization. As developing countries become industrialized, they increasingly rely on FDI as a source of growth; and in so doing they have begun to seek to implement some of the regulatory strategies that their developed country counterparts instigated in the twentieth century, even as these are in some cases contrary to economic liberalization. These strategies include not only membership in multilateral organizations like the WTO and the International Monetary Fund (IMF), nor simply the signage of international investment agreements, but also the inclusion of provisions restricting the powers of their trading and investing partners to interfere with FDI. During the so-called "second wave" of globalization, marked by the ascendency of the large emerging markets, the rise in prominence of services in the global economy may have rendered the use of traditional performance requirements, such as local content rules, largely self-evidently counterproductive. At the same time, however, the more recent period of globalization has shown a distinct increase in a broad array of governmental incentives instigated in order to increase the inward flow of FDI in what has become a competitive global marketplace for wealth-generating firms. As such, performance requirements increasingly appear to take the form of conditions attached to incentives, rather than as simple limits on the extent of FDI.

Indeed, performance requirements can be accurately described as conditions imposed on foreign investors that they must achieve certain goals with respect to their commercial activities in host countries. This is why they are sometimes referred to as "conditional investment incentives". They are used along with other policy tools, such as traditional investment incentives, to attain certain economic development objectives. Investment incentives can be defined as any measurable advantages accorded to specific firms or categories of firm by a host government in order to encourage them to engage in operations of a certain variety; typically, this means FDI of a certain quantity or in a certain sector. This book will adopt a consciously broad definition for both performance requirements and investment incentives in order to provoke a critical assessment of the existing treatment of these instruments under international economic law. The understanding of these concepts, rooted in the notion of discrimination based on national origin, will embrace a wide range of measures and accordingly engage many disciplines.

Performance requirements and investment incentives are among a wide range of policy tools that may address some of the concerns associated with unbridled FDI, including uncompetitive domestic markets and over-reliance on foreign capital, allowing them to optimize the positive impact of FDI. Yet despite their importance to the economies of host states, the use of investment incentives has attracted remarkably little attention by scholars (especially from a legal perspective), with performance requirements faring even worse, receiving virtually no attention whatsoever from the academic legal community. Moreover, although performance requirements and many incentives are employed by governments throughout the world, there remains profoundly limited information about their impacts as tools of economic as well as (often less-recognizably) social policy. Furthermore, since performance requirements are now regularly used in conjunction with investment incentives, it is misleading to consider investment incentives without also discussing performance requirements. The interrelated nature of performance requirements and investment incentives is captured by the fact that the former may be negotiated as a quid pro quo for the latter. Moreover, as incentives tend to be designed to compensate for certain disadvantages that have resulted from performance requirements, the prohibition of entrenched performance requirements might well reduce the need for incentives over the long term.

Some varieties of investment incentives, including most notably fiscal, have been criticized by international organizations as inefficient because they are too expensive relative to their benefits, especially when taking into account their long-term effects on the environment and other social issues. Some of the most advantageous forms of incentive, such as those tied to performance requirements like the provision of infrastructure or knowledge exchange, may not be used as widely as they should be. Investment incentives can be further problematic because, while they may help specific firms or under-performing industries, on a macroeconomic level they can distort markets and result in an efficient allocation of both public and private resources that would be more productively spent elsewhere. Over-use of fiscal incentives diminishes the public funds available to provide essential public goods and services. Likewise, firms receiving assistance may have otherwise directed their resources at more efficient production lines or more profitable markets overseas. On the other hand, incentives can be a vital method of achieving crucial economic goals such as addressing underserved markets. The need for incentives to attract FDI is grounded in the reality that market failures exist in which mutually beneficial investment activities are not fully appreciated by foreign investors. Such failures are tied to information asymmetry between firms and host states as well as externalities associated with foreign investment, including in some cases suppression of the development of an entrepreneurial class and the over-reliance on foreign capital. Incentives can foster positive outcomes that may not be possible through the normal operation of the market. It can stimulate the production of public goods, such as infrastructure, underemployment and research and development. Moreover, incentives, particularly when linked with performance requirements, can help mitigate negative externalities, such as environmental damage.

The capacity of host governments to enact policies to tailor the nature and extent of the FDI they receive is founded upon the principle that states are fundamentally entitled to assert sovereignty over their own economies even as they participate in economic globalization. The principal of permanent sovereignty over natural resources (PSNR) embodies the right of states and their peoples to dispose of their natural resources as they see fit. Since the state has the legitimate discretion to regulate in the public interest, this supreme right can potentially result in conflict with the rights of foreign investors under international investment law. Under public international law, the state should not relinquish its sovereignty for any reason. The General Assembly of the United Nations sought to establish a link between resource-sovereignty and development by elaborating on the foreign-investment-related provisions of PSNR. This was captured in the General Assembly's resolution on PSNR, Resolution 1803. This resolution states that nations must be able to exercise sovereignty over their natural resources in the interests of their national development and well-being, which overrides individual private interests, both domestic and foreign.[1] This principle is also reflected in Resolution 3281 of the Charter of Economic Rights and Duties of States, which confirms that every state shall freely exercise full permanent sovereignty including possession, use and disposal over all of its wealth, natural resources and economic activities, supplemented by the duty of states to compensate any private parties which suffer deprivation as a consequence. States may accept commitments not to exercise certain sovereign rights for a time in order to attract foreign investment, but this does not mean that the state is abandoning the doctrine of PSNR. In other words, the recognition of a state's right to offer investment incentives should not be seen as a derogation of a state's sovereignty because international law also recognizes a state's capacity to commit itself internationally, just as it empowers a state to control its natural resources.

The prohibition of performance requirements addresses trade in goods and services, and it does so at the point where the disciplines of trade in goods, trade in services, and investment intersect. The major regimes under international economic law which restrain state's sovereign capacity to use performance requirements and investment incentives are those of the WTO and the many thousands of international investment agreements (IIAs) which operate either bilateral or regionally. The WTO is a member-driven and rules-based international organization with a

1 UNGA Res. 1803 (XVII) (14 December 1962).

membership of 161 countries worldwide that promotes the free movement of goods and services across international borders through the elimination or reduction of regulatory protectionism instigated at the domestic level. Established in 1995 but effectively operating through the stand-alone General Agreement on Tariffs and Trade (GATT) since the 1940s, the WTO now has specific disciplines relating to non-tariff barriers to trade such as subsidization, anti-dumping, safeguards, as well as intellectual property and technical barriers to trade. It also maintains its own dispute-settlement mechanism, the WTO Dispute Settlement Understanding, which facilitates the resolution of disputes among its member states as to the interpretation and implementation of its covered agreements.

While the WTO has a mandate of liberalizing trade (in both goods and services) and not investment, laws that prevent unnecessary barriers to trade may also affect barriers that can be imposed on foreign investment. The primary regulatory sphere of the WTO in this regard is the Agreement on Trade Related Investment Measures (TRIMs). Similarly, the WTO's control of subsidies as an unfair distortion to global trade through the Agreement on Subsidies and Countervailing Measures (SCM) may have an impact upon the extent to which states can offer assistance to foreign firms in order to encourage FDI. For their part, the de-decentralized network of IIAs, most of which consist of highly standardized language, contain direct prohibitions on performance requirements but tend to say very little about investment incentives. Yet some of the protections found within these instruments could themselves be viewed as incentives, particularly where they ensure that continued advantageous treatment is forthcoming. In addition to the binding laws imposed on host countries by the WTO and IIAs, there are several soft-law instruments promulgated by international organizations such as the Organisation for Economic Co-operation and Development (OECD) and the World Bank that can influence if not the ability then at least the willingness of states to implement these policy tools to achieve economic developmental or social aims.

This book will demonstrate that international economic law has failed to regulate performance requirements and investment incentives effectively, often resulting in market distortions on both a national and global scale as well as lost opportunities for the stimulation of productive FDI in certain situations. It will do so by examining the approach taken to the control of these instruments by both trade-based regimes (the WTO and regional trade agreements) and investment-based regimes (IIAs). The division of the book into performance requirements and investment incentive is self-explanatory: it reflects the different objectives and regulatory approaches to two vastly different but related economic policy tools. The division between trade and investment, while somewhat artificial, is not meant to indicate a separation between two varieties of subsidy as much as it is to demark the two chief regulatory methods of regulating all types of performance requirement and incentive. Clearly some types of performance requirement and investment incentive will involve both trade and investment elements because investment and trade are often highly interrelated. As this book focuses on law rather than on finance or economics, the distinction that will be made here is therefore a legal one. There are trade laws (mainly promulgated by the WTO) and there are investment laws (mainly promulgated by IIAs). These are both used to varying degrees to address policy tools that in reality are cross-disciplinary.

The structure of this book is as follows. Chapter 1 will explore the phenomena of performance requirements and investment incentives in greater detail, outlining some of the policy justifications behind these tools and conveying the economic arguments for and against their implementation. Chapter 2 will focus on the theme of performance requirements and investment incentives as manifestations of discriminatory treatment based on nationality either against foreign firms in the case of performance requirements, or in favour of them in the case of investment incentives. In so doing this chapter will examine the national treatment requirement as it is captured in both trade and investment law. Chapters 3 and 4 will consider the trade-based controls of performance requirements and investment incentives respectively under international economic law. This will involve an analysis of WTO agreements such as the TRIMs and the General Agreement on Trade in Services (GATS) as well as provisions in IIAs such as the prohibition of performance requirements. Chapters 5 and 6 will examine how international economic law has limited the capacity of states to use investment incentives through a discussion of WTO disciplines on subsidies as well as various provisions of IIAs that could affect the use of incentives, including those which could be used to ground claims for the revocation of incentive packages by host states. Chapter 7 will conclude by offering recommendations for the improvement of the regimes that regulate performance requirements and investment incentives. In particular it will focus on the need to address imperfect information and information asymmetries, as well as the crucial importance of tying the regulation of these instruments in policies of non-discrimination. A unified regime governing both performance requirements and investment incentives will be contemplated, allowing for the evaluation of these policy tools in more comprehensive and systematic way. It will draw on reflexive governance theory to suggest that access to ever greater quantities of information through the global digital commons can help facilitate mass collaboration between investment-promotion agencies and multinational enterprises (MNEs) to arrive at efficient decisions regarding the structure of FDI.

1. Performance requirements and investment incentives: an overview

The purpose of this introductory chapter is to offer a broad picture of the types of performance requirements and investment incentives that are typically used by host states and in so doing also provide a deeper understanding of many of the economic concerns that are raised in conjunction with these instruments. This chapter is divided into two parts, following the structure of the book: the first covers performance requirements, and the second deals with investment incentives. Again, this should not be taken to convey that these two varieties of policy tools necessarily operate in isolation: they are often employed by host states in tandem. Nor does this separation imply that the same measure cannot simultaneously be construed as both a performance requirement (an impediment on FDI) and as an investment incentive (a stimulus for FDI). One of the central themes of this chapter, and indeed of this book as a whole, is that it is exceedingly difficult to establish discrete definitions of these concepts, a reality that often exacerbates both identifying as well as regulating these kinds of measures.

1. PERFORMANCE REQUIREMENTS

(i) Definitions and Categories

There is no universally adopted definition of performance requirements. Some materials describe performance requirements as all "host state control techniques on operational level".[1] Other studies referred to them simply as "host country operational measures".[2] These definitions reflect an understanding of performance requirements as a variety of regulatory measures imposed by host state governments on the activities of foreign

[1] C. Wallace, *The Multinational Enterprises and Legal Control* (2nd edn, Kluwer Law International, The Hague 2002) 326.

[2] 'Host Country Operational Measures' (UNCTAD, 2001) <http://unctad.org/en/docs/psiteiitd26.en.pdf> accessed 11 June 2014.

multinational enterprises (MNEs) within its territory. Performance requirements are therefore conditions which host countries impose on MNEs, requiring them to meet certain specified goals with respect to their business activities in the host country.[3] Indeed, they are often termed "conditional investment incentives", a phrase which can also be applied to relocation incentives within states implemented by sub-national governments. At a very general level, performance requirements are intended to oblige MNEs to conduct their investment activities in ways considered beneficial for the host state's economy.[4] Much as there is no commonly accepted definition of performance requirements, there is also, perhaps somewhat more problematically, no exhaustive list of what type of measures would be captured by such a definition. A wide range of foreign investment regimes exist from country to country in accordance with their investment policies and developmental strategies. Performance requirements could take the form of various conditions imposed upon the mode of the foreign investor, such as a joint venture with a local partner or a requirement that they possess a certain quantity of foreign capital to fund their operations. In the post-establishment stage of investment, performance requirements could dictate the way the foreign investor undertakes its commercial activities within the territory of the host state. This could include, for example, rules relating to the use of domestic materials and inputs in manufacturing or that a certain amount of production is exported. Local content-based performance requirements are one of the most commonly used performance requirements.[5] Such measures have been widely used by some of the emerging market countries such as Indonesia, India, Malaysia, China, Brazil, Argentina, and others in the automotive industry.[6] Generally speaking, performance requirements have been used extensively by many countries at different stages of development. The incidence of performance requirements have varied across countries, depending upon their development strategy, their endowments of natural resources as well as skilled labour, and the market size of the host state.

---

[3] 'Foreign Direct Investment and Performance Requirements: New Evidence from Selected Countries' (UNCTAD, 2003) iii <http://unctad.org/en/Docs/iteiia20037_en.pdf> accessed 6 June 2014.

[4] 'World Investment Report. FDI Policies for Development: National and International Perspectives' (UNCTAD, 2003) 119 <http://unctad.org/en/Docs/wir2003light_en.pdf> accessed 5 June 2014.

[5] UNCTAD (n 3) 7.

[6] ibid. 13.

The United Nations Conference on Trade and Development (UNCTAD) divides performance requirements into three categories, based on the way in which they are regulated under international law: the first consists of those which are explicitly prohibited by the WTO Agreement on Trade Related Investment Measures (TRIMs) because they are inconsistent with Articles III (national treatment) and XI (prohibition on quantitative restrictions) of GATT 1994; the second includes requirements that are explicitly prohibited, conditioned or discouraged by interregional, regional or bilateral (but not by multilateral) agreements, typically concerning investment but also found in regional trade and economic integration agreements; and the third category covers requirements that are not subject to control by either the WTO or under any IIA, because they address social, environmental or other public-interest concerns.[7]

Local content rules which mandate that firms use a specific percentage of local materials are among the most popular performance requirements. Such measures have been used by a wide range of developed and developing states for decades as part of the strategy for assisting domestic industry by providing ready markets for their manufactured goods.[8] Similarly, a product mandate requirement compels an investor to manufacture a specific product that may be of economic interest to the host state. This can result in an increase in exports if there is insufficient demand in the local market for the mandated product.[9] Some states impose laws that are aimed at artificially increasing exports. A foreign investor subject to an export requirement must export a certain amount or percentage of its production, normally ascertained either by value (as a percentage) or by quantity (numerically or by weight). This has the potential advantage of freeing up local firms to serve internal markets, possibly with more lucrative returns. Export performance requirements also attempt to guarantee that the foreign currency earned by the host state as a consequence of the presence of the foreign investor exceeds the revenues which foreign investors earn through their sales on local markets.[10] Though not as widespread as local content rules, export

[7] UNCTAD generally (n 3).

[8] G.C. Hufbauer and J. Schott, *Local Content Requirements: A Global Problem* (Peterson Institute for International Economics, Washington DC 2013).

[9] R. Edwards and S. Lester, 'Towards a More Comprehensive World Trade Organization Agreement on Trade Related Investment Measures' (1997) 33 *Stanford Journal of International Economic Law* 169, 202.

[10] M. Sornarajah, *The International Law on Foreign Investment* (3rd edn, CUP, Cambridge 2012) 205.

performance requirements have been implemented by some newly industrializing countries as a consequence of the shift in their developmental strategy from manufacturing within the country (a strategy itself which was aimed at reducing reliance on imports) towards securing profits by means of export of goods.[11] Such export-oriented developmental strategy can be seen, for example, in some of the Association of Southeast Asian Nations (ASEAN) states, which initially concentrated on import-substituting industrialisation, gradually transitioning to export-oriented industrialisation. Similar to export and local content requirements are trade-balancing performance requirements. These are restrictions placed on foreign investors which limit the amount of purchases or use of imported products by foreign MNEs to a proportionate amount of the volume or value of local products that the company exports.[12] They also restrict the importation by an enterprise of products which are used in, or related to, its local production in general or to an amount related to the volume or value of local production that it exports.[13] Such restrictions have the effect of compelling firms to use local substitutes.

Price controls are another performance requirement that can be placed on foreign firms. These are limits that host states impose on the prices that a foreign investor can charge the public for the products or services that it sells. The price may be fixed by a governmental ministry or a designated administrative agency for various policy goals, including notably allowing less-competitive local firms to remain viable in a given market. Over time, the costs of labour and other inputs will require that such set prices will have to be re-assessed in order for the investment to remain profitable, such that foreign investors may find themselves in a constant state of renegotiation. Transfer pricing – the prices charged between affiliates for commodities or services – may also be subject to host-state regulation.[14] This has the effect of apportioning a foreign firm's income tax to the host state rather than to another jurisdiction.

Local equity requirements mandate that local investors hold a certain percentage ownership of a company created by foreign investment. Such performance requirements may take the form of other financial restrictions including minimum equity requirements, prescribed debt equity ratios, limits of profit repatriation, requirements for reinvestment of profits and prohibitions on financing from local sources. In a similar

---

[11] ibid. 111.

[12] TRIMs Agreement, Annex, 1(a).

[13] ibid. 2(a).

[14] J. Salacuse, *The Three Laws of International Investment* (OUP, Oxford 2013) 104.

vein, local collaboration rules specify that a foreign firm is permitted to enter the host state only in collaboration with a local partner, allowing local firms to benefit from the commercial expertise and profitability of the foreign partner. This type of performance requirement was used by many developing countries, including Eastern European states during the Communist era and prior to the formal installation of free market economics.[15] The use of local collaboration with a state entity allowed socialist states, which saw the benefits of foreign investment by MNEs, to combine their theory of economic governance with the expansionary capitalistic strategy of FDI. This model proliferated to the communist states in Asia such as China, Vietnam, Laos and Cambodia.[16] Another way in which local equity requirements can be imposed on foreign multinationals is through requiring the establishment of a joint venture with local firms. These have remained popular in Asia. Requirements which advantage firms owned by nationals (or particular ethnic groups) are referred to as indigenization measures.

Minimum capitalization performance requirements are controls implemented by the host state demanding that the foreign investor should bring in all or a certain percentage of their capital from abroad, rather than raising it from local sources. This can help ensure that there is a sufficient quantity of local capital to invest in domestic firms. In a related fashion, host states can ensure that there is sufficient capital available in domestic banks for future re-investment by restricting or limiting the repatriation of profits. This is achieved via various tools, including taxing remitted dividends, limiting debt: equity ratios, and restricting the use of various types of equipment. Foreign exchange controls, which can also be viewed as a kind of performance requirement controlling the conduct of firms, are instigated by countries where the available amount of foreign currency is limited. Limiting a foreign firm's capacity to repatriate profits can significantly impact on its profits.[17]

Employment and training requirements may also be imposed on foreign firms. This could involve a quota of host country nationals being employed, or might require a training plan for the development of local personnel so that over time indigenous employees will occupy more positions within the project.[18] Employment or training requirements have been applied by a number of countries. For example, employment

---

[15] Sornarajah (n 10) 106.
[16] ibid. 106–7.
[17] Salacuse (n 14) 105.
[18] ibid.

requirements were introduced in Malaysia in the 1970s with the introduction of the Labour Utilization Relief incentive. It provided increasingly generous tax exemptions for pioneer-status industries the greater the number of full-time employees. Illustrating the intersect with investment incentives, tax deductions for training expenses were given for approved employee training in Malaysia's manufacturing sector in the 1990s in order to raise productivity. In Singapore, the Skills Development Fund gives financial assistance to companies for training their workers.[19] In a similar fashion, host states may instigate management controls to ensure that the managers or other employees of the investment project will encourage the transfer of expertise and technology. Mandatory technology transfer is itself a leading form of performance requirement, although unlike conventional employment and training targets, it is less easy to measure.

It must be recognized that host states do not always apply all performance requirements consistently or evenly. Host states may relax some of their demands on foreign investors if the foreign firm undertakes other commitments which may address the country's developmental strategy more effectively, often in conjunction with the imposition of other types of performance requirements. For example, local equity requirements may be relaxed by host states, allowing foreign investors to set wholly-owned enterprises in industries which are of particular interest to the host state. Equity requirements may be suspended if the investor is willing to locate its operations in an underdeveloped region of the host state or if it exports a larger percentage of its manufactured goods.[20] Given that these strategies allow for the transgression of rules like local equity participation, such policies bear a close resemblance to investment incentives.

(ii) Justifications

Performance requirements are used to obtain the type of investment that a host state needs for its economic needs, improving the distribution of any gains from FDI towards the host country. Governments tend to impose performance requirements to achieve macro- (the whole country) or micro-economic development (one industry or region) goals or to alter the distribution of benefits among regions or the population at large. This will include not only assisting local firms, providing employment and

---

[19] Z. Boroo, 'Effective Use of Performance Requirements and Investment Incentive' (2012) 17 *Mongolian Journal of International Affairs* 97.

[20] Sornarajah (n 10) 114.

training but can also address a state's desire to guard against any balance of payment problems caused by the remittance of profits from FDI back to the home state.[21] As performance requirements do not create unimpeachable barriers to FDI, but simply make it conditional on certain conduct, they are not necessarily hostile to liberalized markets. Indeed, some commentators have suggested that there is nothing inherently unjust about the imposition of economically distortive performance requirements, because promoting the development of the national economy is a valid objective of any government.[22] Some see them as legitimate tools by which governments seek to distribute the gains engendered by foreign firms more evenly across a broader socio-economic spectrum.[23] Most of the literature on the value of performance requirements has focused on the economic effectiveness of these tools to achieve various economic objectives, including GDP and employment. There has been very little emphasis on the potential for performance requirements to advance social or other policy goals, such as the advancement of indigenous peoples or the protection of the environment.[24]

The case for support of trade-related controls on FDI performance requirements essentially amounts to a justification of government intervention in markets. So called "strategic" trade theory suggests that some non-market forces can have a significant positive impact on trade flows in a way that the traditional theories of free trade cannot explain. This is because there are certain key sectors where labour and capital are more productive than other sectors as a consequence of advantages engendered by economies of scale as well as experience and innovation. So some trade-based restrictions on FDI can actually enlarge national income even in situations where the country lacks a comparative advantage in those sectors. Government intervention in the form of restrictions on free trade can accordingly correct market imperfections.[25]

---

[21] P. Muchlinski, 'Policy Issues' in P. Muchlinski, F. Ortino and C. Schreuer (eds), *Oxford Handbook of International Investment Law* (OUP, Oxford 2008) 32.

[22] B. Legum, 'Understanding Performance Requirement Prohibitions in Investment Treaties' (2007) 53 *Contemporary Issues in International Arbitration and Mediation* 53–4.

[23] D. Schneiderman, *Constitutionalizing Economic Globalization* (CUP, Cambridge 2008) 27.

[24] J. VanDuzer, P. Simons and G. Mayeda, *Integrating Sustainable Development into International Investment Agreement*, (Commonwealth Secretariat, London 2013) 204.

[25] Edwards and Lester (n 9) 175–6.

One example where performance requirements appear to have been economically justified is in support for "infant industries". According to the infant industry theory, developing countries have a potential advantage in manufacturing, but new manufacturing industries in developing countries cannot initially compete with well-established manufacturing in developed countries. This is especially so if the manufacturing sector is faced with direct competition at home in the form of FDI. The economic rationale for governmental intervention in these circumstances is that, over time, per-unit production costs will fall as experience in production increases, enabling the industry's goods to become more competitive in the future.[26] So by protecting a relatively weak domestic industry from foreign competition at the outset (either via trade or through direct investment), the host-state government allows the industry to accumulate experience in production, ultimately generating productivity gains. The WTO itself has acknowledged that performance requirements could assist in economic development.[27]

Some countries, especially in the developing world, also employ a wide range of performance requirements in order to combat the restrictive business practices used by foreign firms, such as monopolization to control a market or transfer-pricing to distort earnings for tax evasion. This will include empowering specific industries such as manufacturing or high technology, reducing unemployment, augmenting the skills of local workers, promotion of regional development, trade balancing away from imports, technology transfer, and in some cases political independence.[28] In some circumstances local content, export, and joint venture participation are imposed by host states to mitigate or pre-empt anti-competitive business practices in the form of monopolization, price fixing, cartels and collusive tendering.[29] It is thought that a number of developing countries resort to performance requirements as a response to the anti-competitive business practices of MNEs, and not necessarily as a means of generating greater domestic resource gains.[30] Restrictions on

---

[26] ibid. 176.

[27] Ministerial Declaration on Doha Work Programme, adopted at Hong Kong, 18 December 2005, Annex F (WT/MIN(05)/DEC).

[28] UNCTAD (n 3) 6.

[29] H. Puri and P. Brusick, 'Trade-related investment measures: Issues for developing countries in the Uruguay Round', Uruguay Round: Papers on Selected Issues (1989) UNCTAD/ITP/10, cited in UNCTAD ibid.

[30] V. Mosoti, 'The WTO Agreement on Trade-Related Investment measures and the Flow of Foreign Direct Investment in Africa: Meeting the Development Challenge' (2003) 15 *Pace International Law Review* 181, 195.

the size or the structure of foreign firms can render them less capable of exerting monopolistic influences on markets, ultimately harming consumers. To the extent that these types of performance requirements are effective, they may be seen to operate as a suitable alternative to the lack of international cooperation in competition law. Likewise, some developing countries in particular have argued that trade-oriented performance requirements consisting of export obligations and foreign currency exchange neutrality are needed to moderate the adverse effects of capital outflows associated with balance-of-payment problems linked to trade deficits.[31] This justification appears more credible in light of some of the problems of capital flight associated with incidents such as the Asian financial crisis of the late 1990s and echoed in warnings issued by the IMF during the global financial crisis.

Studies have demonstrated that local content requirements can be a useful tool for economic growth, although this may depend on the specific conditions of their application in each context.[32] Beneficial effects have been observed when these tools are used in conjunction with offsetting measures designed to ensure that local firms continue to face some competitive pressures and still have access to technology and skills to improve their capabilities. Local content, when coupled with technology transfer rules, may promote the establishment of industrial linkages with suppliers and consumers, assisting in the development of the host state's economy. Without these requirements, foreign firms would be more likely to source their production inputs from abroad, which could undermine the establishment of beneficial local clusters in host states.[33] For their part, export-oriented requirements were imposed on foreign firms because of the inability of the import-substitution model of industrialisation to generate consistent growth in manufacturing output and employment. Numerous studies demonstrated that import-substituting industrialisation was inefficient whereas, export-oriented strategies were economically advantageous. Export performance requirements safeguard the domestic market for local firms. In the absence of export performance requirements, local firms have to compete with foreign multinationals which sell their goods domestically and which are often able to produce goods at a lower cost. The emerging local industry

---

[31] India's submission to the WTO: WT/WGTI/W/152 (19 November 2002).

[32] UNCTAD (n 3).

[33] K. Singh, 'India. Foreign Investors' Paradise: The Devastating Impacts of the EU-India Free Trade Agreement' (Global Research, 2011) <www.globalresearch.ca/india-foreign-investors-paradise-the-devastating-impacts-of-the-eu-india-free-trade-agreement/23036> accessed 12 June 2014.

is at risk of being suppressed without such controls. In this way, the avoidance of the crowding-out effect is another justification for export performance requirements.[34] Export-oriented industrialization strategies resulted in remarkable growth in Asian economies including Malaysia and the Philippines.[35]

The purpose of minimum capitalization performance requirements is to preclude multinational corporations from exhausting capital that may be available through the host state's domestic financial institutions, freeing up domestic capital for domestic uses. Accordingly, in the absence of such restrictions, if the foreign firm is permitted to raise capital on local markets, local funds would be depleted in satisfying the needs of the foreign investor instead of being directed at local projects that might more clearly favour the host state or public interest.[36] In other words, if host states did not impose capitalization requirements on incoming foreign investors, it is quite possible that one of the main benefits of FDI, namely capital inflows to host country, would be nullified.[37] The IMF's acceptance of a wide range of capital controls as a legitimate buttress against rapid capital inflows, both of which have the potential to destabilize an economy, is evidence of support for this variety of performance requirement.[38]

Local equity performance requirements can serve a number of purposes including allowing parties to pool resources and technological competences. They also permit the diversification of risks associated with the project. Joint ventures formed between foreign and domestic investors may conduct their business activities in a manner that is more economically beneficial to the host state than that of a wholly foreign owned enterprise. For example, an MNE with foreign affiliates may be more likely to import a greater proportion of raw materials and other production inputs than necessary, simply because these firms are more familiar with foreign suppliers than they are with local suppliers. Foreign affiliates might suffer from a lack of information on the capabilities of local suppliers. The presence of a local partner in a joint venture could

---

[34] Sornarajah (n 10) 206.

[35] T.K. Wie, 'Export-Oriented Industrialisation and Foreign Direct Investment in the ASEAN Countries' in E. Aryeetey and ors (eds), *Asia and Africa in the Global Economy* (United Nations University Press, Hong Kong 2003).

[36] Sornarajah (n 10) 108.

[37] ibid.

[38] 'The Liberalization and Management of Capital Flows: An Institutional View' (International Monetary Fund, 14 November 2012) <www.imf.org/external/np/pp/eng/2012/111412.pdf> accessed 2 December 2014.

assist in overcoming these information gaps concerning the potential of local suppliers.[39] Perhaps most importantly, a joint venture with a local partner would be more inclined to undertake research and development to establish new technologies. Such arrangements may accordingly be viewed as more advantageous in terms of fostering local skills and know-how which may be of long term benefit to host states. Imposition of the requirement of entry via a joint venture enables the more efficient transfer of technology and management, capturing the traditional benefits of FDI. Joint ventures are believed to benefit the host state more so than other structures because they ensure that only a minor portion of the MNE's revenues are repatriated overseas.[40]

Furthermore, equity joint ventures between foreign and local enterprises make it possible to preserve local managerial control over the business with the participation of foreign multinationals. Some joint venture laws go beyond simply local equity rules, in that the local partner not only owns a share of the joint venture but also participates in its management, ensuring greater control over the investment. Of course use of joint ventures does not guarantee local control, as local managers may sometimes be unable to manage the project effectively. Even in these situations, joint ventures are believed to facilitate the improvement of domestic managerial skills and knowledge.[41] Likewise, employment and training requirements placed on foreign firms aim not only to reduce local unemployment, but also to induce foreign investors to engage more actively in training and human resource development activities and to encourage the expansion of skill-intensive operations. More complete and rewarding employment can result in both tangible economic gains as well as less measurable social improvements.

At a more general level, the need to regulate MNEs through performance requirements has arisen because a significant portion of FDI in the developing world has been in the extractive industries, leading to issues of natural resources depletion and the possibility of environmental damage.[42] This may be one reason why developing countries are convinced that imposition of performance requirements, dictating the nature

---

[39] UNCTAD (n 3) 99–100.

[40] C.B. Choi and P. Beamish, 'Resource Complementarity and International Joint Venture Performance in Korea' (2013) 30:2 *Asia Pacific Journal of Management* 561.

[41] P. Muchlinski, *Multinational Enterprises and the Law* (2nd edn, OUP, Oxford 2007) 191–2.

[42] Wallace (n 1) 326.

and extent of commercial activities, enhances the value of FDI.[43] It is often pointed out that since developed countries adopted performance requirements during their periods of industrialization, developing countries should have the right to use the same tools as they seek to diversify their economies.[44] This is precisely why a number of commentators view the efforts of developed countries to prevent the use of performance requirements as unfair, because such policies were among the tools used by these countries to achieve prosperity in the first place.[45] The use of these policies by developed states during their periods of industrialization along with their subsequent removal and prohibition, has been condemned by some for its apparent hypocrisy. In this regard, conditioning the acceptance of inward FDI in extractive sectors on the provision of infrastructure appears to have been a useful policy for some developing states. For instance, China is widely recognized to have provided significant transportation facilities for many African states as a condition of its FDI.[46]

The purpose of ownership-based controls on foreign investment, such as those encouraging indigenous ownership and those requiring joint ventures, are thought to contribute to the emergence of a local "entrepreneurial class",[47] which may have social as well as economic benefits. Such measures seek to ensure that foreign investors contribute to the economic advancement of groups which may have been traditionally disadvantaged. If FDI benefits are enjoyed solely by elite groups within the host state, this could lead to increased inequality and ultimately engender social tension. Ethnicity may be taken into consideration when host states determine the nature of permissible FDI within its territory. In Malaysia, for example, there is a prescribed structure of shareholdings, where preference is given to indigenous Bumiputera people of Malaysia.[48] South Africa implemented its Black Economic Empowerment programme in order to spur the advancement of a particular racial group. This led to tensions with some foreign investors

---

43 Sornarajah (n 10) 205.

44 ibid. 206.

45 E.g. H.J. Chang, *Bad Samaritans: Rich Nations, Poor Policies and the Threat to the Developing World* (Random House, London 2007) 84–103.

46 See e.g. U. Ofodile, 'Trade, Empires, and Subjects – China-Africa Trade: A New Fair Trade Arrangement or the Third Scramble for Africa' (2008) 41 *Vanderbilt Journal of International Law* 505.

47 S. Picciotto, *Regulating Global Corporate Capitalism* (CUP, Cambridge 2011) 163.

48 ibid. 107.

who suffered regulatory discrimination as a consequence of the policy, which arguably had a legitimate social justification.[49] While such types of performance requirement may invite conflict with foreign firms, such measures may become less invasive once the process of indigenization has been completed and the visible dominance of foreign investment has diminished.[50]

(iii) Criticisms

Despite the fact that many developed countries used performance requirements in the past, many are reluctant to accept the right of developing countries to use performance requirements on the grounds that they distort international trade,[51] associating these tools with ineffectual statist interventionism.[52] The damaging effect of performance requirements is believed to be one of the reasons that most nations around the world favoured direct stimulus packages in order to address the global financial crisis of 2008–09 rather than via discriminatory trade provisions.[53] In the long term, trade-based performance requirements have are thought to be damaging to both the MNEs as well as the host states which impose them. Trade-related performance requirements distort international trade flows, undermining the welfare effects of free trade.[54] UNCTAD's World Investment Report has in the past indicated that the economic advantages of performance requirements are not clearly empirically demonstrated.[55]

Commentators have distinguished between protections in IIAs that are rooted in concepts of natural justice, like the fair and equitable treatment standard or the guarantee against expropriation without investment, and prohibitions on performance requirements, which are grounded upon

---

[49] *Piero Foresti, Laura de Carli & Others v The Republic of South Africa* ICSID Case No. ARB(AF)/07/01.

[50] Sornarajah (n 10) 114.

[51] ibid. 206.

[52] UNCTAD (n 3) iii.

[53] R. Leal-Arcas, I*nternational Trade and Investment Law* (Edward Elgar, Cheltenham 2010) 19–20.

[54] C. Fontheim and M. Gadbaw, 'Trade Related Performance Requirements Under the GATT-MTN System and US Law' (1982) 14 *Law & Policy of International Business* 129, 139.

[55] UNCTAD World Investment Report 2014, 112 (linking performance requirements with investment incentives) <http://unctad.org/en/Publications Library/wir2014_en.pdf> accessed 2 December 2014.

economic efficiency.[56] Indeed performance requirements are often criticized as an unwarranted interference in the process of economic decision-making by investors, resulting in an inefficient allocation of resources. Performance requirements accordingly represent a deadweight cost on production that can impose significant burdens on foreign investors and traders.[57] To frame this allegation in more simple terms, if it was profitable for a firm to engage in the behaviour that was required by the performance requirement, then the firm would do so of its own accord. Alternatively, if the investor does not wish to behave in the manner dictated by the performance requirement, then it can be inferred that the performance requirement is inefficient, imposing an unnecessary cost on economic activity.[58] Of course, this view presumes that the firm and the government have interests (as well as understandings of efficiency) that are aligned, which may not always be the case. Performance requirements are seen as fundamentally inconsistent with the principle of liberal markets.[59] Generally speaking, where applied in a protectionist manner, with limited competitive stress, performance requirements can result in inefficient suppliers that burden consumers with high prices and low quality goods or services.[60] This is why they have largely been abandoned in favour of more widespread acceptance of liberalization.[61]

The conventional case against trade-based performance requirements, as well as against trade and protectionism generally, is derived from the theory of comparative advantage and the resulting gains from international trade. Successive generations of economists have elaborated on the simple model of comparative advantage originally articulated by David Ricardo in the early nineteenth century.[62] These affirm the basic conclusion that both national and global welfare are maximized when governments allow market forces to direct trade flows.[63] The same theory could be applied to the flows of FDI. Liberalizing the movement of

---

56 Legum (n 22) 57.

57 D. Rodrik, 'Economics of Export Performance Requirements' (1987) 102:3 *Quarterly Journal of Economics* 633.

58 VanDuzer et al. (n 24) 194.

59 R. Dolzer and C. Schreuer, *Principles of International Investment Law* (2nd edn, OUP, Oxford 2012) 90 and Edwards and Lester (n 9) 170.

60 UNCTAD, World Investment Report 2002: Transnational Corporations and Export Competitiveness at 169 <http://unctad.org/en/Docs/wir2001_en.pdf> accessed 2 December 2014.

61 Schneiderman (n 23) 27.

62 D. Ricardo, *Principles of Political Economy and Taxation* (John Murray, London 1821) ch. 7.

63 Edwards and Lester (n 9) 174–5.

capital allows it to be channelled to the places where it can be put to the most productive use, generating wealth and income that can then be used as a basis for further production and trade. In addition to its role as a complementary strategy to trade, FDI is often viewed as an alternative to trade where tariffs and other trade barriers are prohibitive. Market-seeking firms locate in foreign states so that their products are no longer considered as exports.[64] This objective is frustrated when there are trade-based performance requirements linked.

For example, local content rules can diminish the value of the investment because the production of goods comes at an increased cost which may not be fully recovered through price increases. The host state may gain from the imposition of a local content requirement on a foreign firm because this transfers wealth to local producers which may not otherwise be able to survive in the global marketplace. But this can lead to an unhealthy dependence in case the foreign investor leaves the jurisdiction, which may often be the case where performance requirements become too onerous (often necessitating other precautionary performance requirements such as capital controls). In some cases, local content requirements will induce foreign firms to increase their own domestic production of the component input and induce capital flows and in so doing advance the process of industrialization of the host country.[65] Local content requirements may also suppress economic development. While such requirements can result in immediate sales for the domestic industry, this industry is also shielded from the beneficial effects of competition, which can be harmful in the longer term. It is also linked to corruption and delays.[66] The foreign firm using mandatory local components is unable to obtain high-quality, low-priced equivalents from other countries, and consequently will be less able to produce internationally competitive finished products. Accordingly, the domestic industry can hope to achieve import substitution, but the likelihood of further development is low.[67] Some studies have shown that local content requirements can actually reduce local employment, undermining one of a government's main objectives in encouraging FDI. Foreign investors

---

[64] E.g. K. Reinert, *An Introduction to International Economics* (CUP, Cambridge 2012) 141–8.

[65] Boroo (n 19).

[66] C. Cimino, G. Hufbauer and J. Schott, 'A Proposed Code to Discipline Local Content Requirements' (Peterson Institute for International Economics, February 2014) 3 <www.piie.com/publications/pb/pb14-6.pdf> accessed 2 December 2014.

[67] (METI, 2010) Boroo (n 19) 101.

will seek to reduce costs associated with more expensive local inputs through automation or by shifting manufacturing to other jurisdictions.[68]

Local content requirements are not always feasible where the imposing state lacks sufficient capacity to satisfy the needs of foreign investors. This has been a persistent problem for Brazil, which traditionally imposed requirements on foreign oil companies to use facilities such as platforms and ships that are constructed locally, while being unable to supply these in sufficient quantity and size. This may lead to delay or even the abandonment of lucrative FDI projects.[69] Local content requirements may be further inefficient because locally produced components in a manufacturing process may not meet standards for export to more rigorously regulated markets. They may also be more expensive than better quality materials produced elsewhere. This can be harmful for manufacturers because the companies adhering to the local content rule may not able to produce goods which can be sold in all markets. Some moderately industrialized developing countries, notably Thailand, were able to adapt to prohibitions on local content rules and even thrive in their absence. Local content rules in Thailand's automobile sector had been imposing unrealistic costs and entrenching inefficient suppliers.[70]

Requirements which mandate that an investor source more inputs locally than the investor would have done otherwise can be detrimental not only to the foreign firms on which they are imposed but also to the host state. This is because, in the absence of local competitive pressures, such rules remove the incentive for local firms to produce materials which would be competitive on a world market, resulting in a short-term transfer of wealth to the host state if the investor decides to leave the jurisdiction. Local content requirements could further result in a decrease in imports into the country applying the requirement because domestic equivalents are used. Such restrictions can therefore have a harmful knock-on effect for suppliers in other jurisdictions, causing scaled-back production and associated negative externalities.[71]

---

[68] C. Davidson, S. Matusz and M. Kreinin, 'Analysis of Performance Standards to Direct Foreign Investments' (1985) 18:4 *Canadian Journal of Economics* 876.

[69] J. Leahy, 'Brazil Oilfield Reveals Local Sourcing Problem' *Financial Times* (London, 30 June 2011).

[70] K. Natsuda and J. Thorburn, 'Industrial Policy and the Development of the Automotive Industry in Thailand' (2013) 18:3 *Journal of the Asia Pacific Economy* 1.

[71] Legum (n 22) 53.

Export requirements, which compel firms to export a given amount of production, are thought to be among the most trade-distorting of all trade-oriented performance requirements. As they often lead to excess supply, these rules can promote dumping in the investor's home market and disrupt trade flows to third countries. Export minima will most likely lead to a higher level of exports from the country applying the rule than would have occurred otherwise, possibly leading to supply shortages and price increases within the domestic market. Foreign firms may have difficulty satisfying the host states' export performance requirements because MNEs often adopt a policy of forbidding export by their subsidiaries into each other's territories.[72] Relatedly, product mandate requirements can result in an increase in exports if there is insufficient demand in the local market for the mandated product. It could also lead to unsold inventory.[73] Export bans, which set maximum levels of export, artificially reduce the supply of goods, inflating prices on global markets and potentially leading to harmful price instability.[74]

Non-trade-based performance requirements may also be harmful to firms as well as states. Requirements placed on foreign investors mandating local partnership with domestic firms which may offer little in the way of genuine expertise, know-how or risk-diversification represent significant barriers to entry for foreign firms. Problems arising from poor coordination and uneven information sharing between foreign and local partners have been identified in some situations.[75] The artificial nature of mandatory joint venture arrangements has seen situations where foreign firms engage in evasive strategies such as the creation of "silent partnerships" with local shell companies. Local partners create companies then let them to foreign managers in order to satisfy local ownership requirements, with the local owner having no control whatsoever over the business. Such practices cause host governments to waste resources on monitoring and enforcement.[76] The impact of a local equity requirement on the activities of the foreign investor is uncertain because

---

[72] Sornarajah (n 10) 112.

[73] Edwards and Lester (n 9) 202.

[74] E.g. G. Welton, 'The Impact of Russia's 2010 Grain Export Ban' (2011) 11:5 *Oxfam Policy and Practice: Agriculture, Food and Land* 76.

[75] See e.g. R.A. Cramb, 'Palmed Off: Incentive Problems with Joint Venture Schemes for Oil Palm Development on Customary Land' (2013) 43 World Development 84.

[76] E.g. in Oman: B. Thomas, 'Omani Firms Face Sanctions for Omanisation Violations' *Arabian Business* (5 February 2014).

it depends on a large number of variables, including percentage ownership of the local investor and the motivations of the individuals in management, in particular whether they favour local companies when sourcing inputs even where this is unsupported by economic logic.[77]

Mandatory technology transfer could prevent investors from using their technology in host states where they may have done so of their own accord, potentially restricting the more gradual and organic transfer of technology. Restrictions on the remittance of profits may have undesirable effects in the long run, causing MNEs to locate to more investor-friendly jurisdictions and leading to unsatisfied dependencies in the original host state. It is difficult to predict ex ante how a restriction on the remittance of profits may affect trade flows. If profits cannot be remitted, they may be used either to purchase more local goods (which leads to a decline in imports), or to purchase foreign goods as inputs for the manufacturing process (which leads to an increase in imports).

2. INVESTMENT INCENTIVES

(i) Definitions and categories

Investment incentives are simply defined as a non-negative per unit subsidy paid to foreign investors in addition to the regular, market-determined rate of return on capital.[78] Put another way, investment incentives are essentially fiscal contributions intended to influence a company's decision on where to invest.[79] Incentives tend to be offered to "mobile investors", meaning those that are able to choose the jurisdiction in which they locate, based on regulatory or economic factors rather than the presence of natural resources. Prior to globalization, the jurisdictional competition for direct investment was primarily focused at the sub-national level within one state, whereas today this competition has a more international dimension as a consequence of the easy mobility of multinationals. With many more countries in need of FDI than there is available, there is a natural market in which states compete to attract the firms that offer the most in the way of economic advantages. There is a

---

77 Edwards and Lester (n 9) 202.

78 E. Blanchard, 'What Global Fragmentation Means to the WTO' *World Trade Organization, Economic Research and Development Statistics* (19 December 2013) 17.

79 Edwards and Lester (n 9) 173.

dearth of information about overall spending on FDI incentives, particularly in developing countries. There remain significant barriers to more complete transparency in this regard, many of which are linked to poor governance generally. Ironically these are the very factors which make investment incentives necessary policy tools.

Investment incentives can take the form of subsidies, also known as state aid. The central idea of subsidization or state aid is that it results in a deviation from the normal course of events. Such a "normal" situation is often understood by reference to the market.[80] In that sense the understanding of subsidies (as with investment incentives generally) may be seen as one rooted in competition-based analysis, rather than trade or investment analysis. Regulatory incentives consist of derogations from national or sub-national laws in a manner which is advantageous to the foreign firm. The common understanding of incentive typically does not include broad non-discriminatory policies, such as the provision of general infrastructure or regulatory and fiscal regimes that apply to all sectors.[81] Regardless of their stage of development, most countries employ a variety of incentives to realize their investment objectives. Subsidies designed to influence the location of investment are a key feature of global competition for FDI. They are used by the vast majority of countries at multiple levels of government, including national, regional and even municipal, and they are applied to a broad range of industries across sectors.

Investment incentives became more popular as tools of economic policy in large developing countries towards the end of the 1990s, as they sought to make themselves more attractive to FDI.[82] Even where the advantages of investment incentives are not clear, many states may be pressured into offering them because of regulatory competition to attract FDI.[83] The fear of increased unemployment, especially among highly skilled workers and the crowding-out of domestic firms in equivalent industries have in the past controlled the extent of FDI incentive measures and other initiatives by host states to promote outward FDI. Home country measures to increase outward FDI by assisting in the

---

[80] L. Rubini, *The Definition of Subsidy and State Aid: WTO and EC Law in Comparative Perspective* (OUP, Oxford 2009) 318.

[81] B.V.R. Subrahmanyam, 'Investment Incentives and Multilateral Disciplines' in S.J. Evenett and B.M. Hoekman (eds), *Economic Development and Multilateral Trade Cooperation* (Palgrave Macmillan and World Bank, New York, NY 2006) 303.

[82] Edwards and Lester (n 9) 177.

[83] Picciotto (n 47) 163.

internationalization of domestic firms tend to have privileged exports because the connection between exports and economic growth as well as the capacity for employment and technology acquisition in the home state is more clearly evident.

Investment incentives tend not to occur in isolation but are usually presented in packages, often tailored to suit the particular firm and the needs of the host state. They may be granted in proportion to the size of the project, its importance to the economy or its geographic location within the host state (such as in an underdeveloped region). It is possible for investors to negotiate special agreements in order to secure additional incentives and privileges beyond those specified in the general investment law of the host state.[84] Importantly, investment incentives are often accompanied by conditions imposed by the host country on the recipient firm. These may be accurately described as performance requirements as discussed above. Indeed, some analysts have used the phrase "performance incentives" to describe this variety of measure, effectively a sub-category of performance requirements imposed on investors.[85] These contemplate financial or other advantages that flow to investors who meet certain performance standards, often inducing the same type of behaviour that is sought by performance requirements. Investment incentives may also be linked to the host state's achieving a particular policy goal, such as environmental sustainability or technological development. While individual packages with conditions are often negotiated with investors on a case-by-case basis, it is common for FDI incentives to be extended much more broadly, with limited restrictions and across a wide range of economic activity in all sectors. It is important to recognize that some investment incentives may be applicable to all investment whether or not it is domestic or foreign, or they may be applied only to FDI.

Commentators have suggested that there are two main categories of investment incentives: those aimed at increasing the return on an investment project (which would capture tax exemptions, subsidies, and agreements to purchase goods or services); and those aimed at reducing risk, which would include guarantees to provide foreign exchange for debt servicing, international dispute settlement through arbitration, guarantees against nationalization and other protections found in IIAs.[86] The former may be used predominately by developed states where elemental political risks are low but profits are uncertain, and the latter by

---

84 Salacuse (n 14) 102.
85 Edwards and Lester (n 9) 173.
86 Salacuse (n 14) 100–101.

developing states where political risk represents a major obstacle to internationalization. The former category also appears to be dominated by trade-based incentives whereas the latter is characterized by more traditional investment-oriented ones.

Investment incentives include measures specifically designed either to increase the rate of return of a particular FDI undertaking, or to reduce its costs or other risks, such as those that relate to non-commercial matters like expropriation without compensation. They consist of fiscal incentives such as tax holidays and lower taxes for foreign investors, financial incentives such as grants, preferential loans to multinational corporations and government insurance at preferential rates, as well as other measures like market preferences and stabilization clauses guaranteeing that existing regulations will not change. The provision of subsidized infrastructure, inputs or services can also be seen as incentives.[87] Since they mitigate some of the risks associated with FDI by providing legal protection to foreign firms, IIAs themselves should be seen as a form of investment incentive.

Taken together, formal FDI incentives and informal FDI promotion initiatives may consist of the following type of measures: improvements to the overall policy framework of the host state, often in conjunction with directed technical assistance from the host state; financial or fiscal incentives such as investment guarantees, insurance, capital or tax relief; preferential market access to the host-state market for goods and services that investors wish to import; the creation of an investment-promotion agency in the host state, with possible discrete external connections in targeted home states, which may include workshops, fairs or information contact points; information exchanges regarding host state investment rules and available opportunities; the more general promotion of linkages between the home and host state; and encouragement of technology transfer between investors and the host state.[88] Some of these measures – as well as activities like attempts to secure the commitment of the home state to provide the host state with technical assistance with the implementation of promotion programmes in the host state – should not strictly speaking be viewed as investment incentives, because they do not necessarily make it easier for specific foreign investment to engage in FDI in the host state; instead, they create a more investor-friendly climate in a more general sense.

---

[87] Boroo (n 19).

[88] VanDuzer et al. (n 24) 493–4.

Tax incentives and grants are the most common variety of investment incentives for both developed and developing host states. The exemption from various taxes is one of the most common forms of incentive, particularly in developing countries, because these types of incentives appear to cost very little to the host government in the short term.[89] Income tax relief exempts the investing firm from local income or other taxation for a specified period of time. The host country may also offer exemptions from taxes on dividends, royalty payments, interest payments, property taxes and various other charges for which the project would be otherwise liable. Tax stabilization may also be granted to foreign investors, guaranteeing that the foreign firm will pay no more than a specified minimum tax rate for a predetermined period of time. This is similar to the stabilization clause found in many investment agreements, ensuring that host governments will not alter their laws in a manner that will damage the foreign investor for a certain specified period of time.[90] Tax-oriented incentives are more sophisticated than traditional investment incentives, in part because they are harder to scrutinize and because their revocation is less confrontational than that of conventional incentives. When the policy approach to FDI is in its downward cycle, the withdrawal of tax incentives for foreign investors tends to be met with less resistance: one of the reasons why this type of reaction against FDI is often described as the "velvet revocation" of incentives.[91]

Technical and business-support-oriented measures are frequently instigated where the host state maintains an investment-promotion agency, and can be deployed in conjunction with other types of incentives or in isolation. These incentives have the purpose of decreasing information asymmetries and administrative burdens associated with a foreign firm's entry into the market of the host country. Technical and business support also facilitates the acquisition of commercial information, such as the location of markets and raw materials. Provision of these types of non-fiscal incentives is often done by investment-promotion agencies. These are an increasingly important component of inward FDI promotional activities. Initially, such bodies were introduced to increase the efficiency of FDI liberalization as a consequence of heavy bureaucratic barriers. They tend to concentrate their efforts on technical issues relating

---

[89] Salacuse (n 14) 102.

[90] ibid. 101.

[91] T. Walde and A. Kolo, 'Coverage of Taxation under Modern Investment Treaties' in P. Muchlinski, F. Ortino and C. Schreuer (eds), *Oxford Handbook of International Investment Law* (OUP, Oxford 2008) 309.

to the dissemination of information on available investment opportunities as well as administrative procedures. Some even provide "aftercare" once an investor has already invested. Distinct from formal incentive programs, investment-promotion initiatives have been described as "light-handed public policies to overcome information asymmetries and other market failures" that hinder both inward and outward FDI. Such policies have been advocated by commentators in order to make available information about investment opportunities to MNEs.[92]

Some host state are willing to grant foreign investors a monopoly over the local market by agreeing either to prohibit other similar investments for a specified period of time or to restrict the importation of competing goods through either high tariffs or quotas.[93] Soft loans are those from the government to private firms at terms more favourable than those obtained on the open market. This type of investment incentive has been very popular, particularly in Japan where a number of these loans have been offered to small and medium-sized enterprises. A similar type of incentive, equity participation by a government involves a financial contribution with a lower expected rate of return than that which would be demanded by private capital markets. This type of investment incentive, popular in some European countries, can be easily disguised through an artificial joint venture.[94] Lastly, as suggested above, international investment agreements themselves may be seen as a kind of investment incentive, in that they offer investors protections that mitigate the risk of commercial operations overseas. Access to specialized dispute settlement (international arbitration) which is not available to local firms is among the most powerful features of such instruments.

Incentives aimed at stimulating outward FDI have been employed by some countries. This is tied to the recognition that domestic firms must be competitive in international markets as a consequence of the rapid pace of globalization. There has been very limited scholarship on the manner in which states encourage the internationalization of their firms and indeed on the phenomenon of outward FDI itself.[95]

---

[92] T. Moran, 'What Policies Should Developing Country Governments Adopt Toward Outward FDI? Lessons from the Experience of Developed Countries' in K. Sauvant (ed.), *The Rise of Transnational Corporations from Emerging Markets* (Edward Elgar, Cheltenham 2008) 293.

[93] Salacuse (n 14) 102.

[94] L. Oxelheim, 'EU–China and the Non-Transparent Race for Inward FDI' (2008) 19:4 *Asian Journal of Economics* 358.

[95] See e.g. D. Collins, *BRIC States and Outward Foreign Direct Investment* (OUP, Oxford 2013) (noting the recent trend in growth of outward FDI from the

Developing countries have shown a strong inclination towards the use of investment incentives.[96] There is now a much greater use of tax incentives to promote research and development initiatives in OECD countries.[97] In the past 20 years, investment incentives have spread to developing countries where before they had been tools associated only with industrialized countries. Whereas developing countries tend to impose performance requirements on foreign investors to suit their economics needs, investment incentives are a more commonly used tool by developed states. Developing countries may not have sufficient capital or financial means to pay incentives to attract firms, just as they may not have sufficiently developed controls over restrictive business practices under their national laws to curtail anti-competitive behaviour of firms.[98] Developing countries are more likely to use tax-relief-oriented incentives. Exemptions from corporate income tax, known as "tax holidays", are popular, particularly among developing countries, because they are do not require extensive administration nor do they consume any governmental resources. For their part, developed countries more frequently employ financial incentives such as grants, subsidized loans or loan guarantees. Incentives are a key policy tool for many sub-national governments seeking to attract investors. This is especially true in the United States where there is a long tradition of state governments creating "enterprise zones" in which tax relief and other forms of assistance are granted to companies so that they locate within the jurisdiction. There is often intense competition among US states to entice firms through these initiatives with a view to stimulating the local economy by employment and infrastructure creation.[99]

The cycle of FDI regulation capturing investment incentives, as well as their withdrawal, has been alluded to by commentators. While initially being neutral or even hostile to foreign firms, host states move to promote FDI aggressively (the so-called "Red Carpet" stage), following which they engage in a period of prolonged privatization, after which the

---

large emerging economies, much of which has been achieved as a consequence of promotional efforts by home states).

[96] K.P. Thomas, *Investment Incentives and the Global Competition for Capital* (Palgrave MacMillan, New York 2011) Ch 7.

[97] S. James, 'Tax and Non-Tax Incentives and Investments: Evidence and Policy Implications' (World Bank Investment Climate Advisory Services, Washington DC September 2013).

[98] Muchlinski (n 21) 32–3.

[99] A. Peters, *Industrial Incentives: Competition Among American States and Cities* (Upjohn Institute, Kalamazoo, MI 2001).

presence of foreign firms begins to raise suspicion and ultimately resistance. This phase is characterized by the revocation of rights that had once been used to encourage FDI but now appear excessive or even indicative of corruption. The next stage is therefore one in which the level of FDI declines.[100] Studies have shown that MNEs have become more responsive to locational incentives, such as tax breaks and free factory space, and that competition between developed and developing countries to attract FDI through these initiatives is intensifying.[101] Comprehensive data on the usage of investment incentives remains elusive, despite incentives' status as some of the most important policy tools employed by countries engaging in FDI.[102]

(ii) Justifications

The use of FDI incentives can be explained by reference to information asymmetry the foreign firm and the host state, with the investor often unfamiliar with the regulatory environment in the host state and the state uncertain as to the precise benefits that the foreign investor can bring to its economy. Furthermore, shortcomings in the investment climate in the host state can be problematic. This can include deficiencies in the infrastructure, a poorly trained workforce and weak domestic governance, including rule of law and protection of private property. As such, the incentive is well-described as a tool of risk mitigation.

The economic rationale for providing incentives to foreign firms is to capture the spillovers associated with FDI, meaning advantages accruing to the wider economy of the host state beyond the recipient firm. In that sense, the benefits of incentives are those that are typically associated with FDI itself, including employment, the transfer of firm-specific assets to the host jurisdiction (such as factories, as well as intellectual property), managerial expertise and technological advancement and the stimulation of competition. These are often described as the "dynamic" effects of FDI, such as the technological improvements to the domestic industry and cost reductions by local firms resulting from gaining know-how through exposure to the production activities of foreign partners or even competitors. Foreign firms can attract anchor investments or clusters, providing multiplier effects by signalling economic prosperity and through the creation of backward linkages in the form of purchase or supply arrangements with the local economy. Many of these positive

---

100 Walde and Kolo (n 91) 309.

101 Moran (n 92) 293.

102 Subrahmanyam (n 81) 301.

externalities create more value to the host country than they do to the investing firm.

If the profits available to foreign investors are not sufficiently high, then the investor will choose not to locate in the host state and these benefits will be lost. Accordingly, incentives intend to account for the difference between private and social rates of return – encouraging socially productive investment that would not have occurred on a purely private, that is, firm level assessment.[103] Incentives have the potential to contribute to an efficient allocation of resources where market prices and private self-interest does not fully capture social benefits. As such, investment incentives may be viewed as an appropriate instrument of governmental policy for the correction of market failures, or, put another way, to address non-market needs, providing benefits for a state or its citizens that are not captured by market transactions. Some examples of this include cultural preservation and environmental protection.[104]

The continued support for FDI incentives by host countries suggests that investment incentives are effective in attracting FDI and that FDI in turn helps achieve economic goals.

Investment incentives remain important for national policymakers seeking to promote local production and employment. Some countries which operate highly focused investment incentive regimes, such as those directed at technology, have implemented these successfully. For example, the investment incentive schemes employed by Austria and Czech Republic have been effective because they are focused on projects that emphasized training of employees and the diffusion of technology as well as efforts to stimulate the development of underperforming regions.[105] The donation of greenfield land to encourage foreign automobile companies to invest was a helpful strategy for Romania, which managed to extract technological know-how from several European firms in the late 2000s.[106] Disregarding the effects of FDI on employment,

---

103 S. James (n 97).

104 D. Petrov, 'Prisoners No More: State Investment Relocation Incentives and the Prisoners' Dilemma' (2001) 33:1 *Case Western Reserve Journal of International Law* 71, 74.

105 'Investment Incentives: The Good, The Bad and the Ugly' (Vale Columbia Center on Sustainable International Investment (13–14 November 2013) 27, citing World Bank Investment Climate Advisory Services (2013) <http://ccsi.columbia.edu/files/2014/01/VCC_conference_paper_-_Draft_Nov_12.pdf> accessed 13 March 2015.

106 K. Hope and T. Troev, 'Manufacturing: Autos Emerge as Driving Force' *Financial Times* (London, 4 December 2012).

which are often difficult to measure because workers employed by foreign firms may have eventually found work at domestic firms, there is strong evidence that FDI leads to higher productivity in industrialized countries. Observed spillovers tend to be enjoyed by other firms located close to the site of foreign direct investment and in the same industry, typically with a similar level of overall technology.[107] One study has shown that sectors targeted by investment-promotion initiatives received twice as much FDI as those sectors which did not receive the promotional assistance and twice as much in the same sector than before the initiatives were instigated.[108]

Incentives may be used to compensate for an unfavourable policy environment in the host state. In developing countries in particular, a significant number of economic activities are either totally controlled by the government or else heavily regulated. In heavily regulated countries, such policies may themselves be viewed as a market distortion; in which case, incentives may be viewed as a corrective device, allowing firms to achieve favourable returns. As such, incentives have a compensatory function. Incentives attempt to achieve some or all of these goals by increasing the rate of return, reducing or redistributing the costs and risks associated with an investment.[109] It can be difficult for over-regulated or high-risk countries to attract FDI in the absence of a structured investment incentive program, particularly in the wake of high profile political upheavals and persistent civil unrest.[110] Countries with a high level of political risk tend to be more likely to use investment incentives as a means of attracting FDI, with incentives compensating for greater risk.[111] The presence of an investment incentive may act as a signal to foreign firms that the donor state is business friendly or that it is eager to provide

---

[107] X. Liu, P. Siler, C. Wang and Y. Wei, 'Productivity Spillovers from Foreign Direct Investment: Evidence from UK Industry Panel Data' (2000) 31 *Journal of International Business Studies* 407–25.

[108] T. Harding and B. Javorcik, 'Roll Out the Red Carpet and They Will Come' 72 *Columbia FDI Perspectives* 18 June 2012.

[109] Subrahmanyam (n 91) 303.

[110] For example, Egypt had difficulty attracting FDI after its revolution in January 2011: I. Kottasova, 'Czechs in Egypt's First Post-Mubarak Foreign Direct Investment' *Financial Times* (London, 21 September 2011).

[111] Y. Zheng, 'Credibility and Flexibility: Political Institutions, Governance and Foreign Direct Investment' (2011) 37:3 *International Interactions: Empirical and Theoretical Research in International Relations* 293–5 (observing a high correlation between political risk and FDI incentives).

an environment that is conducive to commercial profitability, even if there is less tangible indication of this.[112]

One of the chief advantages of investment-promotion programs is mitigating information and communication barriers.[113] Perhaps most interesting, investment-promotion efforts tend to work best in terms of attracting FDI in countries with less effective governments, higher corruption and a greater number of administrative hurdles involved in commercial activities.[114] As such, the chief advantage of investment-promotion schemes may be seen as the reduction of red tape, the degree of which is captured by indicia such as the World Bank's annual *Doing Business* reports.

Investment incentives are often used to counterbalance performance requirements, with some countries using a combination of both performance requirements and investment incentives to control the nature and extent of inward FDI, with investors forced to accept both as part of an overall package of conditions.[115] Studies have shown that a firm's receptiveness to investment incentives is dependent on the stage that it is in during its life-cycle, and the extent to which the incentive that is offered matches its needs at that moment. Newer firms may seek incentives that lower their initial expenses during the start-up phase, whereas more established firms wishing to internationalize are more likely to prefer tax-oriented incentives that will raise their profits. Investors at all stages of their life cycle want incentives that are transparent and understandable. Certainty in investment incentives is highly valued by foreign investors, as this facilitates forward planning and capital acquisition.[116]

(iii) Criticisms

Like classic trade-oriented subsidies, investment incentives tend to be economically inefficient. The utility of investment incentives as part of the economic strategy of a country is tied to the benefits that are engendered by FDI, which are by no means certain. For example, foreign

---

[112] Petrov (n 104) 80.

[113] Harding and Javorcik (n 108). This study involved US investors, so it could be concluded that the same effects would be observed wherever the host state's language and culture differs from that of its inward investors.

[114] ibid.

[115] S. Amarasinha and J. Kokott, 'Multilateral Investment Rules Revisited' in F. Ortino and C. Schreuer (eds), *Oxford Handbook of International Investment Law* (OUP, Oxford 2008) 145.

[116] James (n 97).

firms may use fewer domestic inputs than the equivalent domestic firm and employment opportunities may be limited to those which do not enhance the skills of workers. Furthermore, foreign firms may repatriate rather than re-invest their profits, meaning that much of the economic benefits may be enjoyed by their home state. This is particularly the case in the extractive industries, where profits tend to be more readily sent to shareholders in the home state after up-front capital expenditures have been made. Such strategies will dictate the nature of incentive packages offered by host states to various industries, often in conjunction with performance requirements to maximize the beneficial impacts on the host economy.[117]

The chief drivers of inefficient incentives are asymmetries in information among many target countries and inequality of bargaining power between the host state and the foreign firm. Host states are often at an informational disadvantage regarding the expected benefits of an FDI project relative to the investor itself. When they are unable to ascertain the investor's capabilities or intentions such information asymmetry can lead to host governments paying too much for investment or granting redundant incentives, meaning that incentives do not feature in the investor's decision to invest. Governments often do not know what incentive schemes are being offered by competing jurisdictions, just as large MNEs are often better able to assess the economic impacts of their investments than host states. Smaller states may not have the capacity to negotiate with large MNEs as to the specific conditions, such as performance requirements, that may be provided in conjunction with a tailored incentive scheme, allowing the MNE to seek exploitative packages. Such asymmetries can be exacerbated by the increasing use of site consultants: individuals who are hired by firms or governments to assess the impact of an investment project and which may misrepresent estimates.

Clearly there are both direct and indirect costs associated with fiscal incentives. The direct costs of a fiscal incentive are the revenue losses that occur as a result of the state granting tax benefits to a foreign investor that would have invested even without the incentive. The indirect costs are often more difficult to measure but can be numerous. There may be market distortions that result from encouraging new investments that undermine the success of existing ones. Firms often spend much time and money in lobbying the government for incentives, which may not be recovered. If the incentives are conditional on firms fulfilling certain

---

[117] Vale Columbia report (n 105) 11.

goals, such as those linked to employment or location, the resources expended satisfying these conditions can be considerable. Tax exemptions may lead to illegal behaviour, where firms that do not qualify for the incentive present false information in order to do so. This can in turn represent government expenditures in investigation and enforcement, not to mention the ongoing cost to governments of administering the incentive scheme.

It is far from certain that FDI incentives are actually effective in inducing foreign investors to locate within the offering state. It is also not clear that FDI itself actually achieves many of the economic benefits with which it is associated. Many factors will influence a firm's decision on where to locate its operations. These can include the natural endowments of the host state and the size of the local market, the skills of the labour force, political stability, the extent of the infrastructure and the quality of the regulatory environment, including regard for private property. A majority of studies indicate that investment incentives play a limited role in investment decisions, and as such they generally fail to stimulate economic growth.[118] Firms which internationalize in order to enter new markets or to acquire raw materials or strategic assets are less inclined to make locational decisions on account of incentives than more mobile and efficiency-seeking firms aiming to reducing costs for products destined for global rather than domestic markets.[119] One survey indicated that incentive packages ranked very low in terms of the factors influencing a firm's locational decision. Economic stability, political stability, costs of raw materials, the local market, transparency of business regulations and legal framework, availability of skilled labour, labour costs, quality of life and the availability of local suppliers were seen as more important for investors.[120] The IMF and the World Bank also tended to advise countries against offering FDI incentives, because they are largely ineffective in achieving economic growth and because a country's institutional infrastructure is a more important determinant in MNE's location decisions than a country's incentive regime.[121]

Exemptions from income tax are heavily criticized by economists. One of the reasons for this is that when tax holidays are granted, the

---

[118] See Petrov (n 104) 79.

[119] Vale Columbia report (n 105) 16.

[120] 'Africa Investor Report 2011: Towards Evidence-Based Investment Promotion Strategies' (UNIDO, 2011) <www.unido.org/fileadmin/user_media/Publications/Pub_free/AIS_Report_A4.pdf> accessed 2 December 2014.

[121] J. Stotsky, 'Summary of IMF Tax Policy Advice' in P. Shome (ed.), *Tax Policy Handbook* (International Monetary Fund, 1995) 292-82.

assessment of the amount of tax revenue that a government will forgo can be problematic. Moreover, income tax holidays tend not to be associated with conditions that could be beneficial for the host state, such as local employment quotas or mandatory reinvestment of earnings. As such, this type of incentive tends not to be paired with a foreign investor's performance requirement. This type of incentive does little to prevent an early departure of the foreign investor when its profits increase relative to the tax revenue that the government has exempted it from. There may come a point where the value of staying in a jurisdiction evaporates as the level of exempted tax becomes insignificant. Tax holidays generally appeal to high profit investment – those where there is major tax liability – rather than those in an early or exploratory phase of their development. FDI-oriented tax incentives work to attract FDI in a minority of instances.[122]

Consequently, there may be a strong likelihood that the MNE would have made the investment in the relevant host state irrespective of the income tax exemption. FDI-oriented tax incentives appear to work to attract FDI in a minority of instances.[123] An additional concern is that tax holidays can lead to more situations where there has been transfer pricing – a strategy by which firms artificially segregate the profit-generating features of their activities to low income tax jurisdictions, an arrangement which can deprive the host state of significant revenue. This is particularly problematic where the foreign investor transfers the profit generating aspects of its business back to its home jurisdiction – effectively channelling the greatest part of its tax out of the host state and in so doing undermining one of the central premises in support of FDI. Such strategies are likely one of the reasons that many countries have actively pursued outward FDI support programmes.[124] Studies have shown that, when FDI is supported by regional aid from the host government, firms are more likely to locate in less economic and prosperous areas, but that their location decision is contingent on ongoing financial aid from government. Accordingly, the entry of FDI does not usually create a self-sustaining local economy.[125]

---

[122] *The McKinsey Report* (2003), as discussed by A. Beattie, 'Report Casts Doubt on FDI Incentives' *Financial Times* (London, 15 October 2003).

[123] ibid.

[124] Vale Columbia report (n 105) 55.

[125] C. Wren and J. Jones, 'Assessing the Regional Impact of Grants on FDI Location: Evidence from UK Regional Policy, 1985–05' (2011) 51 *Journal of Regional Science* 497.

In addition to their dubious economic benefits for the states that impose them, these types of international economic policy tools are criticized for their discretionary and secretive nature.[126] Investment incentives often reflect political machinations, in as much as the economic advantages they entail are disproportionate to their costs, or the benefits to be gained are distributed unevenly, typically on the basis of perceived political advantage. From a political standpoint, extending investment incentives only to foreign firms tends to please small interest groups who benefit disproportionately from FDI. These are likely to be domestic suppliers, distributors or partners of foreign investors. These groups are more likely to dominate when institutional factors are weak, such as a democratically elected government and independent courts. This explains why foreign-only incentives tend to be higher in countries with poor governance than in countries that have stronger institutions.[127] When political institutions are robust, governments are more likely to offer broad based incentives that benefit the economy at large.

Failure to ensure that investment incentives are dispensed in a transparent manner can lead to an invidious situation of disguised favouritism or cronyism.[128] Studies conducted in the US have demonstrated that investment incentives allow politicians to take credit for firms' decisions to locate in specific areas. Similarly, failure to provide adequate incentives allow politicians to minimize the blame associated with firms' decisions to leave the jurisdiction.[129] Regardless of their effects on either national or global economies, because of their strong political overtones, investment incentives also represent an opportunity for government corruption. Governmental officials entrusted with wide discretionary powers could enact legislation offering assistance to foreign firms in order to advance their own personal or business interests, irrespective of whether the assistance is in the public interest.[130] Even in the absence of

---

[126] Picciotto (n 47) 163.

[127] Y. Zheng, 'Credibility and Flexibility: Political Institutions, Governance and Foreign Direct Investment' (2011) 37:3 *International Interactions: Empirical and Theoretical Research in International Relations* 293–5.

[128] As has been associated with India, for example: A. Dubey, 'Key Tasks for a Strong Modi Government' *Financial Times* (London, 15 May 2014).

[129] N. Jensen, E. Malesky, M. Medina and U. Ozdemir, 'Pass the Bucks: Investment Incentives as Political Credit-Claiming Devices: Evidence from a Survey Experiment' (Working Paper, Washington University in St Louis, 30 June 2010) <https://pages.wustl.edu/files/pages/imce/nathanjensen/passthebucks workingpaper.pdf> accessed 2 December 2014.

[130] A. Nov, 'The "Bidding War" to Attract Foreign Investment: The Need for a Global Solution' (2005) 25 *Virginia Tax Review* 835, 842–3.

full-on corruption, the need to earn the support of influential interest groups may be viewed as a subversion of the democratic process, particularly in jurisdictions with a strong lobbying culture or without sufficient safeguards against political donations.

It is widely recognized that financial incentives are a direct drain on government budgets. Tax incentives diminish the tax base, depriving the host state of revenue, but also complicate tax administration. There can be significant costs associated with designing and implementing a coherent investment-promotion strategy or establishing an investment-promotion agency. Even improvements in transparency can place significant burdens on states with limited resources.[131] In some instances, incentives are given for investments in which there are carrying costs that governments themselves are not in a position to manage due to limited resources. Such costs are foisted onto foreign investors, who are in turn compensated through incentives.[132] This explains why they are not offered by developing countries. It can also represent serious financial costs to governments. It is often thought that the country which wins the incentive bidding war and ultimately attracts the foreign firm is most probably the one that has held the most unrealistically optimistic view of the benefits likely to be achieved.[133] A state that grants an incentive may have fewer resources to spend on education or infrastructure, which may render it less appealing to investors seeking skilled employees or a sophisticated transportation network. It may also result in a waste of governmental funds that would have been better deployed elsewhere because the benefits associated with FDI may be negated by the cost to the government of providing the incentive in the first place.[134]

Often the presence of an incentive indicates that there is an absence of strict regulations in many spheres, which can be attractive to foreign firms. This can in turn lead to the potential for environmental degradation and abuse of employees. Investment incentives may encourage investment, but the nature of the incentive may lead the investor to behave in undesirable ways when it is engaging in its investment project. For example, government subsidies on inputs such as water and electricity may cause the investor to waste resources or worse, prevent them from

---

[131] VanDuzer et al. (n 24) 495.

[132] Subrahmanyam (n 91) 302.

[133] M. Daly, 'Investment Incentives and the Multilateral Agreement on Investment' (1998) 32:2 *Journal of World Trade* 5, 6.

[134] Amarasinha and Kokott (n 115) 145.

implementing the very technologies that had made them attractive as investors in the first place.[135]

There can be a misalignment of the costs and benefits associated with investment incentives with the benefits of an investment project being captured by the government in office at the time, with the costs foisted onto future governments – a situation which can be worsened if inappropriate discount rates are used to gauge future impacts. The cost–benefit calculus can be problematic where there is no counterfactual that can be properly evaluated: the government cannot know what would have happened had the particular incentive package that it offered had not been offered, or if it had been less generous. Difficulties in setting the optimal incentive scheme to attract investors may be inevitable as a consequence of the increasing mobility of capital, meaning that even where attractive incentive packages are granted, global firms may easily locate elsewhere to respond to a more desirable scheme in another location after a short period of time.[136]

In a competition among host states to attract foreign investment, the state that succeeds may achieve short-term benefits, but this may be unnecessarily costly. The government is forced to offer a package that is better than that of other jurisdictions or else it will lose the competition. This could create a situation in which the use of investment incentives becomes normalized, conferring an advantage on investors at the expense of the general welfare. As such, competition for incentives may be described as a problem of collective action. This is a situation where multiple individuals would benefit as a group from a certain choice, but this choice has a cost which makes it irrational for any one individual to bear and resolve on its own. The action should be undertaken in a manner in which the cost of the action is shared by all. An individual government does not wish to limit its capacity to employ incentives to achieve an advantage over a competing jurisdiction where there is no indication that other jurisdictions have shown any willingness to restrain their own use of these tools. The self-interest of each state encourages a "race to the bottom" towards the most generous and often excessive incentive packages – playing into the hands of the foreign firms.[137]

At a global level, the proliferation of various varieties of investment incentives may severely distort the global distribution of FDI without necessarily increasing its total supply. Consequently, the main argument

---

135 Salacuse (n 14) 102–3.

136 Vale Columbia report (n 105) 73–4.

137 Thomas (n 96) ch 2.

against the use of investment incentives as mechanisms to attract foreign investment is that they can lead to FDI going to jurisdictions where it achieves less utility from an efficiency perspective. The international dimension of investment incentives is controversial, because of the understanding that host state assistance for foreign investors represents a form of international competition that can lead to damaging outcomes. The OECD in particular has described the strategy of seeking to outdo other countries in offering the most attractive incentives as one that is individually rational; but on a collective, global scale there are unintended consequences, namely subsidization of inefficient firms to the detriment of public resources.[138] Some countries are pressured into offering assistance packages to foreign investors that they would not otherwise extend out of fear that the investor will lose interest and go elsewhere. As such, the offering of incentives for FDI is a classic example of the race to the bottom scenario. Bidding wars among jurisdictions to appeal to the best firms through increasingly generous incentives (notably tax relief) have been condemned by commentators as a serious market distortion in which governments overpay – meaning that they offer more in incentives than they ultimately gain by way of economic advantage, leading to the so-called "winner's curse".[139] The state that manages to succeed in attracting the foreign investor tends to be the one that has offered the most in concessions, which may ultimately be damaging relative to the gains that the foreign investor can offer because such generous packages are required to beat out other jurisdictions, even if this may seem to be economically irrational behaviour. Losing states also suffer because they often expend resources in courting investors that are never recovered. States compete for investors, rather than the opposite, because there are comparatively few large investors compared to the number of governments who seek them, especially when sub-national governments are considered.[140] In the words of the OECD: "competitive investment incentives support industries for political rather than economic reasons … they tend to be offered to the most mobile producers and not to 'captive' producers".[141] In other words, governments tend to offer incentives to firms that are in a position to pick and choose

[138] OECD, 'Incentives-Based Competition for Foreign Direct Investment: The Case of Brazil' (OECD Working Papers on International Investment No. 2003/1, 2003) 8.

[139] Nov (n 130) 842–3.

[140] K. Thomas, 'EU Control of State Aid to Mobile Investment in Comparative Perspective' (2012) 34:6 *European Journal of Integration* 567, 570–71.

[141] OECD (n 138) 10.

among target destinations, not to firms that would be willing to make long term commitments to the host state, or which may already be located there and would therefore be unwilling to bear the cost of re-locating. There is clear evidence that "incentive competition", as it is often termed, does take place, although much of the research into this phenomenon has focused on regional competition at the sub-national level within particular countries.[142] The economic integration brought about by globalization is believed to have tightened the conditions of competition for FDI, creating a situation in which countries rush to establish tailor-made packages to attract foreign investors, rather than by establishing a favourable business environment in the long term. Much of these initiatives are non-transparent, meaning that they are arranged bilaterally between host governments and target companies with little input from the electorate or through open competition.[143]

Developing countries are often in direct competition with wealthier countries for a particular investment. There are often situations where developing countries end up offering much more generous incentives than those paid for in developed countries. The unfortunate consequence of such arrangements is the reduction of available resources for infrastructure and education. It is often asserted that the capacity to offer such advantages to foreign firms privileges wealthier countries, some of which are able to extend public funds to support research and development or to make sure that the foreign investors operations are located in a region of high unemployment. Poorer states are often relegated to extending incentives in the form of tax relief or generous depreciation allowances which, unlike direct grants, do not require an immediate expenditure even though they diminish future government revenue.[144]

Finally, as the protections enshrined in IIAs are viewed as a form of incentive that minimizes some of the risks associated with FDI, criticisms levied at these instruments should be noted. Chief among these is the allegation, of particular relevance in conjunction with the ongoing negotiation of the Transatlantic Trade and Investment Partnership (TTIP), that investor–state dispute settlement is unfairly discriminatory against local investors because it offers a means of dispute settlement that is available only to foreign firms. This has been depicted by some as a

---

[142] Predominately among US states: see e.g. M. Taylor, 'A Proposal to Prohibit Industrial Relations Subsidies' (1994) 72 *Texas Law Review* 669.

[143] L. Oxelheim, 'EU–China and the Non-Transparent Race for Inward FDI' (2008) 19:4 *Journal of Asian Economics* 358.

[144] Picciotto (n 47) 163.

violation of the principal of equality before the law.[145] The potential for massive damages awards levied against host states, some of which are ill-positioned to satisfy them because of their developmental status, is similarly problematic both from a perspective of global equity as well as questionable incentive strategy for states seeking beneficial FDI.

3. CONCLUSION

The nature and purpose of performance requirements and investment incentives as applied by host states in conjunction with their regulation of foreign investment presents a complex picture of numerous advantages and drawbacks, some of which cannot be readily quantified and which remain a source of debate for economists and politicians. Their implementation requires the careful consideration of various competing policies, including the need to stimulate FDI while ensuring that the ensuing competition does not adversely affect the local economy. Negotiation over the FDI incentives and any conditions imposed thereon between host states and firms can be fraught with information asymmetries often resulting in a situation in which the government ends up surrendering more than it gains. From a regulatory standpoint, investment incentives, whether conditional or traditional, can risk discriminating against certain firms based on their nationality, compromising one of the central pillars of international economic law. It is this second issue that will be the focus of the next chapter.

---

145 Speech by J.C. Juncker, Strasbourg, 22 October 2014.

2. The national treatment standard and differential treatment of foreign investors

1. INTRODUCTION: PERFORMANCE REQUIREMENTS AND INVESTMENT INCENTIVES AS DISCRIMINATORY TREATMENT

As outlined in the previous chapter, the central premise of this book is that international economic law has paid insufficient regard to the control of performance requirements and investment incentives. This has resulted in the potential for economic inefficiencies, expressed as market distortions, as well as insufficient regard to legitimate social aims where these contradict the principle of competitive equality among economic actors as a normative foundation of international economic law. As performance requirements imposed by host states tend to be placed upon foreign investors, but not upon domestic investors in equivalent situations, they are inherently discriminatory.[1] To be sure, some investment incentive packages do not distinguish between foreign or domestic investors, but are offered instead based on the commercial activities of the particular beneficiaries. Still, foreign firms are quite often better placed to take advantage of certain incentives (especially those with conditions such as performance requirements attached) because they are more flexible in terms of their location choice, and are more likely to engage in research and development and to invest in strategic sectors of importance to the granting state.[2] In addition to the economic distortions tied to discrimination against local firms, if foreign firms are given preferred treatment

[1] M. Sornarajah, *The International Law on Foreign Investment* (CUP, Cambridge 2010) 202.

[2] 'Background Paper for the Eighth Columbia International Investment Conference on Investment Incentives: The Good, The Bad and the Ugly' (Vale Columbia Center on Sustainable International Investment, 13–14 November 2013) 26, citing World Bank Investment Climate Advisory Services (2013)

relative to domestic investors, then this can undermine the continued political support for international agreements as a tool of integration into the world economy.[3]

Thus as a starting point of the analysis of the manner in which these discriminatory policies are regulated under international law, performance requirements can be said to conflict with the national treatment guarantee found in most IIAs, as well as several agreements of the WTO that have an impact on FDI. This chapter will introduce the national treatment standard through a preliminary examination of how it has been applied in trade and investment law as a means of defeating discrimination. The extent to which these concepts inform international economic law's engagement with performance requirements and investment incentives will be addressed in later chapters. This chapter is therefore premised on the assertion that an understanding of the national treatment standard from both the trade and investment perspectives is essential to grasp the tension between these policy tools and the legitimate expectations of foreign investors.

National treatment is a relative standard, prohibiting states from treating local firms better than foreign firms when applying their laws and procedures. This guarantee necessitates a comparison between the regulatory conditions faced by equivalent domestic and foreign investors, as well as or often in conjunction with an assessment of the goods or services which they produce and to whom they are sold. In a related but antithetical fashion, investment incentives offered by governments to foreign investors in order to encourage them to locate within host states or to engage in certain varieties of economic activity may also be viewed as discriminatory, because they extend favourable treatment to foreign investors over domestic investors. This is also a departure from the general principle of equality of competitive conditions within markets that is embraced by international economic law. In such circumstances better-than-national treatment, which may be available to foreign investors as a consequence of the promise of treatment "no less favourable" contained in some IIAs, can be an essential way to augment FDI flows to host states where the regulatory infrastructure is deficient even for local businesses. While still relative because it establishes a comparator to the treatment enjoyed (or not enjoyed) by the equivalent domestic investor,

---

<http://ccsi.columbia.edu/files/2014/01/VCC_conference_paper_-_Draft_Nov_12.pdf> accessed 2 December 2014.

[3] B. Hoekman and R. Newfarmer, 'Preferential Trade Agreements, Investment Disciplines and Investment Flows' (2005) 39:5 *Journal of World Trade* 949, 969.

such a guarantee sets a baseline of regulatory treatment by reference to the bare minimum of acceptable measures that are imposed by the domestic government on the equivalent local firm.

Despite the overarching importance of the national treatment standard as the guardian of equality among economic actors in international trade and investment law, the capacity of this obligation to control performance requirements and investment incentives is undermined by the lack of clarity in terms of the manner in which it is implemented in international treaties and interpreted by judicial bodies, especially international investment tribunals. As we will see later in this book, the interaction between national treatment and performance requirements and investment incentives is consequently often complicated and unsatisfactory from the perspective of predictability as well as efficiency. The national treatment standard may therefore be seen as a blunt instrument for addressing the challenge to competitive markets that are presented by performance requirements and investment incentives. This weakness is the result of indeterminacies in means of comparison between foreign and local investors, in particular the lack of sufficient economic analysis in the investment disputes, the provision's limited scope of coverage in IIAs to post-establishment interference by host states, and insufficient supervision by policy-oriented exceptions in IIAs to control protectionism. Taken together, these shortcomings undercut national treatment's utility as a guardian of competitive equality in international economic law. This insufficiency necessitates more direct, formal and comprehensive treatment of performance requirements and investment incentives, methodology which will be explored throughout the rest of this book.

As indicated above, this chapter will illustrate the nature and purpose of the national treatment standard as it has been implemented in international economic law. It will consider the way in which non-discrimination against investors and their investments on the basis of national origin has been approached by trade and investment tribunals, illustrating the doctrinally uncertain instrumentation of this standard from the perspective of safeguarding competitive markets and controlling protectionism. It will conclude by suggesting that international investment tribunals should adopt a more economically rigorous analysis of the effects of nationality-based discrimination, one that is more in keeping with the more concrete competition-focused evaluations seen in the national treatment jurisprudence of the WTO. This would help engender economic efficiencies while permitting regulatory transgressions that do not have a disguised purpose of advantaging uncompetitive local firms. Before embarking on this analysis it is first necessary to consider briefly the origins and purpose of the national treatment standard in international economic law.

2. ECONOMIC JUSTIFICATIONS FOR NATIONAL TREATMENT OF FOREIGN INVESTORS

National treatment is not a principle of international law that exists independently of the treaties in which it is found. Rather, it is a standard of treatment that is extended to aliens by states expressly through written agreement. It cannot be read into a treaty where it does not appear and its precise effect depends upon the wording that has been used in the relevant instrument and how this is subsequently interpreted by a tribunal. National treatment is therefore a relative standard in two senses: first, it is contingent upon the equivalence between two investors, one of which is domestic and one foreign; second, it depends on the interpretive approach of the adjudicator applying the standard in a given context, an exercise which is itself coloured by the lack of consistent treaty language, at least in the investment context.[4] In curtailing nationality-based discrimination, national treatment is both at the root of the aversion that international economic law has shown for performance requirements and the attractiveness of investment incentives as an aid to inward FDI.

National treatment is linked to the notion of state responsibility for injury to aliens, found for example in the United Nations Charter of Economic Rights and Duties of States.[5] This was linked to the Calvo Doctrine, which posited that foreign investors were required to use local courts, rather than those of their home country, effectively precluding diplomatic protection.[6] The national treatment standard grew in prominence throughout the late twentieth century as developing country host states began to exceed the minimum standards of treatment understood by customary international law. This rendered the treatment of foreign investors relative to local investors a vital mechanism for safeguarding

---

[4] See e.g. A. Bjorklund, 'The Standard of National Treatment' in K. Yannica-Small (ed.), *Arbitration Under International Investment Agreements: An Analysis of the Key Jurisdictional, Substantive and Procedural Issues* (OUP, Oxford 2010).

[5] United Nations A/Res/29/3281 (entered into force 12 December 1974) Art. 2(2)(c).

[6] S. Montt, *State Liability in Investment Treaty Arbitration* (Hart, Oxford 2009) 38–45.

the expectations of high-risk commercial projects overseas.[7] In that sense it is quite correct to suggest that national treatment has its origins, at least in the investment context, as an instrument of diplomatic protection.[8] While it purports to eradicate discrimination against foreign investors on the basis of the origins of the products they use or their nationality of ownership and in so doing should encourage FDI, the national treatment standard has the potential for deep encroachment on national sovereignty. Laws that may have a legitimate social purpose but which inescapably place a disproportionate burden on foreign firms can be called into question by international authorities, such as WTO panels or investment tribunals. Precluding favouritism towards local firms can undermine a host country's capacity to govern not simply its own economy, but possibly many aspects of domestic social policy that may be affected by the presence of foreign firms, such as national security, culture, the environment and even indigenous rights. As such it could be said that the national treatment standard derogates from that which is achieved by host states through their imposition of performance requirements on foreign investors. It follows that the standard should be applied in a manner that is sensitive to overarching purposes of the agreements in which it is found such as "economic development"[9] and "promoting prosperity"[10] of the states which grant it, as dictated by the Vienna Convention on the Law of Treaties.[11]

In international trade law the purpose of national treatment is focused on the prohibition of discrimination by WTO members against products and services originating from foreign countries.[12] These rules can impact strongly on foreign investors as well as on traders. National treatment in WTO law originated primarily in order to ensure that tariff concessions, secured over many decades of multilateral negotiations under the GATT, would not be circumvented by the use of discriminatory internal measures, like taxes or regulations such as those governing the conditions on

7 N. DiMascio and J. Pauwelyn, 'Non-discrimination in Trade and Investment Treaties: Worlds Apart or Two Sides of the Same Coin' (2008) 102 *American Journal of International Law* 48, 67.

8 R. Howse and E. Chalamish, 'The Use and Abuse of WTO Law in Investor–State Arbitration: A Reply to Jurgen Kurtz' (2009) 20:4 *European Journal of International Law* 1087, 1090.

9 Preamble of the WTO Agreement (1 January 1995).

10 Preamble to the Japan–Iraq BIT (7 June 2012).

11 Art. 31(1) (signed 23 May 1969).

12 GATT Art. III. The GATS protects the suppliers of the service as well as the service itself, whereas GATT only protects the product itself: see below.

the sale or distribution of foreign products.[13] Accordingly, it has been stated by the WTO Appellate Body that the purpose of national treatment (at least under the GATT) is to avoid protectionism, restore equality of competitive conditions and protect expectations of equal competitive relationships.[14] National treatment therefore represents the foundation of the WTO's foundational principle of comparative advantage: nations should specialize in the production of that which they are relatively best at and trade for everything else, a doctrine that works only when goods from overseas do not face regulatory barriers that alter their appeal to domestic consumers, primarily because they are artificially more expensive. This ethos is in turn premised on the now widely-accepted premise that the most efficient use of the world's resources is achieved by eliminating discrimination-based distortions in the international markets for goods as well as services.[15] Under the WTO, however, certain non-economic matters are given primacy over the guarantee of non-discrimination, provided that they are not implemented as a strategic means of suppressing international trade.[16] Moreover, article III(8)(b) of the GATT provides that the national treatment requirement does not prevent the payment of subsidies exclusively to national producers, facilitating some forms of economic assistance. The scope of this carve-out is relatively limited because, as will be explored further in Chapter 5, a Member may not make the receipt of a subsidy contingent upon the purchase by the recipient of domestic over imported goods

In international investment law, national treatment requires that the host state make no negative differentiation between foreign and national investors when applying its rules and regulations. This ensures that the foreign investors and their investments enjoy the same level of treatment as nationals, allowing them to compete on an equal footing in a given domestic market. Thus a company can survive and prosper because of the quality of its goods and services, not because of regulatory favouritism at the hands of the state in which it operates. Recognition of the importance of equality in commercial opportunity led UNCTAD to describe national treatment as the "single most important standard of treatment enshrined

---

[13] S. Lester, B. Mercurio and A. Davies, *World Trade Law: Text: Materials and Commentary* (Hart, Oxford 2006) 266.

[14] Appellate Body Report, Korea – Alcoholic Beverages WT/DS75/AB/R (adopted 17 February 1999) [120].

[15] E.g. S. Beugeldijk, S. Brakman, H. Garretsen and C. Van Marrwijk, *International Economics and Business* (2nd edn, CUP, Cambridge 2013) 137–41.

[16] As in Art. XX of the GATT and Art. XIV of the GATS. These issues will be revisited in Chapters 3 and 4.

in international investment agreements".[17] While the goal of averting protectionism is not explicitly stated in the text of IIAs, this objective can be inferred from the value placed on attracting FDI and how this can be suppressed through domestic regulations that give advantages to domestic suppliers of capital.[18] In contrast with the WTO regime, few IIAs constrain national treatment by reference to explicit social policy goals like the environment or culture, although this may be changing.[19]

So it would seem that from the perspective of enhancing FDI flows, the purpose of national treatment, in either international trade or investment law, is to ensure that there is a degree of equality among firms within domestic markets. The economic concept of competitive markets, outlined briefly in the previous chapter, can therefore be understood as one of the central doctrinal constructs upon which the concept of non-discrimination on the basis of national origin is based. In WTO law this permits traders to export their goods to foreign markets and sell them there as if they had been produced locally. In IIAs national treatment guarantees the protection of foreign investors from targeted attacks by host states as a consequence of their foreign character. National treatment thus eliminates distortions caused by unevenly applied laws, achieving economic efficiency by allowing the best producers to supply consumers based on the quality and price of their goods and services, which is itself achieved either by selling to new markets or lowering production costs abroad.[20] The national treatment standard facilitates FDI by assuring foreign investors that their often considerable ex ante resource commitments are relatively safe from arbitrary state action, mitigating the chilling effect of excessive and unpredictable state interference after the decision has been taken to invest.

---

[17] UNCTAD, National Treatment, UNCTAD Series on Issues in International Investment Agreements (United Nations, New York and Geneva 1999) 1.

[18] J. Kurtz, 'The Merits and Limits of Comparativism: National Treatment in International Investment Law and the WTO' in S. Schill (ed.), *International Investment Law and Comparative Public Law* (OUP, Oxford 2010) 252–3.

[19] See e.g. J. Gaffney and J. Sarvaranthanam, 'Achieving Sustainable Development in International Investment: Could Future IIAs Impose Sustainable Development-Related Obligations on Investors' Columbia FDI Perspectives, No. 108, 11 November 2013. These issues will be explored further in Chapters 5 and 6.

[20] K. Reinert, *An Introduction to International Economics* (CUP, Cambridge 2012) 146–8.

In a few IIAs, notably those of the US and Canada[21], national treatment goes further by permitting foreign investors to access local markets on equal terms, precluding the imposition of conditions such as the nationality of the investor or the origin of the products which they use. Such a "right of entry", which is often subject to significant restrictions, further promotes FDI because it effectively eliminates national regulatory boundaries. This pre-establishment national treatment can therefore be rightly viewed as one of the basic policy instruments of economic globalization. It should be said that the effectiveness of national treatment, or indeed of IIAs generally, in augmenting global FDI flows remains questionable, but compelling statistical evidence has shown a positive correlation between IIA signage and inward FDI flows.[22] In other words, the promise of receiving national treatment, even only at the post-establishment stage, acts as an incentive for firms to internationalize.

A second, perhaps somewhat less important economic justification for extending equal regulatory treatment to domestic and foreign firms through the national treatment standard is that it is costly for a government to maintain two (or more) distinct regulatory regimes, one for locals and one for aliens. Having one system of rule-making and enforcement for all commercial actors regardless of origin can lead to administrative efficiencies and the conservation of often scarce resources.[23] This is one of the reasons why commentators have suggested that differences in treatment among foreign and local firms should be expected to progressively disappear on their own, irrespective of treaty-based guarantees.[24] This is of course provided that any welfare gains from imposing a discriminatory burden on a foreign firm does not itself finance the cost of the two-tiered regulatory system.

Still, in many states without a tradition of administrative efficiency, equality of competitive opportunities may offer limited comfort to foreign investors where there is unpredictable and arbitrary governmental interference in the commercial affairs of the state's own citizens. Clearly

---

21 E.g. Canada–Latvia Art. II.3 (26 April 1995); United States–Jordan Art. II.1 (2 July 1997).

22 T. Buthe and H. Milner, 'Bilateral Investment Treaties and Foreign Direct Investment: A Political Analysis' in K. Sauvant and L. Sachs (eds), *The Effect of Treaties on Foreign Direct Investment* (OUP, New York NY 2009) 171–3.

23 K. Nadakuvakaren Schefer, *International Investment Law: Text, Cases and Materials* (Edward Elgar, Cheltenham 2013) 303.

24 S. Schill, *The Multilateralization of International Investment Law* (CUP, Cambridge 2009) 372.

in states lacking institutions such as independent courts and democratic elections, local businesses may suffer at the hands of their own governments, regularly facing expropriations or other damaging regulations. This is not discrimination on the basis of national origin, but simply a lack of due process or absence of the rule of law. In these situations some international minimum standard of treatment of aliens, drawn from customary international law rather than a specific treaty, is required to safeguard investors' property, a notion in many ways oppositional to formal national treatment.[25] Such reverse discrimination, while potentially damaging to local companies and contrary to the notion of equality of competitive opportunities, may be viewed as the first step towards improvements in governance capacity generally. This is thought to be one of the advantages of a liberalized stance towards FDI that is captured in twenty-first-century international economic law. China is often cited as an example of a state in which domestic economic governance has been reformed as a consequence of modifications to the domestic legal system aimed at attracting foreign investment.[26] If this is true, then it is arguably justifiable that domestic firms suffer relative to their foreign counterparts for some initial period before reforms take effect. This idea will be revisited again in Chapters 5 and 6 on investment incentives.

Finally, while economic justifications of national treatment tend to focus on the advantage of competitive equality which it accords supplying firms, it also has a significant positive secondary impact on consumers. National treatment, like its sister doctrine most favoured nation treatment, empowers consumers by giving them access to a greater range of goods and services at prices that are not artificially set to advantage particular producers. By ensuring that citizens are free from unnecessary state interference in transactions (either the product or its price), national treatment can be seen as an instrument of individual liberty,[27] at least as far as liberty can be captured in the freedom to participate in market transactions. This key but often overlooked function of the standard is

---

[25] S. Subedi, *International Investment Law: Reconciling Policy and Principle* (2nd edn, Hart, Oxford 2012) 72.

[26] S. Schill, 'Tearing Down the Great Wall: The New Generation Investment Treaties from the People's Republic of China' (2007) 15 *Cardozo Journal of International and Comparative Law* 73, 117.

[27] F. Garcia, *Trade, Inequality and Justice: Toward a Liberal Theory of Just Trade* (Transnational Publishers, Ardsley, NY 2003).

seen most clearly in GATT jurisprudence which focuses on consumer taste and preferences as well as concepts such as elasticity of demand.[28]

Having outlined the economic rationales for national treatment, this chapter will now consider how the standard has been developed in international trade law as it impacts upon foreign direct investment. This will then be contrasted with the somewhat less refined approach of international investment arbitration.

3. THE NATIONAL TREATMENT STANDARD IN INTERNATIONAL TRADE LAW

(i) National Treatment in WTO Agreements

National treatment is a cornerstone of WTO law and is found in numerous WTO agreements, including the original GATT of 1947. National treatment provisions may have a direct impact on FDI and can structure the use of a host state's performance requirements and possibly also investment incentives. The link between non-discrimination and the imposition of trade-based performance requirements and investment incentives will be explored further in Chapters 3 and 4 respectively. The nature of national treatment in Free Trade Agreements (FTAs) will not be explored in this chapter, with Chapters 3 and 5 also examining the role of various key FTAs in controlling performance requirements and investment incentives.

There are several instances of national treatment protection found in WTO Agreements that are important for the regulation (protecting of existing) as well as liberalization (facilitating new) FDI. The chief national treatment obligation for measures affecting trade in goods are Articles III:2 and III:4 of the GATT. Article III:2 states that products originating from one WTO Member that are imported into another Member cannot be subjected, either directly or indirectly, to internal taxes or charges of any kind that are in excess of those applied to like domestic products. Article III:4 provides more generally that the same obligation applies with respect to all laws, regulations and requirements affecting the internal sale, purchase, transportation or use of imported products. In addition to these two substantive guarantees, Article III:1 establishes an overarching principle of the prevention of protectionism of

---

28 E.g. Appellate Body Report, *Philippines – Taxes on Distilled Spirits* WT/DS396/AB/R (adopted 20 January 2012) [118].

domestic production (purposeful favouritism towards local suppliers) through internal regulations. Taken together, the national treatment obligations of the GATT prevent Members from treating imported products less favourably once the imported product has entered the domestic market, meaning once it has been cleared through customs and any tariffs have been paid. As suggested above, the essential function of GATT national treatment is to ensure that any benefits engendered by tariff concessions are not unravelled through the imposition of discriminatory internal regulations, such as sales taxes or special conditions dictating the way in which imported goods must be sold.

As outlined in Chapter 1, the WTO TRIMs prohibits the imposition of certain performance requirements on foreign investors in conjunction with their use of certain goods, re-iterating the national treatment obligation in the GATT. The TRIMs specifies that WTO Members may not apply a trade-related investment measure that is inconsistent with the GATT obligation not to discriminate against a good on the basis of that good's nationality of origin.[29] The TRIMs and its limited case law will be discussed in greater detail in Chapter 3 as the chief instrument through which the WTO aims to regulate performance requirements.

A national treatment guarantee can also be found in the WTO's Agreement on Trade-Related Aspects of Intellectual Property Rights (TRIPs). Article 3 of the TRIPS Agreement requires Members to accord treatment no less favourable than it accords to its own nationals with respect to the protection of intellectual property. In this context, "protection" includes matters affecting the scope, maintenance and enforcement of intellectual property rights. Assessments of national treatment under TRIPs may be viewed as more directly analogous to those in IIAs because the comparator under TRIPs is the owner of the intellectual property right, not the right itself; TRIPs requires a comparison between foreign and national firms. Additionally, the WTO's Agreement on Technical Barriers to Trade (TBT) controls the use of regulatory barriers placed on foreign goods that can make it difficult for these products to compete on equal footing in the domestic market. Article 2.1 of the TBT contains a national treatment obligation: Members must ensure that technical regulations shall not be applied to give more favourable treatment to products of national origin over like products of foreign origin. Moreover, the WTO's plurilateral Government Procurement Agreement (GPA) contains a national treatment guarantee that is relevant to FDI. Article III:2 of the GPA states that signatories "shall not treat a

[29] Arts 2.1 and 2.2.

locally-established supplier of a governmental service less favourably than another locally-established supplier on the basis of their degree of foreign ownership or affiliation". This provision ensures that host states do not unfairly prejudice foreign-owned firms seeking to supply goods or services to governments. The GPA is structured in a positive-list manner that allows signatories to list which sectors or industries they are willing to extend to commitments under the agreement, often by reference to specific agencies within the central and sub-central government. None of these agreements (other than the GATT) directly references the need to preserve equality of competitive conditions, nor does it speak of preventing protectionism, although it may be possible to infer an anti-protectionist intent behind these agreements by reference to the GATT as a consequence of the conceptualization of the entire suite of WTO agreements a single undertaking.[30]

Finally and most crucially from the perspective of liberalizing FDI, the WTO's GATS contains a national treatment obligation that is relevant to FDI under Mode 3 or the "commercial presence" mode of supply of services.[31] Non-discrimination based on foreign origin is granted under the GATS to the suppliers of the service (foreign investors) but crucially it is extended only to the extent that a Member is willing to make commitments with respect to particular sectors and modes of delivery, such as commercial presence. In this sense GATS extends pre-establishment national treatment, structured as a right of entry to foreign investors on the basis of their commercial presence when delivering services, but only in those sectors that Members have included in their schedules and subject to any restrictions.[32] GATS national treatment also covers both measures that affect the suppliers of the services in addition to, or instead of, the services itself.[33] In that sense, the relevant comparator is also the investors and not only their investments, a situation more closely analogous to the standard's role in international investment law. Importantly, national treatment under the GATS is different from that seen in the GATT because the text of the GATS expressly refers to modifications of the conditions of competition as

---

[30] This was indicated by the Appellate Body in *Argentina – Footwear* WT/DS121/AB/R (adopted 12 January 2008) 81, in which it described the WTO agreements as: "an inseparable package of rights and disciplines which have to be considered in conjunction". This would not include the plurilateral agreements like the GPA.

[31] Art. I.2 c).

[32] Art. XVII.

[33] Art. XVII.

indicative of less favourable treatment.[34] This language has been described as a codification the national treatment case law developed under the GATT.[35] Thus the GATS (drafted almost 50 years after the GATT) is imbued with the normative value of a competitive marketplace to inform the understanding of nationality-based discrimination.

(ii) The Application of the National Treatment Standard in WTO Jurisprudence

Allegations of breach of the national treatment guarantee found in some of the instruments noted above have been a common feature of WTO dispute-settlement cases, especially those involving Article III of the GATT and trade in goods. Indeed, tests employed for the purposes of evaluating the national treatment obligation of GATT have been adapted by panels and the Appellate Body to fit analysis that is called for under the other agreements. As will be discussed below, investment arbitration tribunals have relied on GATT jurisprudence to inform their analysis of national treatment provisions in IIAs. A full discussion of the manner in which national treatment has been evaluated by the WTO panels and Appellate Body is beyond the scope of this chapter, but a brief introduction to some of the key themes in this process is warranted.

The Appellate Body has clarified that national treatment under the GATT applies to both de jure (less-favourable treatment clearly linked to nationality in the text of the measure) and de facto (not clearly stated in the text of the measure) discrimination.[36] Without this extension its effectiveness as a means of controlling the damaging effects of protectionism could be impaired through strategic drafting of laws to provide formally identical treatment that still yielded harmful market distortions. This was the situation in the *Japan – Alcoholic Beverages* dispute[37], where higher tax was imposed on vodka (irrespective of whether it was imported or domestic) than on *shochu* (irrespective of whether it was imported or domestic) where *shochu* was effectively the domestic equivalent of vodka. The purpose of Article III was articulated in the *Korea – Alcoholic Beverages*[38] dispute where the Appellate Body explained that

---

34 Art. XVII:3.

35 Lester, Mercurio and Davies (n 13) 665.

36 Appellate Body Report, *Korea – Various Measures on Beef* WT/DS161/AB/R (adopted 10 January 2001).

37 Appellate Body Report, *Japan – Alcoholic Beverages (II)* WT/DS8/AB/R (adopted 1 November 1996).

38 WT/DS75/AB/R (adopted 17 February 1999).

the provision aimed to avoid protectionism and in so doing required equality of competitive conditions, in that case between the Korean beverage *soju* and similar foreign drinks which had been taxed at a higher rate. The Appellate Body added that in preventing protectionism, GATT's national treatment provision was also intended to protect expectations of equal competitive relationships, meaning that foreign products with which local consumers are not yet familiar should have the opportunity to replace local equivalents, emphasizing the dynamic nature of the marketplace.[39] A further purpose of the national treatment clause in GATT, as illustrated by the Appellate Body in *Japan – Alcoholic Beverages*, is one of safeguarding tariff commitments made under Article II. Members should not attempt to reverse gains made by foreign suppliers through lower tariffs by imposing internal taxes or other regulatory measures. National treatment should be seen to extend beyond tariff commitments, applying even to products where no tariff commitments have been made.[40]

In terms of applying the standard in practice by panels and the Appellate Body, a three-tiered test has been established for evaluating whether Article III:2, sentence one, has been violated. This sentence refers to internal taxation in excess of that applied to "like" domestic products. The second sentence of Article III.2 concerns internal taxation in excess of that applied to "directly competitive and substitutable" products (as explained by an interpretive note contained in Annex I of the GATT – these words do not appear in the text of Article III itself). With respect to the test under the first sentence, this exercise involves assessing whether the measure in question is an internal tax or other internal charge on products, whether the imported and domestic products are "like" and whether the imported products are taxed in excess of domestic products.[41] If this test is satisfied then protectionism can be presumed.[42] Of these three components, the "likeness" test is perhaps the most controversial and the one which has attracted the most attention from the WTO panels and Appellate Body. This is because the concept of "likeness" is fact-dependant and therefore requires analysis on a case-by-case basis. In the recent decision of the Appellate Body in *Philippines – Distilled Spirits*, it was reiterated that relevant factors to consider when evaluating

---

[39] ibid. [120].

[40] ibid. [16].

[41] Appellate Body Report, *Canada – Periodicals* WT/DS31/AB/R (adopted 30 July 1997) [468] and Appellate Body Report, *China – Auto Parts* WT/DS339/AB/R/WT (adopted 12 January 2009) [181].

[42] *Japan – Alcoholic Beverages* (n 37) [111]–[112].

"likeness" include the products' properties, meaning their physical characteristics, as well as their end uses.[43] These issues should be relatively straightforward, essentially calling for a common sense analysis of factors like ingredients, for example, sugar or alcohol content of a certain drink. However, the additional criterion of consumers' tastes and habits[44] appears to demand a somewhat more economically-minded approach because it draws on the logic of substitution and therefore competition within a marketplace. In this regard, the Appellate Body concluded in the *Philippines – Distilled Spirits* dispute that, as long as the differences among the products tied to their raw inputs (for example, sugar cane, cereals and fruit) leave fundamentally unchanged the competitive relationship among the final products, then the existence of the superficial physical differences do not prevent a finding of "likeness".[45]

The importance of maintaining the competitive relationship between products in terms of their capacity to satisfy consumers is tied to the phrase "directly competitive or substitutable", which like "likeness" was not defined in the GATT. In *Korea – Alcoholic Beverages* the panel found that the traditional local beverage *soju* was directly competitive or substitutable with Western-style drinks like whisky and vodka even though it was not held to be like.[46] The Appellate Body explained that "like products" is a narrower concept than directly competitive or substitutable – all like products are directly competitive or substitutable, but not all directly competitive or substitutable products are like.[47] Products will be construed to be directly competitive or substitutable when they are interchangeable with one another or when they offer alternative ways of satisfying a particular need held by the consumer even if they lack common physical characteristics such a colour, composition or even taste.

In *Japan – Alcoholic Beverages* the Appellate Body recognized the appropriateness of using the economic concept of elasticity of substitution to evaluate the marketplace in which particular goods are traded in order to distil the existence of discrimination rooted in competition for the same consumers.[48] As noted above, a fluid understanding of substitution has been implemented in some national treatment disputes, with

---

[43] *Philippines – Distilled Spirits* WT/DS396/AB/R/ (adopted 20 January 2012) [118].

[44] ibid. [118].

[45] ibid. [125].

[46] para. 6.32.

[47] para. 118.

[48] *Japan – Alcoholic Beverages* (n 37) [129].

like or directly competitive or substitutable being linked to products that could potentially be in competition with each other at some point in the future.[49] In that sense, national treatment safeguards the legitimate expectation of competitive opportunities rather than simply actual ones. The panel in *Philippines – Distilled Spirits* brought some objectivity to the evaluation of competition by considering the affordability of a certain product by reference to the disposable income of an average consumer, which dictated whether or not two products could be satisfying the needs of the same market.[50] Further refinement of the concept of competition was seen in the Appellate Body's inquiry into the products' channels of distribution as well as the price at which the product was sold in the importing country.[51] Despite the overarching principle of flexibility, these incidences disclose a relatively precise, empirically-grounded test for "likeness" and in so doing reveal the purposeful, competition-focused foundation of the national treatment principle for the international trade of goods. This method of judicial scrutiny into national treatment has been praised by commentators, in particular for its contrast to a more literalist or formalist approach wherein the relevant goods are evaluated simply on the basis of similar characteristics, without reference to the underlying objective of maintaining functioning markets.[52]

As noted above, under the GATS the "likeness" test is tied to the comparison between imported and domestic services and focuses on the suppliers of the service as well as simply the services themselves. In this sense the judicial assessment of the GATS-based national treatment obligation more closely resembles that which is conducted for national treatment analysis under IIAs. This is true also of the TRIPS, for which scrutiny of the national treatment provision has concentrated on modifications to the effective quality of opportunities in a given market, including also future opportunities in markets which the foreign investor has not yet entered.[53] Commentators have cautioned that the "likeness" test for national treatment under the GATS raises even more difficult conceptual problems than that of the GATT. This is primarily because services are intangible and the firms which supply them may have

---

[49] E.g. Appellate Body Report, *Thailand – Cigarettes* WT/DS371/AB/R (adopted 15 July 2011) [135].

[50] *Philippines – Distilled Spirits* (n 43) 7.59.

[51] ibid.

[52] E.g. M. Trebilcock, *Understanding Trade Law* (Edward Elgar, Cheltenham 2011) 59.

[53] E.g. Panel Report, *EC –Trademarks and Geographical Indicators* WT/DS174/R (adopted 20 April 2005) 7.140.

radically different structures even if they are formally operating with the same sector or industry.[54] The comparison is exacerbated by the fact that the four modes of service supply are themselves artificial constructs created for the purpose of evaluating international services and not ones that exist in national legal systems.[55] As in the GATT context, the test under GATS for likeness of both services and service suppliers should be done on a case-by-case basis.[56] More importantly, the evaluation should be based on evidence that pertains to the competitive relationships of the services being compared.[57] This emphasis discloses the purposeful, market-based mind-set of WTO services adjudication. There remains very little WTO case law regarding the meaning of "likeness" for the purposes of national treatment analysis under the GATS. More fruitful jurisprudence may be developed in the future as the WTO panels and Appellate Body are called upon to adjudicate in an increasingly services-dominated global economy. It should be noted that, under GATS national treatment, the obligation of ensuring conditions of competitive equality does not, however, require the Member to compensate the foreign services provider for any inherent competitive disadvantages which result from the foreign character of the services.[58] Of course, this provision does not prevent Members from so doing should they wish, as per investment incentive policies, which may transgress a literal reading of the national treatment guarantee. Many types of incentives, such as tax exemptions or licensed monopolies may well be intended to combat precisely this type of disadvantage.

4. THE NATIONAL TREATMENT STANDARD IN INTERNATIONAL INVESTMENT LAW

(i) National Treatment in IIAs

National treatment is an essential principle of international investment law found in many if not most IIAs. It is also one of the least-well

---

[54] P. Van den Bossche and W. Zdouc, *The Law and Policy of the World Trade Organization* (3rd edn, CUP, Cambridge 2013) 410.

[55] Lester, Mercurio and Davies (n 13) 665.

[56] Panel Report, *China – Electronic Payment Services* WT/DS413/R (adopted 31 August 2012) para. 7.701.

[57] ibid. para. 7.702.

[58] Fn 10 to Art. XVII:1 as clarified in Appellate Body Report, *Canada – Autos* WT/DS139/AB/R (adopted 19 June 2000) 10.300.

developed standards in terms of doctrinal coherence as embodied by the rulings of arbitration tribunals. As it appears in IIAs, national treatment has been accurately described as "minimalist" in its style.[59] While some FTAs use more expansive language, which is often inspired by that of the GATT, the national treatment standard in most IIAs tends to be captured in one short sentence with very little instructive context. There is typically no guidance as to the purpose of non-discrimination as an interpretive norm. This can be problematic in terms of the way it is understood by investment tribunals. In terms of its capacity to regulate the discriminatory element in performance requirements and investment incentives, the national treatment standard, as it has been interpreted by international investment arbitration tribunals, lacks sufficient emphasis on the economic dimension of nationality-based favouritism. In particular there is a lack of focus in the jurisprudence on the underlying goal of ensuring competitive markets. This, along with the standard's limited application to post-establishment investments, is one of the reasons why the national treatment guarantee in international investment law does not effectively address the advantages or, crucially, curtail the disadvantages associated with performance requirements and investment incentives as market distorting devices.

Preferential treatment to foreign investors in the form of investment incentives may be viewed as a form of reverse discrimination, and as such could fall within the sphere of a national treatment obligation; however, this would not amount to a violation of the national treatment provision because domestic investors have no rights under IIAs. Phrasing in IIAs which indicates that foreign investors are entitled to enjoy treatment that is "no less favourable" than domestic investors opens the possibility that foreigners may be eligible for treatment that is better than that received by locals.[60] While no arbitration tribunal has ever confirmed this view, it is worth nothing that some older IIAs use language requiring the "same" or "as favourable as" treatment, which appears to preclude preferential treatment for foreign firms.[61] Similarly, IIAs which contain clauses granting foreign investors the better of national treatment or most favoured nation may create a situation in which local investors will suffer discriminatory treatment compared to foreign entrants.[62] It has been

[59] Kurtz (n 18) 249.

[60] 'National Treatment' *UNCTAD Series on Issues in International Investment Agreements* (UNCTAD, New York and Geneva 1999) 5.

[61] E.g. Agreement on Investment and Free Movement of Arab Capital Among Arab States (signed 29 August 1970) Art. 4.

[62] UNCTAD (n 60) 11.

suggested that positive differentiation of this nature could even be obligatory where the general standards of customary international law are higher than those applying to domestic entities.[63] In such situations, local investors suffering at the hands of corrupt or incompetent governments may be able to challenge discrimination in favour of foreigners under their own national constitutional provisions.[64] The notion that foreign investors may be entitled to greater rights than local investors provoked a particularly harsh reaction among domestic citizens in relation to the North American Free Trade Agreement (NAFTA)'s guarantee against expropriation without compensation. Although this provision lacked a reference to national treatment, some felt that it had a discriminatory effect against US investors because the NAFTA guarantee against expropriation was arguably stronger than that available under US domestic law (as embodied in the Fifth Amendment of the US Constitution and associated jurisprudence[65]) yet formally complied with NAFTA's national treatment clause. This situation, which along with complaints about the availability of investor–state dispute settlement led to the enactment of the US Trade Act of 2002, a statute intended to ensure that in future IIAs concluded by the US foreign investors would not enjoy greater substantive rights than those available to US investors.[66] The US Trade Act influenced the substantive provisions of a number of recent US IIAs, including those with Singapore and Australia, although it has not retroactively affected NAFTA itself. It also did not lead to a change in US domestic law on expropriation, an interesting counterpoint to the often argued claim that international investment law is meant to effect improvements in domestic governance. The change in US foreign investment policy has been viewed as indicative of somewhat of a revitalization of the Calvo Doctrine in international investment law generally, especially in Latin America.[67] This instance of reverse discrimination is instructive, because US domestic law on expropriation offers considerably greater protection than that available under many domestic legal

---

[63] R. Dolzer and S. Schreuer, *Principles of International Investment Law*, (OUP, Oxford 2008) 178.

[64] UNCTAD (n 60) 35.

[65] Notably that established under *Penn Central v New York City* (1978) 438 US 104.

[66] US Trade Act 2002, Art. 2102(b)3.

[67] See e.g. W. Shua, 'From North-South Divide to Private–Public Debate: Revival of the Calvo Doctrine and the Changing Landscape in International Investment Law' (2007) 27:3 *Northwestern Journal of International Law and Business* 631–2.

systems around the world. Still, the protection of private property is not unlimited and it is invidious to contemplate a situation in which a US investor would lose a claim brought before the US Supreme Court but win against a developing country government through international arbitration.[68] It is far from certain whether a foreign investor's ability to win a claim brought against the US government would ameliorate or exacerbate this problem. The resurgence of the Calvo Doctrine in international investment law as a guardian against this type of conflict as well as the related issue of resource nationalism and investment incentives will be discussed further in Chapter 6.

The guarantee of non-discrimination on the basis of the national origin of the investor has a wide-ranging impact on the capacity of host states to implement policies that advantage the local economy, such as performance requirements and incentives to attract FDI. Under national treatment, domestic governments at all levels are not entitled to prefer local economic interests over the needs of foreign investors who have located in the host state.[69] Consequently, states often impose boundaries on their commitments of non-discrimination. The chief limitation of the national treatment obligation in IIAs is a temporal one. In most IIAs, national treatment normally only extends to the post-establishment stage of an investment, meaning after the foreign investor has entered a host country and begun its operations there. Restricting the standard in this critical manner allows governments to dictate which forms of foreign economic activity it is willing to permit within its borders, according to its own economic and social requirements. This is perhaps the single most significant limitation on the effectiveness of the national treatment standard in policing the imposition of performance requirements. In this regard, *GEA Group Aktiengesellschaft v Ukraine*, a dispute brought under the German–Ukraine BIT, the arbitration tribunal held that an additional administrative burden placed on foreign investors by the Ukrainian government that did not apply to local firms was not discriminatory because the investor had not yet been admitted.[70] In contrast, the much rarer granting of pre-establishment national treatment, as in NAFTA and number of US as well as Canadian IIAs[71], effectively removes barriers to entry that are faced by foreign firms, allowing full market access. It can

---

[68] Montt (n 6) 76.

[69] D. Schneiderman, *Constitutionalizing Economic Globalization* (CUP, 2008) 31.

[70] ICSID Case No. ARB/08/16 (31 March 2011) [344].

[71] E.g. Canada–Latvia Art. II.3 (26 April 1995), United States–Jordan Art. II.1 (2 July 1997).

therefore be viewed as one of the chief mechanisms for the liberalization of FDI. Given that this extension of national treatment can expose many sectors of the domestic economy to a level of competition for which it is unprepared, some IIAs use a negative-list style of national treatment, in which various sensitive sectors, including those that may represent risks to national security (such as transportation and telecommunications), are excluded from the non-discrimination guarantee. The ASEAN Comprehensive Investment Agreement employs this structure.[72] China has indicated a potential willingness to have pre-establishment national treatment with a negative list in its future IIAs.[73] This latter development could mark a significant shift in favour of the liberalization of FDI globally.

In addition to controlling the application of national treatment by reference to the stage of the investment process (often restricted therein to particular sectors or industries), and to key sectors, guarantees against discrimination on the basis of the nationality of the investment may be further specified by various exceptions contained in the text of the IIA. In this way, host states may structure IIAs to grant them the power to deny national treatment in any industry at any stage of investment. While it remains rare, a few IIAs contain lists of the types of matters that are excluded from the coverage of the instrument's protection, allowing the host country to enact discriminatory laws because of justifications linked to health, national security, public order or the environment.[74] Such limitations can expose investors to a wide range of ostensibly discriminatory treatment, such as that entailed by the imposition of performance requirements, on the basis of such policy justifications – in which case such unequal treatment is arguably not a manifestation of genuine discrimination. The facilitation of performance requirements through general exceptions in IIAs will be explored further in Chapter 4.

(ii) The Application of the National Treatment Standard by International Investment Arbitration Tribunals

The investment arbitration jurisprudence regarding the national treatment standard obligation offered by IIAs lacks clarity with respect to a number

[72] Art. 9 (signed 26 February 2009).

[73] 'Ministry of Commerce: China Using Global Approach in Investment Talks with US' (*People's Daily On-Line*, 12 July 2013) <http://english.peopledaily.com.cn/90778/8323785.html> accessed 2 December 2014.

[74] Many IIAs, notably RTAs, specifically adopt the language of the General Exceptions contained in the GATS Art. XIV and GATT Art. XX, e.g. NAFTA (Art. 2101) and ASEAN Ch 15 Art. 1.

of key issues, including most notably the role of competitive markets as a means of comparison between investors. This renders non-discrimination based on nationality less workable as a means of directly controlling performance requirements and investment incentives, both of which tend to be predicated on economic justifications. There is limited arbitral practice on national treatment, which is striking because of the comparative depth of inquiry associated with other IIA standards, such as fair and equitable treatment (FET), in both arbitral practice and in scholarly commentary.[75] Unlike international trade law, there have been very few investment disputes that have engaged national treatment provisions in IIAs. This is possibly because it is often difficult to identify a violation of national treatment as there tend to be very few laws that formally discriminate against foreigners. Furthermore, the limited coverage of national treatment in most IIAs to the post-establishment stage means that market-access-oriented complaints are often framed as trade disputes. A less obvious but compelling reason for the lack of national treatment based jurisprudence in investment law is that the much broader and more widely-claimed fair and equitable treatment standard may be seen to include a non-discrimination obligation,[76] just as claims of illegal expropriation are often rooted in discriminatory treatment of foreign property.

In order to understand how investment arbitration tribunals have approached the national treatment standard in IIAs, it is important to explore the nature of the comparison between treatment accorded to foreign investors and domestic investors by host states. For this relationship to be legally meaningful, the relevant investors or their investments (depending upon the wording of the treaty) must be in similar or "like" circumstances: language that resembles that seen in the WTO national treatment regimes, although some IIAs do not use a linking comparator at all.[77] Some older IIAs had used the phrase "situations" instead of

---

[75] E.g. Nadakavukaren Schefer (n 23). But see e.g. A. Bjorklund, 'National Treatment' in A. Reinisch (ed.), *The Standards of Investment Protection* (OUP, Oxford 2008) and L. Choukroune, 'National Treatment in International Investment Law and Arbitration: A Relative Standard for Autonomous Public Regulation and Sovereign Development' in A. Kamperman Sanders (ed.), *The Principle of National Treatment in International Economic Law* (Edward Elgar, Cheltenham 2014).

[76] This similarity was noted recently by the tribunal in *Tulip Real Estate and Development Netherlands BV v Republic of Turkey* ICSID Case No. ARB/11/28 (10 March 2014) [445].

[77] E.g. Russia–Mongolia BIT (29 November 1995) Art. 3.

"circumstances" although it is not clear that there is a difference between the two concepts.[78] Thus the association between the foreign and the local appears to rest upon context in a broad commercial sense rather than as a description of some intrinsic feature of the firms or the products they produce. As discussed below, it remains unclear however whether "like circumstances" requires that foreign and domestic investors sell the same goods, are in the same business, or simply operate in the same industry or even sector. This lack of coherence reflects the difficulty in the application of the economic logic of equality of competitive conditions between foreign and local firms.

It is not clear from investment jurisprudence that the concept of competition between investors will be viewed as a criterion for foreign and domestic actors to be held in "like circumstances" and therefore deserving of the same treatment. In *Pope & Talbot v Canada,*[79] a dispute brought under NAFTA, (the instrument from which much of our understanding of the jurisprudence on national treatment is derived), the tribunal rejected the use of GATT (and GATS) jurisprudence on the modification of competitive conditions in order to defeat Canada's allegation that the claimant must show a disproportionate disadvantage in order to ground a de facto breach of national treatment. The tribunal justified this rationale on the basis of the lack of reference to competitive conditions in the text of NAFTA, as well as NAFTA's contemplation of a single investor seeking damages, in contrast to the WTO regime where it is the national government bringing a claim under GATT or GATS on behalf of a whole sector.[80] The logic appeared to be that modification of competitive conditions may be presumed where the discrimination has harmed a single investor, whereas it must be proactively demonstrated where the complainant is effectively an entire sector. Given that injuries born by a diffuse collective of enterprises as represented by their government would tend to be more opaque than those suffered by one company seeking to maintain profitability, this view may have some merit. On that latter point, the *Pope & Talbot* tribunal (also considering NAFTA) conceded that by their nature "circumstances" are context dependent and have no invariable meaning outside the particular facts. The tribunal went on to say that, as a useful starting point, "like circumstances" will be taken to be investors that are within the same

[78] Dolzer and Schreuer (n 63) 179.
[79] Award on the Merits, 7 ICSID Reports 102 (10 April 2001).
[80] ibid. [56], [57].

business or economic sector,[81] unhelpfully failing to appreciate the major distinction between the categories "business" and "sector". The *Pope & Talbot* claimant did not win on NT. Also, no other tribunal has followed the *Pope & Talbot* approach.

The NAFTA tribunal in the *Feldman v Mexico* dispute held that like circumstances would be established if investors were in the same business[82], whereas the *Occidental Exploration v Ecuador* tribunal (under the US–Ecuador BIT) ruled that like circumstances could apply to local producers in general, regardless of the type of commercial activity.[83] This reasoning has been defended by commentators on the grounds that non-discrimination in the investment context has historically been linked to the notion of diplomatic protection of aliens, which says nothing about competing businesses,[84] a guarantee that is arguably more effectively enshrined in the more general FET standard which the *Occidental* tribunal did not explore. This non-economic view of national treatment is predicated on the understanding that the much more widely-claimed fair and equitable treatment standard itself contains a promise of non-discrimination, which is by no means certain given the notorious indeterminacy of that standard. In *Occidental* the tribunal did consider whether the concept of directly competitive or substitutable was relevant to the analysis of the likeness comparator. Unfortunately, the tribunal merely reiterated that the relevant comparison is between the firms themselves and not goods, and did not explain why the concept of market distortion under GATT case law must be inapplicable to the investment context, other than the unhelpful re-iteration that NAFTA does not speak directly of modifications to competitive conditions or market distortions. The *Occidental* tribunal did appear to make a distinction between market distortion and unequal competition in its dismissal of the relevance of the WTO case law. If a difference between these concepts does exist and is legally meaningful, which it may well be under a technical economic analysis,[85] this was not explored by the tribunal.[86] More specifically, it is not evident why the concepts of competition and substitution could not be readily applied to firms, as they have been to products, at least in the

---

[81] ibid. [78].

[82] Award, 16 December 2002, 7 ICSID Reports 341 (16 December 2002).

[83] *Occidental Exploration v Ecuador*, Award, 12 ICSID Reports 59 (1 July 2004).

[84] Howse and Chalamish (n 8) 1092.

[85] See e.g. ambiguities in definition of "market" in R. Whish and D. Bailey, *Competition Law* (7th edn, OUP, Oxford 2012) 27–8.

[86] *Occidental Petroleum* (n 83) [175].

GATT context, as a means of unpacking the dangerously vague "like circumstances" comparator. In other words, the tribunal could have inquired more closely as to whether the two investors were in competition with each other for customers in the same fields to which the regulation applied, ideally using the principles of economics or competition law.

In assessing whether the relevant investors were in like circumstances, the *Methanex Corp v USA*[87] tribunal was unwilling to apply the concept of direct competition to the companies themselves because of the lack of use of these words in NAFTA's investment chapter, expressly rejecting trade-based arguments in that regard made by the claimant.[88] In considering like circumstances of investors rather than competition between the products they produce, the tribunal emphasized that if an identical (or at least more similar) comparator is available, as it was in *Methanex* because there were local producers of the same fuel additive, then this is the comparison by which the understanding of like circumstances should be constructed.[89] Like circumstances, in this case methanol producers, should be construed as narrowly as is possible given the class of available local investors that may have been affected by the measure in question, not through approximation to an arguably inappropriate one.[90] While the firms in *Methanex* were clearly identical in that they were both producers of methanol, it is unfortunately that the tribunal did not offer much insight into precisely how appropriate or as-near-as-possible comparators will be identified, other than by implicit reference to their use of competitive products, a test which they ironically declined to consider formally.

The *Occidental* and *Methanex* tribunals' attenuation of a competitive opportunities test for likeness have been condemned by commentators for their lack of economic rigour relative to the trade GATT-based analysis.[91] Others have praised them for their judicious integration of a shared standard (competing products under GATT) into the diffused system of multi-tribunal arbitration.[92] It is somewhat surprising that arbitration tribunals, other than *Pope & Talbot*, have not drawn upon the national treatment standard found in the more analogous GATS for inspiration in their comparison analysis. Not only does GATS refer explicitly to the

---

87 Award, 44 ILM (2005) 1356 (3 August 2005).
88 ibid. [33].
89 ibid. [17].
90 ibid. [19].
91 Kurtz (n 18) 257–60.
92 Howse and Chalamish (n 8) 1094.

empirically grounded concept of modification of competitive conditions, national treatment under the GATS refers to likeness of the suppliers of services as well as services themselves, and as such more naturally links with the investment context where it is the foreign and local suppliers, rather than their products, that is in question.[93] Admittedly there is limited GATS case law from which to draw inspiration and indeed it may transpire that WTO panels turn to the more abundant arbitration jurisprudence when they are called upon to consider the GATS national treatment provision.

The challenge of applying "like circumstances" or "like situations" to disclose discriminatory treatment against foreign investors was explored in the *Loewen v United States*[94] case. The tribunal ruled that it could find no violation of NAFTA's guarantee of national treatment because the circumstances of the two litigants at the trial (the Canadian and the American companies) were not sufficiently similar to engage the treaty's injunction against discriminatory treatment. Implementing a narrow application of the "likeness" test, the tribunal concluded there was no comparator in like circumstances which the tribunal could use to make the necessary comparison in order to identify discrimination.[95] It seems that only facts that disclosed treatment consequent to virtually identical fact scenarios would have allowed the tribunal to engage the standard, and these had not been demonstrated. The *Loewen* tribunal seems also to have missed the point that de jure and de facto discrimination contemplate different types of comparators. Unfortunately it is not clear from the tribunal's analysis precisely on what basis likeness could have been derived, nor was there a discussion regarding the role that a competitive relationship between investors would play in this analysis. *Loewen* is unsatisfactory because it fails to shed light on how the concept of likeness should be construed instrumentally, other than its emphasis that it will be heavily fact-based (as in trade) and restrictive, conclusions that are also seen in the *Methanex* decision. In attempting to distil a principle from the *Loewen* judgment, it may be sensible to conclude that a narrow understanding of like circumstances means that even firms which do compete directly with each other in some capacity may not be sufficiently alike to warrant a finding of discrimination if there are what might be termed "superficial" differences, such as the sector of operation or the investor's size and structure. In this instance the Canadian

---

[93] See further, N. Diebold, *Non-Discrimination in International Trade in Services* (CUP, 2014).

[94] Award, ICSID Case No. ARB(AF)/98/3 (26 June 2003).

[95] ibid. [140].

company was much larger than the American one, although the tribunal insisted that it was not ruling on that basis. The *Loewen* tribunal also unhelpfully indicated that they could not compare the plaintiff to the defendant in a trial because in any dispute one party wins and one loses and as such the winning party will always have more favourable treatment.

This is not to suggest that size of business is not itself a meaningful economic indicator. It could be asserted that differential treatment between large and small entities should not truly be viewed as discrimination,[96] even where companies compete for the same customers. A large company arguably places greater strain on local infrastructure than a smaller firm, possibly legitimizing higher contributions in the form of taxes. Even more so, the size of a business entity often signifies its capacity to engage in abusive market practices. Discrimination based upon an investor's size, while not necessarily intending to disadvantage foreign investors, may result in a national treatment violation because the large investors will most likely be exclusively foreign, especially in developing country host states. In this regard it appears that de facto discrimination should be sufficient to find a national treatment violation.[97]

One way of injecting greater coherence into the national treatment analysis in the investment context might be to emphasize the nature of the national treatment guarantee as encapsulated in the relevant IIA. Recall that the Vienna Convention on the Law of Treaties instructs that the interpretation of treaty provisions must have in mind the overall purpose of the particular instrument in which they appear. In this regard, the narrow readings of "likeness" in *Methanex* and *Loewen* could be explained on the basis of NAFTA's broad grant of national treatment to the pre-establishment stage among signatories of similar economic development. This represents a deep commitment of significant economic implication that is substantially beyond that seen in many traditional IIAs between developed and developing countries that grants simple post establishment national treatment, allowing foreign investors to act in markets that may not be fully competitively mature. In the case of NAFTA's pre-establishment guarantee by the US to Canadian and Mexican firms, it could be argued that foreign investors should not expect to be completely discrimination-free in anything other than the most egregious situations of favouritism – meaning those where the investors are

---

96 Sornarajah (n 1) 203.

97 E.g. *Feldman v Mexico* (n 82).

operating in almost identical conditions, for example, size, structure, and some understanding of competition for the same consumers. It is noteworthy that in its analysis of national treatment, the tribunal in *SD Myers v Canada*[98] was motivated by the reference in Article 102(2) a of NAFTA to promote the conditions of fair competition in the free-trade area,[99] highlighting the relevance of a functioning marketplace in the encouragement of foreign investment and trade. It is important to recognize that in *SD Myers* there had been a statement in Parliament by the Canadian Minister of the Environment that the Canadian waste disposal industry needed to be protected from competition, making it very difficult for Canada to argue that there was no protectionist intent.

A somewhat more illuminating analysis can be found in the ruling of the tribunal in *Sergei Paushok v the Government of Mongolia*,[100] a dispute brought under the Russia–Mongolia BIT. In deciding that there was no evidence of nationality-based discrimination against the Russian investor, which was in part framed as a violation of the fair and equitable treatment standard as well as national treatment itself (which were both contained in the same provision of the treaty), the tribunal claimed that the test for discrimination involved an assessment of the sectors in which the relevant investors (foreign and local) operated, in this case the Mongolian gold sector. Interestingly, the concept of sector was itself linked to competitive and substitutable products as developed in WTO jurisprudence – in other words, shared sector of operation implies that the products in which the firms deal compete with one another for customers.[101] The tribunal appeared to resort to WTO economic-oriented tests on which to ground its analysis of discrimination paradoxically because of the lack of reference to "likeness" of any kind in the text of the Mongolia–Russia BIT, freeing it to use interpretations based on the expansive, although unspecified principles of the Vienna Convention, which in turn took it to the WTO regime.[102] This discloses a telling preference for the somewhat more concrete competition-based analysis of product substitutability in situations where tribunals do not feel shackled by the NAFTA's ambiguous "like circumstances" heritage.

It may be possible in the investment context to inject some more coherence into the national treatment analysis at the compensation stage rather than at the stage where the tribunal merely assesses whether or not

---

98 First Partial Award, 40 ILM (2001) 1408 (13 November 2000).
99 Partial Award (13 Nov 2000) 198.
100 Award, UNCITRAL, 28 April 2011.
101 ibid. [315].
102 ibid. [313].

a national treatment violation has occurred. In this regard, the *SD Myers* tribunal used an empirical competition-based analysis to structure the extent of damages payable to the injured investor as a consequence of several breaches of NAFTA, including national treatment consequent to a border closure imposed by the Canadian government affecting a chemical disposal industry. The tribunal considered the extent to which prices charged by competing investors in Canada would have been lowered had there been competitive pricing (and not non-competitive ones, which resulted from the Canadian border closure).[103]

Identifying protectionist purpose may be another way of understanding the national treatment obligation in international investment law that results in a more predictable and workable manner that underscores the economic purpose of non-discrimination. In this regard, the *Pope & Talbot* tribunal explained that while crucial, a competitive relationship between the relevant investors is not enough on its own. There must also be evidence of a protectionist purpose to show that there has been a breach of national treatment.[104] The *SD Myers* tribunal also drew attention to the need to establish intent, which it viewed as necessary but not decisive to a finding of national treatment violation.[105] Arbitration practice, at least under NAFTA, indicates that it is sufficient for the investor to show that there was less favourable treatment accorded to it than to domestic investors in like circumstances in order to succeed in a claim of national treatment; the investor does not have to show that the discrimination is motivated by nationality, despite the fact that all three NAFTA governments have argued vigorously that the discrimination must be based on nationality.[106] It is also supported by commentators who argue that the relevant test for the breach of the national treatment standard under international investment law is whether the alleged discrimination is effectively based upon nationality rather than some other policy reason,[107] capturing both de facto as well as de jure discrimination.

Framed from the perspective of the respondent, the usefulness of showing that discriminatory treatment is not motivated by the preference for domestic producers in order for the host state to escape liability under the national treatment clause is enhanced when the measure is a form of de facto, i.e. facially neutral, discriminatory treatment. Such national

---

103 *SD Myers v Canada* (n 98) [255].
104 *Pope & Talbot* (n 79) [79].
105 *SD Myers v Canada* (n 98) [254].
106 *Feldman v Mexico* (n 82) [181].
107 DiMascio and Pauwelyn (n 7) 76.

treatment violations, while more common as sources of complaint, are by their nature more elusive and therefore more needful of precise methodology of identification. This additional requirement for de facto discrimination reflects a somewhat narrower if not insurmountable understanding of likeness. Indeed the *Pope & Talbot* tribunal was quick to clarify that there should not be seen to be a stricter test for de facto breaches of national treatment than de jure ones as this would be inconsistent with the objectives of NAFTA to promote FDI.[108] The requirement of protectionist intent (as distinct from protectionist effect) for internal taxation on like products was explicitly rejected by the WTO's Appellate Body in *Japan – Alcoholic Beverages* as overly restrictive in part due to evidentiary difficulties, the rationale being that a protectionist aim can be inferred from the design of the measure.[109] The need to discern the host state government's motivation of protectionism (which the *Pope & Talbot* tribunal helpfully framed as the intent to alter the nature of the competitive relationship in favour of the local firm) was emphasized despite the fact that the relevant IIA (again NAFTA) had no express reference to controlling protectionism (either as a motivation or an effect), as do few if any IIAs. This is a somewhat troubling conclusion given that it is naturally very difficult if not impossible to isolate the purpose of a given measure despite the *Japan – Alcoholic Beverages* logic of inference, particularly when investment regulations, unlike internal taxes, are often promulgated by a number of different government agencies acting in concert, or worse, where there is no culture of political transparency, as in many developing states. Still, a protectionist purpose may be more readily identifiable in the case of discrimination against foreign firms than against foreign goods, where foreign firms tend to be more conspicuous to voters, politicians and regulators than the products which they produce. This latter point rests on the admittedly tenuous assertion that political rewards for favouring local companies over foreign ones may be greater in the context of investment, because of the gains associated with satisfying well-organized corporate lobbying groups rather than those linked to disparate consumers who tend to benefit from lower-cost traded goods. It may accordingly be useful to shift the burden on the host state to disprove protectionist intent.

Finally, it should be kept in mind that the manner in which the national treatment obligation in IIAs is interpreted by tribunals can also be coloured by other provisions in the treaty, such as general or specific

---

[108] *Pope & Talbot* (n 79) [70].

[109] *Japan – Alcoholic Beverages* (n 37) 120.

exceptions. In this sense, a narrower understanding of the national treatment obligation may be warranted as a consequence of the lack of a general exception type provision in most IIAs, along the lines of GATT Article XX and GATS Article XIV, which would allow measures that fulfil certain public policy aims as long as they are not used as a disguised restriction on trade (an assessment which itself arguably contains an element of non-discrimination).[110] Such clauses could act as a contextual guide to prevent the over-extension of the non-discrimination guarantee by inserting a purpose-oriented qualifier, such that only measures that lacked a specified policy justification would be caught by the standard.[111] Furthermore, expectations of equal treatment must be viewed in light of the current trend of protectionism consequent to the global financial crisis.[112] Regulatory responses to such emergencies (if they may be viewed as such)[113] may suggest that the concept of a functional, competitive market itself is flexible and tied to the overall health of the economy in question.

In light of the treaty-specific context of each national treatment provision, commentators have cautioned against the reliance on WTO jurisprudence in order to inform the analysis of national treatment obligations in international investment law. Such an exercise, it has been argued, is fraught with interpretive difficulties because of the very different context of the WTO's multilateral forum and individually negotiated investment treaties, the latter of which may form part of more comprehensive economic integration projects like NAFTA or bilateral instruments between two states of vastly disparate negotiating power.[114] Again, the context of the instrument in which the national treatment appears is instructive. Mindful of these very different arenas of economic integration, investment tribunals appear to be somewhat timid in their approach to national treatment in IIAs, making sure that they distinguish

---

[110] But see Art. 17.1 of the ASEAN Comprehensive Investment Agreement (signed 26 February 2009), which uses the same language as GATT Art. XX.

[111] Kurtz (n 18) 274.

[112] Howse and Chalamish (n 8) 1090.

[113] As argued by Argentina in a series of investment treaty arbitrations including: *LG&E Energy Corporation v Argentina* Decision on Liability, ICSID Case No. ARB/02/1 (3 October 2006); *CMS Gas Transmission v Argentina* Award, ICSID Case No. ARB/01/8 (12 May 2005); *Sempra Energy International v Argentina* Decision on Annulment, ICSID Case No. ARB/02/16 (29 June 2010); and *Enron Corporation v Argentina* Award, ICSID Case No. ARB/01/3 (22 May 2007).

[114] Howse and Chalamish (n 8) 1089.

between the context of the GATT and that of the relevant IIA.[115] Acknowledging this divide is warranted. Clearly the national treatment test in trade law (at least under GATT) focuses on the nature of the goods themselves rather than the companies which use or supply them.[116] The national treatment trade jurisprudence may be further distinguished from the investment jurisprudence because of the former's focus on consumers (their tastes and preferences) with the latter's focus on suppliers (the sector in which they operate, sometimes their size), possibly for the political economy reasons noted above. Still, others have urged that it is impossible to evaluate critically the national treatment obligation in IIAs without a grasp of the analysis of the standard seen in the WTO cases.[117] Such synthesis may be particularly important in the context of performance requirements and investment incentives which can blur the distinction between trade and investment law. An investor's capacity to trade in the goods that it produces may represent a key component of its commercial strategy abroad. Indeed, this is precisely the advantage sought by host states imposing trade-based performance requirements on foreign investors. Moreover, a finding of a national treatment violation with respect to a trade-oriented measure under WTO law by a panel or the Appellate Body could potentially strengthen an investor's claim in international arbitration that the same measure undermined its national treatment entitlement under an IIA.[118]

5. CONCLUSION

This chapter has introduced national treatment as one of the foundational principles of international economic law. The standard ensures that governments do not discriminate against foreign goods or the firms which produce them through the application of their domestic laws. This has particular relevance for both performance requirements and investment incentives which tend to be applied on the basis of a firm's nationality: in the case of performance requirements, typically against foreign firms; in the case of incentives, typically against local firms. The national treatment standard protects foreign investors from interference

---

115 E.g. *Occidental Exploration* (n 83) [176].

116 Dolzer and Schreuer (n 63) 184–5 and Sornarajah (n 1) 203.

117 Kurtz (n 18) 244.

118 A. Davies, 'Scoping the Boundary Between the Trade Law and Investment Law Regimes: When Does a Measure Relate to Investment?' (2012) 15:3 *Journal of International Economic Law* 793, 794.

with their commercial operations on the basis of their nationality, and in some cases it grants foreign firms access to domestic markets on equal footing with local investors. Whether these rights are overtly construed through the WTO's lens of avoiding protectionism, the underlying logic of the national treatment standard is aptly described as one of equality of competitive conditions, an economic concept rooted in the need to allow markets to function free from inefficient distortions. The standard's capacity to protect local firms who cannot benefit from incentives is dubious, given that local firms cannot bring claims under IIAs; however, it may facilitate a foreign firm's claim for better treatment than locals in the event that an incentive regime was discontinued on the basis of its discriminatory nature.

The national treatment standard appears in several agreements of the WTO and in most IIAs. The manner in which it has been interpreted by the judicial bodies of the WTO and investment tribunals is far from predictable, in large part because of the indeterminacy of the comparator by which the non-discrimination guarantee is applied, as well as the overall context of the relevant instrument in which it appears. In one sense the uneven application of the standard should not be viewed as problematic, because it allows a degree of useful flexibility to the adjudication of nationality-based discrimination claims. Allegations of nationality-based discrimination tend to be highly contextualized and fact intensive, necessitating a legal concept that is accordingly malleable. On the other hand, the lack of clarity in the judicial tests for national treatment can lead to commercial uncertainty as well as abuse by governments, just as it can suppress the use of legitimate policy tools such as those which are the focus of this book.

It has been suggested that the approach taken by some investment tribunals in applying the national treatment standard without a more substantive assessment of the extent of the competitive relationship between foreign and domestic firms is both formalist and artificial. This technique risks excluding a broad range of discriminatory treatment from the protective scope of the standard.[119] Since performance requirements are typically imposed only upon foreign investors, the national treatment standard in an IIA may be engaged to prohibit such conditions as a requirement of establishment in host states (where the standard is extended to the pre-establishment phase). It could also protect foreign investors against unfair treatment linked to performance requirements that are implemented after establishment. Likewise, certain iterations of

---

[119] Kurtz (n 18) 262.

the national treatment standard could be used to justify investment incentives aimed at encouraging FDI which could be harmful to local firms. However, the national treatment standard on its own is a weak instrument for controlling the implementation of either performance requirements or investment incentives, necessitating other regulatory mechanisms which will be examined throughout this book. This shortcoming is not only the consequence of the reality that performance requirements and investment incentives are not always discriminatory in their application, but also partly because of the lack of more robust economic analysis in the application of the national treatment standard by investment tribunals as well as its limitation to certain stages of investment or to certain listed industries. The national treatment standard then should be viewed as a rather blunt instrument, in terms of its capacity to control performance requirements and investment incentives.

The next four chapters of this book will explore how the fundamental concept of non-discrimination – encapsulated primarily by the national treatment standard introduced in this chapter, but also seen in other spheres of international economic law – informs the regulatory efforts to contain the damaging effects of performance requirements and investment incentives, many of which are tied to the national origin of the investor or which expressly benefit local or foreign firms.

3. Performance requirements and international trade law

1. INTRODUCTION: TRADE-BASED PERFORMANCE REQUIREMENTS AND FOREIGN DIRECT INVESTMENT

This chapter will consider the controls on performance requirements that have been instigated by the WTO. With its ambit on the liberalization of trade in goods and services, the WTO has played a significant role in the restriction of certain varieties of performance requirements that may be placed on foreign investors in conjunction with their use, production, or export of certain goods or services. Other spheres of WTO law could impact upon host state policy towards the behaviour of foreign firms, including its disciplines on intellectual property and government procurement. The WTO's engagement with these issues is founded upon the link between FDI and international trade. For example, performance requirements imposed on foreign firms may form part of a state's trade policy as a way of displacing imports or increasing the level of exports. Such performance requirements are designed to cause foreign investors to produce goods for export while minimizing the competitive effects they can have on the domestic industry as much as is feasible. The ultimate purpose of this type of strategy is to raise the foreign exchange earnings of the state imposing the requirements as well as to increase employment in the export sector, ideally without imposing additional competitive pressures on equivalent domestic firms. As discussed in Chapter 1, there are a number of trade-related performance requirements. In this chapter it will be shown how these may transgress WTO law.

2. WTO AGREEMENTS AND PERFORMANCE REQUIREMENTS

Depending on the definition of performance requirement that one adopts, a wide range of the WTO's agreements could be said to regulate the use of performance requirements in some way. Given the definition and indicative categories of measures that were discussed in Chapter 1, this chapter will demonstrate that there are four chief instruments through which the WTO imposes disciplines on the use of performance requirements by its Member states. The first and most important of these is the TRIMs, which prohibits a certain sub-set of performance requirements that are essentially linked to the use by investors of local goods in their production activities. The second agreement, which has potentially vast but as yet for the most part unrealized implications for a wide range of performance requirements, is the GATS. This agreement guarantees that FDI in services will enjoy non-discrimination and market access, to the extent that WTO members have been prepared to make commitments in this area – guarantees which could operate to preclude performance requirements. The TRIPS has a similarly broad potential to control performance requirements that may be imposed on the creation and enforcement of intellectual property rights belonging to foreign firms, such as trademarks and patents. Finally, the optional GPA disciplines discriminatory practices imposed by signatory states in terms of their government purchasing activities prohibiting requirements which favour the use of local goods or services, which could be otherwise unduly restrictive on foreign firms. Each agreement will be considered in turn.

(i) The Agreement on Trade Related Investment Measures (TRIMs)

It is important to recognize first of all that the TRIMs does not prohibit performance requirements generally. Rather, it controls a sub-set of these measures which it labels "trade-related investment measures", a term which is undefined in the agreement. These are essentially performance requirements related to goods that directly impact upon foreign firms by imposing direct or indirect quantitative restrictions on imports or exports. In other words, the agreement limits the way WTO Members can require foreign firms to use certain types of goods. The TRIMs provides that no Member may apply a trade-restrictive investment measure that is inconsistent with the GATT's prohibition on national treatment (Article III) or on quantitative restrictions (Article XI).[1] Direct and indirect quantitative restrictions and discriminatory conditions on the use of goods are properly described as investment measures because they dictate the conditions under which foreign firms are able to do business. For example, a foreign manufacturer of machinery may be allowed to

---

[1] TRIMS Art. 2(1), (2).

establish itself in a host state only if uses steel that was produced in that country, a violation of the national treatment's provisions injunction against discrimination of a good based on its origin.

Given that the prohibition of trade-related investment measures may be seen to offer assistance to the foreign investor beyond that which is available if states were free to regulate incoming firms as they wished, the TRIMs may be thought of as a form of incentive to encourage FDI, especially in goods-intensive manufacturing. This is reflected in its preamble which specifies the objective "facilitat[ing] investment across international frontiers". In that sense it is the WTO's only agreement that has a true investment focus. Put in the language of international investment law and IIAs, the TRIMs covers "pre-establishment" FDI, meaning that its obligations apply to all foreign firms (originating from WTO Member states) whether or not they have already established themselves in host-WTO Member states. In other words, its guarantees apply whether or not the firm in question has yet been granted permission to enter the host state.

Covering only a narrow sub-category of trade restrictive measures that impact on FDI, the TRIMs is further limited in that it applies only to trade in goods,[2] so it cannot control measures associated with FDI in services, except to the extent that such activities also relate to the use of goods. Other trade-distorting performance requirements, such as those relating to local employment for example, which arguably violate the intent and spirit of the GATT, are still permitted by the TRIMs. These could be seen as essential policy tools from a developmental perspective.[3] Put another way, TRIMs controls only those performance requirements that might be of interest to an industrialized economy. Nor does it control the use of export requirements – one of the most trade-distorting types of measure – except to the extent that it prohibits restrictions on quantities of exports that are tied to a proportion of local production.[4] This is one reason why some IIAs tended to expand upon the TRIMS through performance requirement prohibitions of a more generalized nature. This will be explored further in the next chapter. Also, as noted above, article 2.1 of the agreement specifies that no WTO Member can apply a trade-related investment measure that is inconsistent with either the National Treatment (Article III) or prohibition on quantitative measures (Article XI) provisions of GATT. The reference to prohibitions found in

---

[2] Art. 1.

[3] Z. Boroo, 'Effective Use of Performance Requirements and Investment Incentive' (2012) 17 *Mongolian Journal of International Affairs* 97, 104.

[4] Annex 2(c).

the GATT discloses one of the chief criticisms of the TRIMs agreement: it is effectively redundant in that it only recapitulates rules contained in the GATT.[5]

While "trade-related investment measures" themselves are not defined under the TRIMs, an illustrative list of trade-related investment measures that are inconsistent with GATT provisions is contained in an Annex to the TRIMs itself. It is thought that uncertainty regarding the definition of a trade related investment measure is a reflection of the political judgement that a certain type of measure reduces economic welfare and should consequently be prohibited. This is one of the reasons why countries that have different policy objectives often disagree as to whether a measure should be regarded as a TRIM. The quantifiable effect of a measure on trade flows is another important factor in ascertaining whether a regulation should be classified as a trade-related investment measure. This can be problematic because the effects of a particular measure are often difficult to isolate.[6]

Commentators have attempted to classify trade-related investment measures as either incentive-based, which tend to subsidize the investor in order to increase its profits, or dis-incentive-based, which tend to restrict the operational discretion of the investor and in so doing decrease the potential profit available on the investment.[7] With this distinction in mind, the illustrative list states that prohibited trade-related investment measures include those measures which are mandatory or enforceable under domestic law or under administrative rulings, or which compliance with is "necessary to obtain an advantage", reflecting the possible overlap between trade-based performance requirements and investment incentives.[8] The Annex goes on to list examples of the requirements which may qualify as trade-related investment measures, noting first those that would transgress national treatment:

> (a) the purchase or use by an enterprise of products of domestic origin or from any domestic source, whether specified in terms of particular products, in terms of volume or value of products, or in terms of a proportion of volume or value of its local production; or

---

[5] S. Quillan, 'The World Trade Organization and Its Protection of Foreign Direct Investment' (2003) 28 *Oklahoma City University Law Review* 875, 891–2.

[6] R. Edwards and S. Lester, 'Towards a More Comprehensive World Trade Organization Agreement on Trade-Related Investment Measures' (1997) 33 *Stanford International Law Journal* 169, 172.

[7] ibid. 171.

[8] Annex 1: 1 and 2.

(b) that an enterprise's purchases or use of imported products be limited to an amount related to the volume or value of local products that it exports.

Followed by those that are inconsistent with the obligation to eliminate quantitative restrictions, specifying restrictions on:

(a) the importation by an enterprise of products used in or related to its local production, generally or to an amount related to the volume or value of local production that it exports;
(b) the importation by an enterprise of products used in or related to its local production by restricting its access to foreign exchange to an amount related to the foreign exchange inflows attributable to the enterprise; or
(c) the exportation or sale for export by an enterprise of products, whether specified in terms of particular products, in terms of volume or value of products, or in terms of a proportion of volume or value of its local production.

While the term "advantage" is not specifically defined in the TRIMs, the Appellate Body in the *Canada – Aircraft* dispute noted that compliance with a trade-related investment measure in order to obtain an "advantage" under the TRIMs may contemplate forms other than a "financial contribution" or "benefit" (such as envisioned by the Agreement on Subsidies and Countervailing Measures, which will be explored further in Chapter 5). This is despite the semantic similarity between these concepts. Furthermore, no comparison with a market benchmark is required in the TRIMs context for the purpose of ascertaining whether an advantage has been conferred.[9] Accordingly for the purposes of the TRIMs, "advantage" is understood to encompass all types of advantages, including tax measures, not simply public financial contributions,[10] evidently contemplating a definition of FDI incentive that is potentially broader than that of the WTO's subsidy agreement.

The TRIMs is further limited in that it notes that all of the exceptions contained in the GATT will apply to its provisions.[11] WTO Members should therefore to be able to impose trade-related investment measures which, for example, serve the purposes of conserving exhaustible natural resources or which have the aim of health protection for humans, plants or animals. National security and balance of payments exceptions in the

[9] Appellate Body Report, *Canada – Measures Affecting the Export of Civilian Aircraft* WT/DS70/AB/R (adopted 20 August 1999) para. 5.208.

[10] M. Daly, 'Investment Incentives and the Multilateral Agreement on Investment' (1998) 38:2 *Journal of World Trade* 5, 17.

[11] Art. 3.

GATT would also apply. A national security-based exception could be contemplated, for example, in conjunction with nationality-based requirements for the managers of firms in sensitive sectors, although many of these tend to be associated with the provision of services rather than goods.

An additional important exception authorized under the TRIMs relates to developing countries. Under Article 4, developing countries are free to deviate temporarily from the TRIMs obligations to the extent specified by GATT Article XVIII, which relates to the preservation of balance of payments: a state may restrict international trade where this is necessary for it to remain solvent, as required by the IMF. This exception could have vital importance for a host state's use of restrictions on the repatriation of profits from FDI projects back to home states in order to curtail economic harms that may be suffered from capital flight. Developed country members of the WTO were required both to notify the WTO of any such trade-related measures that they maintained and to eliminate them within two years of entry into force of the WTO Agreement (1 January 1995), with developing countries allowed five years and least developed countries seven years respectively.[12] The WTO's Council for Trade in Goods is empowered to extend these transition periods for developing country members upon request of the member, provided that the country demonstrates particular difficulties in implementing the TRIMs requirements. The agreement specifies that in considering these requests, the Council will take into account the individual development, financial and trade needs of the relevant member.[13] Transitional entitlements are restrained by the requirement that Members must not modify the terms of any trade-related investment measure which they notify to the Council in a manner that increases the degree of inconsistency with Article 2: namely, incompatibility with national treatment or the requirement to eliminate quantitative measures. Any measures that benefited from the transitional regime had to be introduced at least 180 days before the entry into force of the WTO in January 1995.[14] There are additional permissions for WTO Members to apply to have their trade-related investment measures included in transition periods if they relate to like products, in order to avoid distorting treatment with respect to the conditions of competition between like new

---

[12] Art. 5.1.
[13] Art. 5.3.
[14] Art. 5.4.

and established investors.[15] The expiry of the transition periods for developing countries to implement their TRIMs obligations has removed the capacity of these countries to use the elimination of performance requirements as a possible bargaining chip in negotiation with foreign investors in order to secure economically favourable FDI: a strategy that had been recommended by commentators as a critical development tool.[16] Such countries may therefore be compelled to negotiate using other types of performance requirements, such as those relating to services.

In addition to the above substantive requirements, the TRIMs also imposes transparency requirements on WTO Members, requiring each of them to notify the WTO Secretariat of publications in which trade-related investment measures may be found. This includes publications used by regional and local governments.[17] These obligations are in line with those found in Article X of the GATT: indeed, regulatory transparency is one of the foundational principles of the WTO. As under GATT, TRIMs transparency requirements specify that each member should attempt to respond to requests for information, subject to the obvious allowance to refrain from disclosing sensitive information, such as that relating to criminal law or which could undermine the legitimate commercial interests of certain firms.[18] Members are required under Article 5.1 of the agreement to notify the WTO of any inconsistent trade-related investment measures which they have in effect. A comprehensive database of these measures is available on the WTO website. Related to the transparency and notification requirements, the TRIMs establishes the Committee on Trade Related Investment Measures, which is charged with the administration of the TRIMs. It also provides information to WTO members on any matters relating to the operation and implementation of the agreement. The Committee reports annually to the Council for Trade in Goods.[19] Article 9 of the TRIMs states that, within five years of the entry into force of the WTO Agreement, the Council for Trade in Goods will review the operation of the agreement and propose appropriate amendments to the WTO's Ministerial Conference (the highest body within the WTO). In particular, the review will consider whether the agreement

---

15 Art. 5.5.

16 V. Mosoti, 'The WTO Agreement on Trade-Related Investment measures and the Flow of Foreign Direct Investment in Africa: Meeting the Development Challenge' (2003) 15 *Pace International Law Review* 181, 195–6.

17 Art. 6.2.

18 Art. 6.3.

19 Arts 7.1–7.3.

should be modified to include material on investment policy and competition policy.

It is noteworthy that the TRIMs does not specifically address trade-related investment measures that may be imposed by sub-national governments, raising the concern that some restrictions imposed on foreign firms by regional and local governments could escape its control. Indeed, the only reference to sub-national governments in the TRIMs can be found in Article 6 on transparency. This omission is problematic because some types of performance requirements falling are carried out at the sub-national government level, as seen in the *Canada Feed-In-Tariff* dispute, discussed below.

The TRIMs has been condemned for the limits it imposes on developing countries' ability to use performance requirements in order to extract benefits from foreign investors.[20] Others have observed that local content requirements in manufacturing were never the effective economic tool that many believed them to be, indicating that the WTO's prohibition of these policies merely allowed some countries to eliminate what were unhelpful programs to begin with.[21] The TRIMs has been further criticized for its lack of efficacy in protecting FDI, notably in relation to the early stages of its existence during the operation of phase-in periods.[22] Perhaps most problematically from a standpoint of development, there are no exceptions under the TRIMs disciplines for so-called "infant industries" for which local content rules may be essential in the short term.

It should be remembered that the parties involved in the TRIMs negotiations generally diverged according to their developmental status. While there were some disagreements among the developed countries, they aimed to prohibit the most severe TRIMs, and bring others into the GATT framework regardless of their legality under existing GATT articles. The developing and least-developed countries wished to restrict the negotiations to a clarification of the applicability of existing GATT articles to TRIMs, in conjunction with an effects test to ascertain whether a particular measure affected trade in a way that transgressed the GATT. Control of export performance requirements in particular was a controversial feature in the Uruguay Round of trade negotiations which

---

20 E.g. D. Rodrik, *The New Global Economy and Developing Countries: Making Openness Work* (Overseas Development Council, Washington DC 1999) 147–8.

21 See e.g. R. Ofreneo, 'Arrested Development: Multinationals, TRIMs and the Philippines Automotive Industry' (2008) 14:1 *Asia Pacific Business Review* 1.

22 Quillan (n 5) 875.

led to the TRIMs (as well as the creation of the WTO itself). Many developed countries insist on the inclusion of such restrictions whereas many developing countries staunchly reject them.[23] The US, which consistently argued against the use of export requirements, in particular sought to exclude export performance requirements from the scope of the TRIMs.[24] The right of host states to impose such export performance requirements on foreign investors was ultimately not prohibited either by the TRIMs or by any other WTO instruments.[25] For their part, developing countries resisted the TRIMs because they feared that the agreement would not adequately protect them from the dominance of multinational enterprises which would exert restrictive barriers on host country markets.[26]

There is no indication that the TRIMs will be expanded in the near future, although a number have commentators have advocated this.[27] Some had hoped that the TRIMS would have been amended to incorporate more comprehensive investor protections, such as those found in IIAs.[28] The potential to expand the TRIMS Agreement at some point in the future, by adding more examples to the illustrative list, has increased the uncertainty concerning which features of a national industrial policy could be challenged at the WTO.[29] Recommendations regarding the enlargement of the TRIMs to address investment incentives will be discussed further in Chapter 7.

The provisions of the TRIMs are subject to the normal dispute settlement procedures of the WTO, as outlined in the Dispute Settlement Understanding.[30] This means that there is no possibility of investment arbitration between investors against host states based on TRIMs violations, as this is not a feature of the WTO's state-to-state dispute

---

23 UNCTAD, 'Elimination of TRIMs: The Experience of Selected Developing Countries' (unctad.org, 2007) 3 <http://unctad.org/en/Docs/iteiia20076_en.pdf> accessed 14 June 2013.

24 M. Sornarajah, *The International Law on Foreign Investment* (3rd edn, CUP, New York 2012) 112.

25 UNCTAD, 'Elimination of TRIMs: The Experience of Selected Developing Countries' (unctad.org 2007) 3 <http://unctad.org/en/Docs/iteiia20076_en.pdf> accessed 14 June 2013.

26 Quillin (n 5) 881.

27 Edwards and Lester (n 6).

28 Quillan (n 5) 892.

29 J. Chaisse, D. Chakrabort and A. Guha, 'India's Multilayered FDI Regulation' in J. Chaisse and P. Gugler (eds), *Expansion of Trade and FDI in Asia* (Routledge, New York, NY 2009) 247.

30 Art. 8.

settlement system. Instead, investors must seek the support of their home state to bring such claims. Some IIAs containing investor–state arbitration provisions, however, explicitly incorporate the obligations of the TRIMs into their text.[31] The TRIMs has been the subject of very little WTO case law, primarily because it does little more than reaffirm the application of GATT Article III.4 to certain forms of FDI.[32] Most of the disputes citing TRIMs provisions have been related to the automotive industry. The impact of TRIMs in this sphere is not surprising, given the significant role that the automotive manufacturing sector plays in the economy of many countries, including notably the US and Japan. Moreover, the automotive industry is known for its use of quantitative restrictions and local content rules, which lie at the core of the TRIMs' prohibitions.[33] Additionally many non-industrialized regions, such as Africa, had already adopted a regulatory approach to FDI that was consistent with the TRIMs Agreement's obligations by the time the agreement was concluded.[34]

In 1996, the European Union, Japan and the US requested consultations through the WTO dispute settlement procedure against Indonesia, regarding its allegedly restrictive policies towards its automotive sector.[35] Indonesia provided firms with import duty exemptions or reductions on required levels of imports on automotive parts, based on the percentage of local content that they used in their manufacturing. It also offered tax and import duty exemptions as incentives to firms, based on the degree of local content, effectively constituting a breach of national treatment against foreign produced components. The complainant countries argued that the measures implemented by the government of Indonesia were inconsistent with GATT Articles I:1 (most favoured nation), III:2, III:4 (national treatment) and X:3a (the reasonable administration of laws) and Article 2 of the TRIMs: the agreement's substantive prohibition on national treatment and quantitative restrictions being used in conjunction with foreign investment laws (as well as various sections of the SCM). The Panel agreed with most of these claims, finding that the relevant

---

31 Costa Rica–Canada, Art. VI (signed 18 March 1998).

32 M. Trebilcock, *Understanding Trade Law* (Edward Elgar, Cheltenham 2011) 128.

33 Quillin (n 5) 890.

34 Mosoti (n 16) 201.

35 Panel Report, *Indonesia – Certain Measures Affecting the Automobile Industry* WT/DS54/R, WT/DS55/R, WT/DS59/R, WT/DS64/R and Corr.1 and 2 (adopted 23 July 1998), and Corr. 3 and 4, DSR 1998:VI, 2201.

measures implemented by Indonesia constituted local content requirements that were TRIMs-prohibited trade-related investment measures, violating both GATT national treatment and TRIMs.[36] Indonesia announced its intention to comply with the Panel recommendations, and by 1999 all of the local content performance requirements were eliminated.

In 1999, the European Union and the US brought TRIMs-based proceedings against India through the WTO dispute settlement procedure for its industrial indigenization policies.[37] The EU and the US complained that several regulations instigated by the Indian government in relation to its automobile industry violated Articles III (national treatment) and XI (prohibition on quantitative restrictions) of the GATT as well as Article 2 of the TRIMs (the prohibition on trade-related investment measures). The relevant Indian laws mandated that imports of complete automobiles and of certain parts and components were subjected to a system of non-automatic import licences. Import licences for these products would be granted only to local joint venture manufacturers that had signed a Memorandum of Understanding with the Indian government. This arrangement obliged manufacturers to conform to specified local content as well as export-balancing requirements. The Panel ultimately ruled that India's imposition of these requirements on automotive manufacturers was in breach of its commitments under the GATT and, having reached this conclusion, it decided that it was not necessary to consider whether the measures also violated Article 2 of the TRIMs. In exercising judicial economy, the panel did not elaborate on the way in which the TRIMs will be interpreted; however, it did note that the TRIMs should not be viewed as a more specific version of the GATT, and as such it was not compelled to consider the TRIMs before the GATT under the principle of the specific agreement illuminating the more general. This may be another reason why there is limited TRIMs case law in favour of decisions being made under the GATT. Implementing the panel recommendations in the *India – Autos* dispute, the WTO Dispute Settlement Body required the Indian government to eliminate all inconsistent measures. To its credit, India had removed all of these local content requirements by September 2001, even before the Panel had circulated its report.[38]

---

[36] ibid.

[37] Panel Report, *India – Measures Affecting the Automotive Sector* WT/DS146/R, WT/DS175/R and Corr.1 (adopted 5 April 2002), DSR 2002:V, 1827.

[38] ibid.

One of the most important disputes relating to trade-based performance requirements brought under the GATT (before the existence of the WTO) was the *Canada – FIRA*[39] case between Canada and the US. In this dispute, which was instigated before the establishment of the WTO and its more formal dispute settlement procedure (and before the TRIMs), the US complained that certain measures relating to local content, that were imposed on foreign investors by the Canadian government under the federal Foreign Investment Review Act enacted in 1973, violated provisions of the GATT. Under this statute, Canada required foreign investors to purchase certain goods from the domestic market, based on specific proportions of local content, or to purchase goods from Canadian sources. The law also obliged foreign firms to export a certain percentage of their final products. The US claimed that these regulations constituted performance requirements that were illegal under the GATT's national treatment provisions. Canada obliged foreign firms to purchase certain goods from domestic market in preference to imported goods, or in definite amounts or proportions, or to purchase goods from Canadian sources, and to export a certain amount or percentage of final products. This constituted both local content and export performance requirements. With respect to local content performance requirements, the Panel concluded that they were inconsistent with Article III:4 of GATT (national treatment to imported goods). The Panel also ruled that Canadian requirement, imposed on foreign investors, to export certain amount or percentage of the manufactured goods was not inconsistent with Canada's obligations under the GATT. In so doing the panel was careful to emphasize that what was at issue in the dispute before the Panel was the conformity of certain trade-related measures undertaken by the Canadian Government with its GATT obligations, but not the right of Canada as a host state to regulate foreign investment per se.[40] It is interesting to note that the FIRA dispute has been described by some as a "subterfuge" in that the US, as complainant, successfully characterized the dispute as one relating to trade and not investment in order to avail itself of the GATT panel system.[41]

Canada faced a high-profile complaint under the TRIMs brought by the EU in relation to Canada's Feed-in-Tariff program, in which it (through

---

[39] GATT Panel Report, *Canada – Administration of the Foreign Investment Review Act,* adopted 7 February 1984, BISD 30S/140.

[40] ibid.

[41] R. Leal-Arcas, *International Trade and Investment Law* (Edward Elgar, Cheltenham 2010) 191.

the sub-central government of the province of Ontario) imposed restrictions on the sale and distribution of equipment for renewable energy generation (including wind and solar) facilities.[42] The EU (along with Japan) alleged that Canada accorded less favourable treatment to foreign suppliers of the equipment than it did to local ones, in violation of the national treatment obligation in Article III:3 and III:5 of the GATT as well as Article 2.1 of the TRIMs. The measure in question required that the renewable energy equipment had to be supplied with a minimum content (25 per cent for wind and 60 per cent for solar power) from firms within Ontario. These were effectively domestic content requirements, affording protection to local producers of such equipment. The Canadian government had maintained that the local content measures were necessary to promote the use of clean energy in Ontario. The panel upheld the EU's claims under Article 2.1 of the TRIMs, as well as under the GATT, ruling that the measure fell within the type of trade-related investment measure described in Article 1(a) of the agreement's illustrative list, namely a local content requirement. The panel considered also whether Canada could rely upon Article III:8(a) of the GATT (which excluded government procurement activities from the scope of the national treatment obligation) to justify breach of Article 2.1 of the TRIMs, ultimately deciding that Canada could not do so because the feed-in-tariff programme implemented by the government of Ontario covered the procurement of electricity that was undertaken with a view to commercial resale, which fell outside the rubric of procurement which contemplated governmental use. The panel's recommendation was appealed to the Appellate Body, which upheld the panel's determination that the local content features of the feed-in-tariff measure contravened Article 2.1 of the TRIMs, further confirming that Article III:8 of the GATT was not applicable to the feed-in-tariff measures because they involved commercial sales rather than procurement activities.[43] In June 2014 Canada notified the WTO that it had complied with the Appellate Body's recommendation, by no longer subjecting large renewable electricity procurement to domestic content requirements under the feed-in-tariff programme. This decision reveals the impact that the TRIMS will have on governments' attempts to promote indigenous technology as well as

[42] Panel Report, *Canada – Certain Measures Affecting the Renewable Energy Generation Sector*; *Canada – Measures Relating to the Feed-in Tariff Program* WT/DS426/R (19 Dec 2012).

[43] Appellate Body Report, *Canada – Certain Measures Affecting the Renewable Energy Generation Sector*; *Canada – Measures Relating to the Feed-in Tariff Program* WT/DS426/AB/R (6 May 2013).

nascent industries (namely renewable energy), which may have broader social as well as economic benefits. In this regard, the panel and Appellate Body's ruling in this dispute should be welcomed because they prohibited the discriminatory element of an environmental policy, not the environmental policy itself. It should be noted that another crucial aspect of the *Canada – FIT* dispute involved allegations of subsidies in favour of local industry. These claims were rejected by the Appellate Body under a narrow reading of "benefit" under Agreement on Subsidies and Countervailing Measures, a topic which will be explored further in Chapter 5. This feature of the decision may please environmentalists seeking support for inefficient but environmentally beneficial programmes, although it has drawn significant criticism from academics for its bias in favour of subsidies that have an environmental aim, despite being trade distortive.[44]

More recently, the EU has accused Brazil of imposing local content requirements on automobile companies, including increased excise taxes of up to 30 per cent of value, based on the amount of imported content in each vehicle. Brazil has resisted this accusation and at the time of writing there has yet to be a panel established to resolve the matter under the WTO's dispute settlement system. Many see this policy as a sign of Brazil's increasing trade (and investment) protectionism, which has resulted in much higher prices for its own consumers.[45] Japan and EU have initiated complaints against Russia under the TRIMs for fees that it has imposed for the recycling of automobiles.[46] There are a number of other disputes relating to the TRIMs currently at the consultation stage.

(ii) The WTO General Agreement on Trade in Services (GATS)

The GATS is the WTO's agreement covering trade in services and has a significant impact on FDI in this sector. Negotiated during the Uruguay Round in the 1990s, as services were becoming a more entrenched and high-value presence in the global economy, the GATS relies on each Member's individual commitments in order to achieve liberalization in

---

[44] See e.g. R. Pal, 'Has the Appellate Body's Decision in *Canada – Renewable Energy / Canada Feed-in-Tariff* Program Opened the Door for Production Subsidies?' (2014) 17:1 *Journal of International Economic Law* 125.

[45] J Leahy, 'EU Steps Up Trade Fight With Brazil Over Local Content Rules' *Financial Times* (London, 31 October 2014).

[46] *Russian Federation – Recycling Fee on Motor Vehicles* WT/DS463 (request for consultations 9 July 2013), WT/DS426 (request for consultations 24 July 2013).

the international trade of services. This piecemeal approach, which differs considerably from the GATT, may be explained in part by the complexities associated with not only the regulation of services, but in the simple definition of what constitutes a service: a far more complicated task than that of goods because of the intangible nature of this type of activity. Accordingly Article I of the GATS defines instead "trade in services" by reference to the four modes of supply of services. Mode 3 of the supply of services through commercial presence – effectively, a firm from one state setting up a branch or office in another state – is relevant to the regulation of FDI. It is important to note that "services" under GATS does not include those supplied in the exercise of governmental authority, which means any service which is supplied neither on a commercial basis, nor in competition with one or more service suppliers.[47] This, along with its positive-list style of commitment, is GATS' most significant limitation.

GATS does not contain any prohibitions on the imposition of performance requirements on foreign suppliers of services, indeed the phrase performance requirement is absent from this agreement, as it is from all WTO agreements – including the TRIMs. The starting point for the analysis of GATS' potential to control performance requirements, then, is its national treatment obligation. Unlike the GATT, national treatment under the GATS only applies to the extent that a member has made specific commitments within particular sectors and in favour of designated modes of services delivery.[48] As such, members are free to discriminate against foreign suppliers of services should they wish to; however, once a commitment has been made and listed in a members' schedule of commitments, it becomes binding and failure to fulfil it could result in a complaint through the WTO dispute-settlement system. The nuances of the national treatment test for GATS were discussed in the previous chapter, but it is worth repeating that the text of GATS expressly includes reference to discriminatory treatment against foreign services or services suppliers that modifies the conditions of competition, effectively meaning that foreign investors cannot compete on an even footing with the equivalent local ones because of the manner in which the services that they supply are regulated by the host state.[49] Accordingly, as alluded to in the previous chapter, in the understanding that there is no settled definition of what constitutes a performance requirement, various types

---

47 Art. I(b), (c).
48 Art. XVII.
49 Art. XVII.3.

of conditions (for example, mandatory local content, local employment or training requirements) that are imposed upon foreign firms that are not imposed upon like local ones could constitute GATS national treatment violations. This feature of the agreement achieves pre-establishment right of entry for foreign firms, far beyond what is contained in most IIAs which focus on protections for foreign firms upon their establishment.

Article XVI of GATS covers members' commitments on market access, which facilitates the investment (through Mode 3 commercial presence) of service suppliers from WTO members into the territory of another member. This provision precludes quantitative limitations on the number and extent of FDI. This obligation only applies to the extent that members have made market-access commitments which they have then included in their schedule of commitments. Market access applies regardless of national origin: when a commitment is made by a member to open up a given services sector, the prohibition on numeric quotas (such as a certain number of firms per industry) is disallowed, whether or not the investor is local or foreign. Given that market access is nationality-neutral, it does not have an FDI specific objective in mind, although enhanced market access undoubtedly has a positive impact on FDI-flows in committed sectors. When market-access commitments are made, a state may limit this provision by adding that the foreign investor will not be allowed to enter if it is subsidized by its home government.

The market-access provisions of GATS prohibit:

(a) limitations on the number of service suppliers whether in the form of numerical quotas, monopolies, exclusive service suppliers or the requirements of an economic needs test;
(b) limitations on the total value of service transactions or assets in the form of numerical quotas or the requirement of an economic needs test;
(c) limitations on the total number of service operations or on the total quantity of service output expressed in terms of designated numerical units in the form of quotas or the requirement of an economic needs test;
(d) limitations on the total number of natural persons that may be employed in a particular service sector or that a service supplier may employ and who are necessary for, and directly related to, the supply of a specific service in the form of numerical quotas or the requirement of an economic needs test;
(e) measures which restrict or require specific types of legal entity or joint venture through which a service supplier may supply a service; and
(f) limitations on the participation of foreign capital in terms of maximum percentage limit on foreign shareholding or the total value of individual or aggregate foreign investment.

In one sense, GATS market-access provisions appear to implicate the control of performance requirements more readily than national treatment because of their emphasis on quantifiable conditions, which recalls the language seen in the TRIMs agreement concerning percentage of local content and percentage of goods for export. In another sense GATS market-access rules seem to be precisely the opposite of performance requirements because they set out prohibitions on maximum levels of FDI, effectively removing a host state's capacity to structure FDI in a manner that it deems desirable. Performance requirements tend not to restrict the quantity of FDI but rather specify the manner in which that FDI is delivered, such as in conjunction with the use of certain categories of goods or by certain categories of people. In that sense the market-access provisions bear little resemblance to performance requirements.

Another provision of GATS that is potentially relevant to the regulation of performance requirements placed on foreign investors is Article VI on domestic regulation. This provision does not impose a binding requirement on WTO Members, but rather indicates a direction that further services liberalization negotiations should take, by encouraging states not to use technical standards as obstacles to trade in services (including via commercial presence FDI) where possible. It is apposite to draw attention to the language used, because it appears to contemplate measures that might be viewed as performance requirements:

> With a view to ensuring that measures relating to qualification requirements and procedures, technical standards and licensing requirements do not constitute unnecessary barriers to trade in services, the Council for Trade in Services shall, through appropriate bodies it may establish, develop any necessary disciplines. Such disciplines shall aim to ensure that such requirements are, inter alia:
> (a) based on objective and transparent criteria, such as competence and the ability to supply the service;
> (b) not more burdensome than necessary to ensure the quality of the service;
> (c) in the case of licensing procedures, not in themselves a restriction on the supply of the service.

In other words, host states should not impose any superfluous requirements on foreign investors that impair their ability to deliver services freely. To the extent that conditions are imposed, such as licensing requirements or qualifications, they have to be reasonably non-burdensome. As such, a performance requirement consisting of a law specifying that foreign lawyers wishing to open a branch office in the host state must obtain legal qualifications in domestic educational institutions might be necessary, because it implies a certain level of competence, whereas a requirement that such foreign lawyers obtain masters degrees and doctorates from local universities in order to practice would be excessive or overly-burdensome. For the purposes of clarity, the implicit analogy in the above example is between a local content rule for manufactured goods (a clear performance requirement) and a local content rule for services (arguably a performance requirement). In other words, qualification-based performance requirements on services FDI are acceptable as long as they can be reasonably justified.

Finally, given the impact of performance requirements on non-economic matters such as labour or environmental concerns, the GATS contains a general exception provision which could allow WTO Members the possibility to justify discriminatory or market-access-based performance requirements relating to trade in services. Thus, Article XIV reads in relevant part:

> Subject to the requirement that such measures are not applied in a manner which would constitute a means of arbitrary or unjustifiable discrimination between countries where like conditions prevail, or a disguised restriction on trade in services, nothing in this Agreement shall be construed to prevent the adoption or enforcement by any Member of measures:
>
> (a) necessary to protect public morals or to maintain public order;
> (b) necessary to protect human, animal or plant life or health;
> (c) necessary to secure compliance with laws or regulations … including those relating to:
>   (i) the prevention of deceptive and fraudulent practices …;
>   (ii) the protection of the privacy of individuals …;
>   (iii) safety;

The GATS general exceptions are slightly different than those contained in the GATT 1947 and which govern the TRIMs. Most notably, the connecting language in GATS is exclusively that of "necessity" which tends to be viewed as more onerous than that of "relating to" seen in conjunction with some of the goods-based policy justifications. There is limited case law on the GATS general exceptions, but the highly indeterminate and potentially broad concept of "public morals" and "public order" could have wide-ranging implications in terms of a member's capacity to impose performance requirements that have non-market implications for policies such as those based on cultural elements as well as addressing severe regional economic disadvantage. Accordingly, it may be feasible for a WTO Member to impose research-and-development-type obligations on foreign services investors as a condition of entry based on these provisions.

As with the TRIMs, jurisprudence on GATS is sparse, and there is less still relating to the commercial presence mode of delivery that is relevant to FDI. In a complaint brought by the US,[50] Mexico was found to have violated its commercial-presence commitments under GATS because it had not taken any steps to ensure access for foreign firms to private telecommunications channels, as per its obligations under the GATS Annex on Telecommunications. Mexico's requirement that foreign telecommunication firms must connect with international gateways, rather than through foreign public telecommunications networks, violated its obligation to ensure that service suppliers of any other Member have access to and use of any public telecommunications transport network or service offered within or across the border of that Member, including privately-leased circuits.[51] As a "performance requirement" (a term not used in the dispute) which was placed on foreign telecommunication companies, this measure effectively induced foreign investors to make use of local services providers, to the advantage of those network providers, in order for them to have full access to the Mexican market. In other words, the nature of FDI into Mexico would need to be modified in order to suit economic objectives of the Mexican government, contrary to WTO law. There is a plausible analogy between the national measure that was prohibited in this dispute and a local content law in the manufacturing context.

A more recent example of an FDI-oriented measure challenged under GATS that could be construed as a performance requirement can be seen in the *China – Electronic Payments* dispute.[52] In this dispute the United States argued that China breached its Mode 3 commercial presence (as well as Mode 1) national treatment and market-access commitments under Articles XVI and XVII of GATS by permitting only a Chinese firm to supply electronic payment services for payment card transactions denominated and paid in renminbis in China. Firms from other Members could only supply these services for card transactions when they were paid in a foreign currency. China also required all payment card processing devices to be compatible with the Chinese firm's system and to show its company logo. The US further complained that the Chinese firm which benefited from the law had guaranteed access to all merchants in China that accept payment cards, whereas foreign firms had to

---

[50] Panel Report, *Mexico – Measures Affecting Telecommunication Services* WT/DS204 (panel report circulated 2 April 2004).

[51] GATS Annex 5(b).

[52] Panel Report, *China – Certain Measures Affecting Electronic Payment Services* WT/DS413/R (16 July 2012).

negotiate for access to merchants. The panel decided that China had made market-access and national treatment commitments for commercial presence relating to payment card transactions on condition that the foreign supplier met certain qualifications related to local renminbi business. The panel went on to find the requirements did not breach China's GATS market-access commitments because there were no explicit limitations on the entry of foreign suppliers. However, the requirement that all payment cards must bear that firm's logo was inconsistent with Mode 3 national treatment because it modified the conditions of competition in favour of the local firm, damaging the competitive opportunities of foreign investors. This decision was not appealed and China is in the process of bringing its measures into conformity with the panel's recommendation. This case demonstrates that conditions controlling the manner in which foreign firms supply services within a host state can transgress the non-discrimination and potentially also market-access components of GATS. China had established performance requirements (again this phrase was not used in the panel report) effectively mandating some local participation in the delivery of certain financial services, and these were incompatible with its services liberalization commitments. Again, the analogy between this law and a local content rule should not be overlooked. This decision is expected to contribute to the further opening of China's financial services market, benefiting US suppliers of electronic payment services in particular.[53]

(iii) The Government Procurement Agreement (GPA)

A key and growing sphere of WTO law that is potentially applicable to the control of performance requirements is that relating to government procurement, captured by GPA. Government procurement is the process through which a public agency purchases a good or service for its own use. In developed countries with well-established public sectors, the expenditure on public procurement represents approximately 15 to 20 per cent of the GDP.[54] Governments had traditionally exercised discrimination against international suppliers when engaging in procurement, as

---

[53] P. Delimatsis, 'The WTO outlaws the privileges of the Chinese payment services giant' No. 31, 16 July 2012 *Insights – American Society of International Law*; Vol. 16, 1–5.

[54] European Commission, 'A Report on the Functioning of Public Procurement Markets in the EU: Benefits from the Application of EU Directives and Challenges for the Future' (Brussels, 2004) <http://ec.europa.eu/internal_market/

this was one of the chief mechanisms by which the local economy could be supported. Indeed, as noted above, GATS contains a carve-out for services normally supplied in the exercise of governmental authority.

Procurement-oriented discrimination is common around the world. The Chinese government, for example, believes the strategy of granting Chinese firms preferential treatment in government procurement is essential to furthering the country's technological development. With favourable procurement terms, this policy appears to be predicated on the belief that companies will thrive when they are given time to innovate and capture sufficient market share to scale up their production.[55] Favouring local suppliers in government procurement is based on the theory that an increase in national income can be achieved by reducing government expenditure on imports.[56] Discrimination in favour of local suppliers may also be based on national security or cultural grounds as well as to assist disadvantaged groups or regions. The rationale for liberalized, non-discriminatory procurement rules is founded in the positive effects of enhanced competition as well as efficiency gains, resulting in lower prices and higher quality. This is why the imposition of performance requirements on foreign investors which supply goods and services to government could represent a sub-optimal allocation of resources; the most efficient supplier of goods and services to governments will not be chosen in favour of one that satisfies given conditions.

As noted above, the GPA is the WTO's core agreement regulating government procurement in member countries. The GPA is a plurilateral or optional agreement, and as of early 2015 it has 43 party countries (including the 28 member states of the European Union), most of which are developed (and therefore for which government procurement markets are significant). Its purpose is to ensure that foreign products and services

---

publicprocurement/docs/public-proc-market-final-report_en.pdf> accessed 31 July 2015.

[55] See D. Ernst, 'Global Production Networks and the Changing Geography of Innovation Systems: Implications for Developing Countries' (2002) 11:6 *Economic Innovation and New Technology* 497. It may be more likely that a country that introduces high-tech production subsidies could see its competitiveness in high-technology products grow initially, but in the long run its rate of indigenous innovation will decline. This is thought to have occurred with Japan, which employed technology oriented subsidies that ultimately benefited its trading partners rather than its own producers and even slowed the global pace of technological through diminished competition.

[56] S. Evenett, 'Multilateral Disciplines and Government Procurement' in B. Hoekman et al. (eds), *Development, Trade and the WTO* (World Bank, Washington DC 2002) 417.

are treated no less favourably in government procurement than domestic ones. As such, its Article IV contains most-favoured-nation and national-treatment provisions:

> (1) With respect to any measure regarding covered procurement, each Party, including its procuring entities, shall accord immediately and unconditionally to the goods and services of any other Party and to the suppliers of any other Party offering the goods or services of any Party, treatment no less favourable than the treatment the Party, including its procuring entities, accords to:
> (a) domestic goods, services and suppliers; and
> (b) goods, services and suppliers of any other Party.
>
> (2) With respect to any measure regarding covered procurement, a Party, including its procuring entities, shall not:
> (a) treat a locally established supplier less favourably than another locally established supplier on the basis of the degree of foreign affiliation or ownership; or
> (b) discriminate against a locally established supplier on the basis that the goods or services offered by that supplier for a particular procurement are goods or services of any other Party.

The reference to "degree of foreign affiliation" in Article IV(2) discloses that the GPA is also an investment-oriented agreement: it directly prohibits discriminatory procurement regulations faced by foreign firms which are established in the relevant party state.

The GPA contains five annexes outlining each signatory's obligations, and each signatory may include exceptions to their commitments in their General Notes. There is considerable scope for discriminatory procurement policies that aim to stimulate local innovation and the development of disadvantaged regions. For example, the US excludes from its GPA commitments: (1) small businesses, which policy enables smaller contracts to be directed to innovative small businesses; and (2) research and development activities, which allows the most innovative governmental contracts to be directed to local firms and start-ups, to use the modern terminology.

Such provisions could embrace performance requirements in situations where host government treaty parties were to look favourably on supplying firms with foreign ownership that fulfil certain conditions such as engaging in research-and-development activities. Commentators have observed that China's indigenous innovation laws, which grant procurement preferences to firms whose intellectual property is owned or registered in China, would likely violate GPA rules prohibiting discrimination in procurement based on nationality.[57] While China is not currently a signatory to the GPA, it has observer status and appears to be interested in acceding to the agreement in the near future. It is possible that the GPA's Article V, on special and differential treatment for developing countries, might allow China and other developing countries to maintain policies like this, because it permits such countries to negotiate special terms with the current signatories that apply only to them. Still, maintaining such restrictions could lead to other GPA parties specifically denying Chinese firms from benefiting from their procurement commitments. Wary of this danger, China has recently discussed removing local content requirements from its wind-power market for the purposes of GPA-accession negotiations.[58]

India is another large emerging market with a history of implementing procurement-based performance requirements that is contemplating accession to the GPA in the near future. While membership to the GPA should be beneficial for Indian firms that are competitive in global markets, such as those which engage in information technology provision, other sectors may lack the necessary expertise to access the markets of the predominately developed country membership of the GPA. This means that gains could be limited, while the risk of foreign suppliers entering the Indian procurement market is great. This is why it is expected that India will attempt to negotiate the inclusion of performance requirements into its GPA commitments in the form of "offsets". "Offsets" refers to any condition placed on supplying firms that encourages local development or improves a party's economic development (in terms of its balance of payments status), such as the use of domestic content, the hiring of local employees or the transfer or licensing of technology to local firms.[59] Such offsets could be phased out over time as agreed by India and the other GPA parties after a certain transition period.[60] In the context of procurement, a set-off or an off-set agreement can also refer to an arrangement in which a foreign supplier agrees to buy

[57] S. James Bomil III, 'China's Indigenous Innovation Policies Under the TRIPs and GPA Agreements and Alternatives for Promoting Economic Growth' (2011) 12 *Chicago Journal of International Law* 755.

[58] G. Dyer, 'China and US Resolve Trade Disputes' *Financial Times* (London, 30 October 2009).

[59] GPA Art. 1 l).

[60] S. Khorana and S. Subramanian, 'Potential Accession to the WTO Government Procurement Agreement: A Case Study on India' (2012) 15:1 *Journal of International Economic Law* 287, 302.

products from the government to which it is selling. Under these types of schemes, the seller often agrees to buy products from firms within the target country in order to win the procurement contract. Crucially, Article IV:6 of the GPA states that a Party, including its procuring entities, shall not seek, take account of, impose or enforce any offset linked to procurement commitments it has made: effectively a prohibition on performance requirements applied in the context of procurement. However, Article V:3 provides:

> … a developing country may adopt or maintain one or more of the following transitional measures, during a transition period … , and applied in a manner that does not discriminate among the other Parties: …
>
> (b) an offset, provided that any requirement for, or consideration of, the imposition of the offset is clearly stated in the notice of intended procurement

This article has limited practical impact because there are currently no developing countries which have signed the GPA (with the arguable exception of Israel). This provision could, however, help countries such as India and China seeking to employ offset arrangements should they ever accede to the GPA.

Procurement policies instigated by sub-central governments can have major impacts upon FDI as well as international trade. Canada's initial reluctance to commit its sub-central provincial governments to the GPA was partly the consequence of the US maintaining discriminatory policies in favour of small domestic firms in government purchasing at the state level through its GPA commitments.[61] As most of the suppliers negatively affected by these rules were located in Canada rather than Canadian owned firms in the US, this restriction was more trade-oriented than it was FDI. Canada and the US were able to negotiate exemptions for Canadian suppliers to these US "Buy American" requirements as well as the special arrangements for discriminatory government procurement contained in the US Recovery Act, especially those relating to the use of steel and manufactured goods in public works and public buildings.[62] As a consequence of these bilateral negotiations, Canada committed all of its sub-central governments to the revised GPA, extending these advantages

---

[61] D. Attwater, 'The Influence of Buy American Policies on Canadian Coverage under the World Trade Organization Agreement on Government Procurement' (2012) 46:1 *International Lawyer* 939, 944.

[62] American Recovery and Reinvestment Act of 2009, Pub. L No. 111-5, 123 Stat. 115.

to all other party states.[63] Thus the US was able to maintain its economic regeneration-based procurement performance requirements with respect to other GPA signatories while allowing special exemptions for Canadian firms. These events illustrate the importance of local content-oriented performance requirements to countries with significant manufacturing and extractive sectors, particularly when their chief trading partner has a substantial public-sector economy. The trade-off is that, while Canadian firms now have greater access to US state-level government contracts, they will be subject to competition from US firms seeking similar opportunities in Canada's sub-central procurement markets. Perhaps more profoundly, all governments which have acceded to the GPA have, through the offset prohibition, sacrificed one of the key instruments by which they can fulfil social and industrial policy, such as regeneration following an economic crisis. Of course, parties are free not to commit various types of procurement activities in their GPA annexes in order to serve these purposes.

Article XVIII:1 of the revised GPA requires signatory states to maintain timely, effective, transparent and non-discriminatory administrative or judicial-review procedure for all government procurement bidding regimes. The same tribunal can, and in many cases, does serve multiple functions under both the GPA or procurement rules contained in regional trade agreements. Chapter 10 of NAFTA, for example, requires signatory parties to maintain an independent bid-challenge authority to review procurement procedures.[64] These rules should allow for the clear identification of any prohibited performance requirement / offsets associated with procurement policies, as described above.

Although procurement rules are uncommon to IIAs, it should be noted that there are a number of regional procurement rules contained in economic integration agreements, such as those found in NAFTA and the Comprehensive Economic and Trade Agreement between the EU and Canada (CETA). In this regard, it is noteworthy that the arbitration tribunal in *ADF Group v US* determined that NAFTA's performance requirements prohibitions contained in its Article 1106 do not extend to the treaty's government procurement rules, at least at the sub-national (state and provincial) level. The tribunal noted further that all three NAFTA members regularly imposed performance requirements as part of

---

63 D. Collins, 'Canada's Sub-central Government Entities and the Agreement on Government Procurement: Past and Present' in S. Arrowsmith and R. Anderson (eds), *The WTO Regime on Government Procurement: Challenge and Reform* (CUP, Cambridge 2011).

64 Art. 1017(1)g.

their government procurement regimes.[65] This is despite the fact that NAFTA's two developed countries (Canada and the US) are GPA members bound by the GPA's no-offset rule.

Finally, discriminatory government procurement policies, such as those imputing performance requirements, may constitute an implicit subsidy to certain investors. In this regard it is important to recognize that the GPA specifically excludes fiscal incentives, loans and grants from its coverage,[66] unless provided otherwise in each party's specific commitment annexes. This would presumably remove tax incentives or other advantages offered in conjunction with procurement contracts from the scrutiny of the GPA. Reporting of any type of procurement-oriented assistance to firms is difficult, because such amounts tend not to be recorded in governmental documents.[67] This issue will be explored further in Chapter 5.

(iv) The Trade-Related Aspects of Intellectual Property Agreement (TRIPs)

TRIPs is the WTO's multilateral instrument that covers trade in intellectual property related materials. It establishes minimum standards of protection relating to various forms of intellectual property, including copyright, trademark, and patents. The TRIPs is relevant to FDI because intellectual property represents an important and valuable form of investment to many foreign companies: investors are more prone to internationalize when they are secure in the knowledge that these types of assets will be protected. The agreement has the potential to implicate performance requirements, because it can control the extent to which host states impose various types of conditions on the registration and or enforcement of intellectual property rights, which are typically covered as a category of investment under the definitions of investment under most IIAs.

Non-discrimination as to the origin of intellectual property is one of the cornerstones of the TRIPs regime. Article 3 of the TRIPs outlines the agreement's national treatment provision.

> 1. Each Member shall accord to the nationals of other Members treatment no less favourable than that it accords to its own nationals with regard to the protection of intellectual property …

---

65 *ADF Group Inc v United States of America* ICSID Case No. ARB(AF)/00/1, Award (9 January 2008) [188].

66 Art. II.3(b).

67 Daly (n 10) 10.

Under this provision a foreign investor should be able to secure the protection of its intellectual-property-related assets in conjunction with its entry or continued operation in a host state that is a member of the WTO. Any attempt by a host state to enact laws that in some way frustrate this ability based on the intellectual-property-owner's national origin, would be contrary to the TRIPs and eligible for removal under the WTO's dispute settlement mechanism.

There is a dearth of case law under Article 3 of TRIPs and it is therefore difficult to assess how a panel would approach a performance requirement placed on the ability of a foreign investor to register or enforce its intellectual property rights. Hypothetically then, a policy such as the Chinese government's indigenous innovation scheme (noted above in conjunction with the GPA) could potentially be viewed as illegal under the TRIPs, because it disadvantages foreign-owned intellectual property rights in favour of locally-owned ones by making the patent registration process easier for locally-produced inventions relative to foreign ones. This rule may be conceived as a performance requirement because it effectively conditions legal protection on the degree of domestic content, paralleling the logic of trade-related investment measures, discussed above. Requiring the input of local content into the creation of intellectual property, while potentially helpful to the development and support of local scientists and engineers, could operate to shift research-and-development projects away from more efficient environments.

In the *Indonesia – Autos* dispute, mentioned earlier in relation to the TRIMs, the panel examined the US's complaint against Indonesia regarding its National Car Program, which required participating vehicles to bear a unique, domestically owned Indonesian trademark. This restriction arguably constituted a performance requirement, in that it made legal protection contingent on the engagement in specified conduct, which in this case related to the use of intellectual property. The US argued that the Indonesian law discriminated against nationals of other WTO members with respect to the "acquisition" and "maintenance" of trademark rights as specified in footnote 3 to Article 3. This provision defines the type of "protection" embraced by TRIPs to include matters affecting the availability, acquisition, scope, maintenance and enforcement of intellectual property rights as well as those matters affecting the use of intellectual property rights, including trademarks. The panel rejected the US's claim regarding an impairment to the acquisition of trademarks, reasoning that the program merely stipulated that only certain signs could be used as trademarks, and there was no evidence that right to trademarks excluded from the program could not be obtained in a non-discriminatory manner under Indonesian law. Despite the fact that it strongly incentivized firms to undertake expensive foreign registration activities (registering trademarks in Indonesia rather than in their home state), the measure was not genuinely discriminatory based on national origin. Furthermore, as to the maintenance of trademarks, in *Indonesia – Autos* the US had argued that partners in the national car program would be unlikely to use their global trademarks in Indonesia out of fear of confusing consumers. It would be more likely, they asserted, that the global trademark would be cancelled for non-use in Indonesia. There is nothing obviously unfair in requiring a firm to register its intellectual property domestically, since this type of system subjects foreign firms to precisely the same rules as it does domestic firms. Full national treatment would allow every firm to seek intellectual property protection in its home country rather than require it to establish such rights in the host state in which it invests, effectively establishing local brands as well as bringing intellectual-property-based claims in the courts of the host state, rather than in its own. This decisions illustrates that, while Article 3 of TRIPS does not prohibit the intellectual-property-related performance requirements or their equivalent outright, if such requirements are genuinely discriminatory then they will be banned.

Following the reasoning suggested above, Article 27 of TRIPs, which covers patentable subject matter, could also operate to delimit the use of performance requirements tied to intellectual property rights by host states. Article 27 states:

> 1. … patents shall be available and patent rights enjoyable without discrimination as to the place of invention, the field of technology and whether products are imported or locally produced.

This provision came under scrutiny by a WTO panel in the *Canada – Pharmaceuticals* dispute.[68] This dispute involved a complaint brought by the European Communities against, inter alia, Canada's regulatory patent review provisions, which permitted the general manufacturers of pharmaceuticals to produce samples of the patented product for use during the regulatory review process. The European Communities had argued that this law was discriminatory because it was aimed at pharmaceutical products which in practice only foreign firms created: essentially a performance requirement imposed on foreign patent holders seeking to

[68] Panel Report, *Canada – Patent Protection of Pharmaceutical Products* WT/DS114/R (adopted 7 April 2000).

register their patents in Canada (although the term performance requirement was not used). Ruling that the European Communities did not demonstrate that the regulatory review provision was discriminatory either de jure or de facto, the panel elaborated that the term "discrimination" potentially encompasses a wide range of meanings and should be construed on a case-by-case basis within the precise context of the issue at hand. There is no indication from the panel's ruling how the phrase "whether products are imported or locally produced" should be interpreted. It may require WTO members to apply exceptions in a non-discriminatory manner in order to ensure that governments do not engage in protectionism where intellectual property rights holders tend to be foreign firms. The provision could also be seen to impose a duty on member states not to deny patents on the basis of the field of technology or the location of the firm that develops it. Measures which impact upon foreign investors' capacity to make profitable commercial use of their intellectual property assets have the potential to result in complaints under IIAs through investment treaty arbitration. This issue will be explored in greater detail in the following chapter.

(v) Rules of Origin

A final field of WTO law that may be engaged in the control of performance requirements is that relating to rules of origin. Rules of origin are the criteria applied to determine the national source of a product. They are important because restrictions such as duties owed depend upon the source of imports. Rules of origin imposed by host states can also be used in a manner that compels the purchase of local goods in the manufacture of assembled products, as such they may be used by host states to dictate the nature of FDI that they receive. For example, low-tariff rates or other preferences extended to goods assembled in low-wage countries by firms exporting components from its home base can be denied by host states in order to stimulate the use of domestic inputs,[69] very much equivalent in effect to a local content performance requirement. The WTO regime does not itself contain any provisions which insist on specific substantive rules of origin, however the Agreement on Rules of Origin attempts to achieve harmonization of non-preferential rules of origin.

---

[69] S. Picciotto, *Regulating Global Corporate Capitalism* (CUP, Cambridge 2011) 163.

Rules of origin often become instruments of political influence and are increasingly used as barriers to trade in order to appease producers that have otherwise been harmed by investment and trade liberalization policies. Stricter rules of origin create greater incentives for producers to use local inputs because, generally speaking, the more local material is used, the greater the likelihood of the firm satisfying origin requirements. Rules of origin are favoured by political leaders because the WTO does not dictate how such instruments are to be applied, allowing more policy flexibility. More practically speaking, rules of origin tend to be easy to hide.[70] Rules of origin are used under the auspice of regional trade agreements in order to raise the local value added. Such rules have an effect that resemble those of local content requirements as long as they prescribe the extent of domestic content that products should contain in order to qualify as an internal product in a regional trading area.[71]

Generally speaking, because the WTO system is intended to foster free trade, while performance requirements are protectionist measures the presumption should, therefore, be against considering any performance requirement (or equivalent measure) valid under GATT or other agreements, absence a strong economic or social justification.[72]

3. INTERNATIONAL MONETARY FUND (IMF) AND PERFORMANCE REQUIREMENTS

With a current membership of 188 countries, the IMF is an international organization that has the objective of promoting international financial stability and cooperation among states in monetary policy. Article IV of the IMF Articles of Agreement specifies that the IMF is charged with overseeing the international monetary system and with monitoring its members' compliance with their general obligations contained in Article IV:1. These obligations require members to foster orderly economic

---

[70] M. Hirsch, 'The Politics of Rules of Origin' in T. Broude, M. Busch and A. Porges (eds), *The Politics of International Economic Law* (CUP, Cambridge 2011) 326–31.

[71] UNCTAD, 'Foreign Direct Investment and Performance Requirements: New Evidence from Selected Countries' 12 (UNCTAD, 2003) <http://unctad.org/en/Docs/iteiia20037_en.pdf> accessed 6 June 2014.

[72] C. Fontheim and M. Gadbaw, 'Trade Related Performance Requirements Under the GATT-MTN System and U.S. Law' (1982) 14 *Law and Policy of International Business* 129 143–4.

growth and promote stability, in part encompassing exchange rate systems. While none of the policies of the IMF expressly control the use of performance requirements, its rules do limit a country's capacity to impose restrictions on access to its currency, which may in turn impair the movement of goods or services, as well as FDI across international borders. As such, its principles can be seen to control trade-based conditions on the FDI policy.

The IMF's role in this regard may be illustrated through the link between the IMF and the WTO's regulation of performance requirements, which can be found in GATT Article XV:9 on exchange controls and restrictions. Clearly, exchange controls or restrictions can make it difficult for an importer to pay for its imports or an exporter to be paid for exports. If a foreign firm faces exchange restrictions that are not imposed on a local firm, then these types of measures operate not only as a barrier to trade, but also to FDI because such a firm may unwilling to internationalize. If such restrictions are imposed, based on criteria such as use of local content or the hiring of local employees for example, then they should be construed as conventional performance requirements, such as those prohibited by the TRIMs. Article XV:9 of the GATT states that Members are allowed to use exchange controls that comply with their obligations under the IMF. The relevant IMF rules are found in its Article IV, which generally requires that members promote a stable system of exchange rates and avoid manipulating exchange rates in order to prevent effective balance of payments adjustment or to gain an unfair competitive advantage over other members.

In addition to ensuring that members observe orderly exchange rates in order to promote trade (and by extension FDI of trading firms), the IMF conducts regular information collection and dissemination activities regarding the global economy and the respective economies of its many member states. It is worth noting that this supervisory role has afforded the organization the opportunity to criticize performance requirements that have been imposed by its various member countries. In that sense, the IMF has the capacity to impose considerable pressure on states against the use of various types of performance requirements, including those that fall more directly under its sphere of influence, namely those relating to currency exchange and capital repatriation (of which more will be discussed in Chapter 6). In this regard, it is notable that the IMF censured Brazil for the local content and export requirements placed on the automobile sector in the late 1990s. Although these policies were arguably defensible because they resulted in an expansion in the automobile trade in the area, this had come at a significant cost to consumers and a distortion to world markets.[73]

4. CONCLUSION

The WTO's sphere of influence over international trade has effected a modest degree of control over the use of performance requirements or their equivalents by host states as a means of tailoring the nature and extent of FDI. Most importantly, the TRIMs restricts the imposition of trade-related investment measures on foreign investors, but it applies only to manufactured goods and it lacks a prohibition of export requirements. Consequently significant varieties of these classic performance requirements which could act as barriers to FDI go unchecked. The lack of protection for infant manufacturing industries (such as Canada's renewable energy industry) through the TRIMs disciplines, as well as the ambiguity of general exceptions as means of permitting discrimination under TRIMs, may rightly be viewed as problematic. Other weaknesses of the WTO's management of performance requirements includes the selective commitment structure of the GATS in which conditions placed on commercial presence delivery of services would be permitted, as well as the uncertain effect of that agreement's general exceptions. The effect of the GPA and TRIPs on performance requirements placed on foreign investors is marginal: in the former case, because of the predominately trade-based focus of the agreement as well as its plurilateral membership structure; and in the latter case, because of the limited overlap between intellectual property and FDI. Still, the GPA's prohibition of offsets is significant. There are other aspects of WTO law that could be relevant in terms of their capacity to delimit member states' ability to use performance requirements, particularly under a wider understanding of that term as used in this book. For example, the desired goals of local content requirements may be achieved through anti-dumping rules imposed at a national level. Restrictions on selling locally assembled products composed of imported components at a below marginal cost prices may drive a foreign firm to source their inputs locally.[74] Clearly the internationalization strategies of firms can be dictated in part by anti-dumping duties imposed by host states. The deficiency of the WTO in disciplining

[73] Independent Evaluation Office of the International Monetary Fund, 'IMF Involvement in International Trade Policy Issues' (2009) 181.

[74] Picciotto (n 69) 163.

these key policy tools, however, has resulted in the need for other international legal instruments to embrace wider controls of performance requirements with a view to eliminating counter-productive selection of certain types of FDI of interest to host states. The control of performance requirements by international investment law will be explored in the next chapter.

4. Performance requirements and international investment law

1. INTRODUCTION

Performance requirements shape the nature of FDI into host states, and as such they directly fall within the sphere of international investment law. This is especially the case for performance requirements that are investment-oriented, rather than linked to trade performance. At the same time, prohibitions on performance requirements tend to be poorly understood by investment arbitrators, because they are uncommon in IIAs and often difficult to discern from the text of these instruments. Indeed, some commentators consider controls on performance requirements to be the least understood of all the substantial provisions contained in IIAs. Given that traditional performance requirements have a trade-oriented pedigree (as in trade-related investment measures under TRIMs) the implantation of a predominately trade-based discipline into an IIA calls for a minor "paradigm shift" which contributes to the difficulty of understanding performance requirements.[1]

Substantive IIAs obligations like fair and equitable treatment and guarantees against expropriation without compensation have developed from customary international law. These broadly-defined concepts are aligned with notions of fundamental justice and are often analogous to provisions common to domestic laws. By contrast, controls on performance requirements are much more technical in nature and have little or no basis in customary international law. Prohibitions of performance requirements in IIAs generally exist not because such requirements offend natural justice, but because these requirements can lead to economic inefficiencies and tend ultimately to be ineffective in achieving expected development goals. Worse, performance requirements can inflict harm on a host state's economy, even if the foreign investor upon which they are

[1] B. Legum, 'Understanding Performance Requirement Prohibitions in Investment Treaties' in *Contemporary Issues in International Arbitration and Mediation* (Brill, New York, NY 2008) 53–4.

placed it is itself uninjured. In that sense, prohibitions on performance requirements may be seen as a way of protecting imposing states from harming themselves. In the words of one expert: "the prohibition of expropriation [for example] accords readily with a lawyer's view of what is or is not just. The prohibition of performance requirements, by contrast, may accord readily with an economist's view of what is or is not efficient, but it does not come naturally to a lawyer".[2] Investment treaty specialists accordingly find performance requirements difficult because of problems associated with expressing the prohibition of such measures in terms that are sufficiently broad to achieve intended goals. The prohibition of performance requirements is a difficult drafting exercise, and the result is IIA text that is often unworkable in practice.[3] This chapter will consider some of these issues, exploring how international investment law has engaged with performance requirements, including those which are not specifically framed as such but which have an equivalent effect of structuring the nature and extent of foreign investment.

2. INTERNATIONAL INVESTMENT AGREEMENTS PROVISIONS

From their origins as tools of post-war economic reconstruction of European powers in the mid-twentieth century, IIAs have grown to more than 2600 globally as of 2015. While they had until recently been primarily used to protect investors originating from highly industrialized, capital rich countries in the West, IIAs are now regularly concluded between developing countries and have led to movements of capital from developing states into what were traditionally capital exporting states.[4] Investment chapters are found in numerous economic partnership agreements along with trade commitments, such as NAFTA and ASEAN as well as upcoming treaties such as the Transatlantic Trade and Investment Partnership (TTIP) and the Trans Pacific Partnership (TPP). In short, IIAs aimed at augmenting FDI now form part of the economic strategy of most governments around the world. The protections enshrined in IIAs are almost universally subject to enforcement through investor–state arbitration, a specialized form of mixed international arbitration which

---

[2] ibid.

[3] ibid.

[4] See e.g. D. Collins, *The BRIC States and Outward Foreign Direct Investment* (OUP, Oxford 2013).

permits investors to bring claims directly against host states, often by-passing domestic courts. These treaties are seen by many as indicative of an evisceration of national economic sovereignty, constricting host states' capacity to regulate to address the needs of their own citizens in favour of the business interests of MNEs. Investor–state dispute settlement is highly controversial also because it is viewed by some as a surrendering of judicial sovereignty by signatory states to unaccountable international tribunals.[5] Others, including organizations like UNCTAD, urge that the protections afforded by IIAs along with access to investor–state arbitration remain important tools to ensure continued growth in FDI, particularly to high-risk developing states.[6]

There is some merit to both arguments. Just as allegations of bias in investor–state arbitration against host governments appears to be unfounded (studies have shown that host countries normally win, successfully defending themselves)[7] it is undeniable that IIAs are one-sided, in that they place obligations exclusively on host governments with none on the investor, which may explain the origins of these instruments as tools of wealthy capital exporting countries rather than the generally poorer capital importing ones. Likewise, although the evidence in support of IIAs role in actually increasing FDI flows remains unconvincing,[8] the fact that IIAs are now part of the policy toolkit of many emerging markets, suggests that their remains strong support for them, much as the increasing presence of sustainability-focused, public-interest concerns in the text of these agreements indicates somewhat of a re-balancing of obligations between investors and host states may be underway.[9] Still, the treatment of performance requirements in these instruments, typically through some form of prohibition, may be one such area where the obligations between investors and the countries in which they locate demonstrates an unfortunate imbalance. Such prohibitions deprive host states from the ability to dictate the nature of the FDI that they seek in

---

[5] E.g. G. van Harten, *Investment Treaty Arbitration and Public Law* (OUP, Oxford 2008).

[6] UNCTAD, World Investment Report 2014 130–32 <http://unctad.org/en/PublicationsLibrary/wir2014_en.pdf> accessed 9 March 2015.

[7] S. Franck 'The ICSID Effect? Considering Potential Variations in Arbitration Awards' (2011) 51:4 *Virginia Journal of International Law* 977.

[8] J. Salacuse and N. Sullivan, 'Do BITs Really Work: An Evaluation of Investment Treaties and their Grand Bargain' in K. Sauvant and L. Sachs (eds), *The Effect of Treaties on Foreign Direct Investment* (OUP, Oxford 2009).

[9] UNCTAD, World Investment Report 2014 130–32 <http://unctad.org/en/PublicationsLibrary/wir2014_en.pdf> accessed 9 March 2015.

exchange for the generous protections that are offered under the IIAs. Non-traditional performance requirements, such as those which do not have a clear link to imports or exports as envisioned by TRIMs, may be similarly curtailed by other features of IIAs.

(i) Performance Requirement Prohibitions

The most obvious feature of IIAs which addresses the use of performance requirements are the performance requirement prohibitions themselves. Many treaties simply incorporate the TRIMs' rules under the heading of "performance requirements" and as such do not control measures beyond those which are envisioned by the TRIMS.[10] The ASEAN Comprehensive Agreement on Investment affirms the TRIMs in its provision on performance requirement prohibitions, but adds that Member States (of ASEAN) will undertake assessments of performance requirements within two years of the date of the agreement in order to review existing performance requirements and assess whether an expansion beyond merely a re-iteration of TRIMs is necessary.[11] This provision remains in effect as is, so no additional limitations were added. Clearly instruments containing such terms would limit a party's capacity to impose performance requirements only to the extent that they were inconsistent with the TRIMs: it would not control a broader range of performance requirements referenced in some IIAs.

Wider performance requirement prohibitions in IIAs are sometimes referred to as "TRIMs-plus obligations" because they are seen to embrace more measures than the trade-related investment measures indicated in the TRIMs. This terminology has become popular in the context of additional requirements in this regard which are placed on some countries newly acceding to the WTO, capturing conditions relating to technology transfer, currency and employment. Similarly broad prohibitions are found in numerous RTAs containing investment chapters.[12] In forbidding a wider range of performance requirements beyond simply those which relate to local content usage, parties to such

---

[10] E.g. New Zealand–China FTA Art. 140 (7 April 2008).

[11] Art. 7(2).

[12] E.g. Korea–Australia FTA Art. 11.9 (17 February 2014) (incorporating the same language of NAFTA, see below).

agreements aim to further liberalize their market for inward FDI, attracting more firms by placing less obligations upon them.[13]

Still, the most common method of dealing with performance requirements in IIAs is not to mention them in the treaty at all. This offers host states much greater latitude to dictate the terms under which they receive FDI. Where IIAs are silent on the issue of performance requirements, then the TRIMs will govern, given of course that the relevant signatory state is a member of the WTO. For non-WTO members, without an express provision regarding the TRIMs (or any other WTO rules which may be relevant for performance requirements, such as GATS), these obligations would not be incorporated into the IIA. Of course, in the absence of an express incorporation of TRIMs or other WTO law into the treaty, there would be no method by which an aggrieved investor could bring a claim against a host state on the basis of these rules through the treaty's investor–state dispute system for imposing a prohibited performance requirement.

Generally speaking, modern IIAs between developing states (concluded within the last five years) tend not to include any reference to performance requirements. This reflects the importance of these tools to the economic policy of countries at this stage of development. Developed states are more likely to include performance requirement prohibitions in their IIAs, including those concluded by Asian states. Economic partnership agreements seem to be more likely to contain these provisions rather than conventional BITs. For example, the Japan–Singapore New Age Partnership Agreement, contains prohibitions on performance requirements including those which are based on labour and environmental standards, arguably a worrying step backwards in terms of the recognition of sustainability principles under international investment law. Still, the concern voiced by some commentators, that IIA performance requirement prohibitions in certain IIAs have undermined a country's capacity to pursue human developmental goals through requirements related to employment and training, has often been misguided, as prohibitions have been narrower in scope than was initially feared. For example, Mongolia's BIT with the US only prohibited performance requirements "such as those" relating to the export of goods and services (effectively recapitulating TRIMs) despite warnings that the instrument

[13] United Nations, 'Towards Coherent Policy Frameworks: Understanding Trade and Investment Linkages, Economic and Social Commission for Asia and the Pacific' (United Nations, New York, NY 2007) 14.

would undermine Mongolia's ability to impose employment- and training-requirement-related obligations on foreign firms.[14]

Generally speaking, prohibitions on performance requirements found in IIAs have evolved from broad, often hortatory phrases to more precise rules. An example of an early provision of this kind is contained in the Turkey–United States BIT of 1985, which states:

> Each party shall seek to avoid performance requirements as a condition of establishment, expansion or maintenance of investments, which require or enforce commitments to export goods produced, or which specify that goods or services must be purchased locally, or which impose any other similar requirements.[15]

As with any "best efforts" obligation, it is difficult to envision how a claim could have been brought under this provision, absence some evidence of bad faith. The reference to the mandatory use of local goods in this agreement appears to foreshadow the TRIMs and its limited goods-based focus rather than the modern, enlarged understanding of performance requirements which covers a wider range of conditions.

A major evolution in the prohibition of performance requirements came in NAFTA, a regional economic integration agreement among Canada, the US and Mexico signed in the early 1990s which contains chapters on both trade and investment. Later US and Canadian treaties largely follow the outline of NAFTA's performance requirement rules. NAFTA provides a definitive list of prohibited performance requirements which expands upon the trade-based approach reflected in TRIMs. In the first paragraph of NAFTA Article 1106, there is a list of seven specific types of host state measures that the state cannot impose or enforce:

> 1. No Party may impose or enforce any of the following requirements, or enforce any commitment or undertaking, in connection with the establishment, acquisition, expansion, management, conduct or operation of an investment of an investor of a Party or of a non-Party in its territory:
>   (a) to export a given level or percentage of goods or services;
>   (b) to achieve a given level or percentage of domestic content;
>   (c) to purchase, use or accord a preference to goods produced or

[14] E.g. Z. Boroo, 'Effective Use of Performance Requirements and Investment Incentive' (2012) 17 *Mongolian Journal of International Affairs* 97, 104 asserts that Mongolia surrendered its ability to impose employment and training-related performance requirements in its BIT with the US (which exceeded Mongolia's subsequent WTO TRIMs obligations), but is not reflected in the actual text of the agreement in Art. II.5 (signed 6 October 1994).

[15] Art. II(7) (signed 3 December 1985).

services provided in its territory, or to purchase goods or services from persons in its territory;

(d) to relate in any way the volume or value of imports to the volume or value of exports or to the amount of foreign exchange inflows associated with such investment;

(e) to restrict sales of goods or services in its territory that such investment produces or provides by relating such sales in any way to the volume or value of its exports or foreign exchange earnings;

(f) to transfer technology, a production process or other proprietary knowledge to a person in its territory, except when the requirement is imposed or the commitment or undertaking is enforced by a court, administrative tribunal or competition authority to remedy an alleged violation of competition laws or to act in a manner not inconsistent with other provisions of this Agreement; or

(g) to act as the exclusive supplier of the goods it produces or services it provides to a specific region or world market.

However, the prohibition is narrowed somewhat with the following:

2. A measure that requires an investment to use a technology to meet generally applicable health, safety or environmental requirements shall not be construed to be inconsistent with paragraph 1(f).

The reference to "general applicability" in this section appears to contemplate measures which are applied equally to domestic investors, possibly suggesting, as alluded to in Chapter 2, that the concept of performance requirement is predicated on nationality-based discrimination.

Importantly Article 1106(5) of NAFTA then provides:

> Paragraph [1] ... do[es] not apply to any requirement other than the requirements set out in th[at] paragraph.

As will be discussed below, this provision severely restricts the interpretation of the rest of the article, a clear indication that other types of performance requirement may be permissible.

NAFTA Article 1106 recaptures the prohibitions on trade-related investment measures found in the TRIMs, adding to them prohibitions relating to services. In light of the expansion to services, it may have been possible for the *Mexico – Telecommunications* dispute discussed in the previous chapter to be framed as a NAFTA-based performance requirement complaint under Article 1106(1)(c). Mexico's requirement of connection to a local network could be construed to require a preference to be accorded a service provided in its territory. NAFTA goes beyond the TRIMs most notably in Article 1106(1)(f) with respect to restrictions on mandatory technology transfer conditions imposed on foreign investors. This feature of NAFTA may be the reason why express prohibitions on performance requirements are found commonly in the IIAs of the US and Canada.[16] For example, Article 7 of the Canadian Model BIT 2004 contains a comprehensive prohibition on a wide range of performance requirements, including those relating to services and technology transfer, repeating NAFTA verbatim.

It is worth noting that NAFTA, like the GPA discussed in the previous chapter, also disallows "offsets", meaning performance requirements imposed as a means of selecting the winning bidder in a government procurement contract:

> Each Party shall ensure that its entities do not, in the qualification and selection of suppliers, goods or services, in the evaluation of bids or the award of contracts, consider, seek or impose offsets. For purposes of this Article, offsets means conditions imposed or considered by an entity prior to or in the course of its procurement process that encourage local development or improve its Party's balance of payments accounts, by means of requirements of local content, licensing of technology, investment, counter-trade or similar requirements.[17]

The examples given in this section reflect a broad understanding of what constitutes a performance requirement – far beyond that which was contemplated by TRIMs.

As noted above, Japan has included exacting performance requirement prohibitions in some of its new IIAs. A recent example can be found in the Japan–Myanmar BIT of 2013 which states:

> Article 6
>
> 1. Neither Contracting Party may impose or enforce any of the following requirements, or enforce any commitment or undertaking, in connection with investment activities of an investor of a Contracting Party or of a non-Contracting Party in its Area:
>   (a) to export a given level or percentage of goods or services;
>   (b) to achieve a given level or percentage of domestic content;
>   (c) to purchase, use or accord a preference to goods produced or services provided in its Area, or to purchase goods or services from natural or legal persons or any other entity in its Area;

[16] 2004 United States Model Bilateral Investment Treaty, Art. 8; 2004 Canada Model BIT, Art. 7.

[17] Art. 1006.

(d) to relate in any way the volume or value of imports to the volume or value of exports or to the amount of foreign exchange inflows associated with investments of that investor;
(e) to restrict sales of goods or services in its Area that investments of the investor produce or provide by relating such sales in any way to the volume or value of its exports or foreign exchange earnings; to restrict the exportation or sale for export;
(f) to restrict the exportation or sale for export;
(g) to appoint, as executives, managers or members of boards of directors, individuals of any particular nationality;
(h) to transfer technology, a production process or other proprietary knowledge to a natural or legal person or any other entity in its Area, except when:
  (i) the requirement is imposed or the commitment or undertaking is enforced by a court, administrative tribunal or competition authority to remedy an alleged violation of competition laws; or
  (ii) the requirement concerns the transfer of intellectual property rights which is undertaken in a manner not inconsistent with the [TRIPs]

  Note: The requirement prohibited under this subparagraph, irrespective of its objectives or effects, shall be deemed to include any requirement by a Contracting Party, either explicit or implicit, that an investor offer or accept:
  (i) a rate or amount of royalty below a certain level; or
  (ii) a given range of period as the term of a licence contract, in regard to any licence contract freely entered into between the investor and a natural or legal person or any other entity in its Area.
(i) to locate the headquarters of that investor for a specific region or the world market in its Area;
(j) to achieve a given level or value of research and development in its Area; ...[18]

This prohibition is interesting for its reference to its coverage of employment conditions of managers of investing firms, which does not appear in NAFTA.

In contrast to a prohibition controlling certain types of performance requirements, an IIA could potentially affirm a party state's right to enact performance requirements, although there is no known treaty that contains this kind of term. Such a provision would simply re-assert the right that a country would have as a sovereign entity in the absence of such a

---

[18] Japan–Myanmar (15 December 2013). This provision is common to many Japanese IIAs.

provision, then its inclusion may well be irrelevant.[19] Even if this type of a provision were included in an IIA, the host state would still be expected to fulfil its WTO obligations, such as the TRIMs and the GATS (provided of course that it is a WTO member). Still, the WTO obligations would likely not be enforceable under the IIA dispute resolution procedures. Of course all of these obligations will also depend on the application of reservations and exceptions contained elsewhere in the treaty.

While developed states such as Canada, the US and Japan have taken a strong stance against performance requirements in their IIAs, a number of emerging markets have been reluctant to include prohibitions on performance requirements in their international investment commitments, reflecting the perceived value of these rules in attracting developmentally-friendly FDI. China, as well as India, has shown an aversion to the prohibition of performance requirements in their IIAs, and as such it is unlikely that either of these emerging market powerhouses would be willing to accept treaties, such as those employed by the US and Canada, denying state parties the use of these instruments to control FDI,[20] other than merely affirming the trade-based TRIMs rules. Allowing some types of performance requirements clearly works two ways. While China's FDI initiatives in Africa are often criticized as exploitative of developing countries because of their tendency to seize control of vital natural resources, none of China's IIAs with African states contain prohibitions on performance requirements, allowing African nations the potential to impose conditions on its inward FDI in a manner that advances their developmental policy needs.[21] This may offer some explanation as to why China has engaged in significant infrastructure projects in conjunctions with its FDI initiatives in Africa, activities which could be construed as economic-development-related performance requirements.

[19] J. VanDuzer, P. Simons and G. Mayeda, *Integrating Sustainable Development into International Investment Agreements: A Guide for Developing Countries* (Commonwealth Secretariat, London 2012) 201.

[20] M. Sornarajah, 'India, China and Foreign Investment' in M. Sornarajah and J. Wang, *China, India and the International Economic Order* (CUP, Cambridge 2010) 151.

[21] U. Ofodile, 'Africa–China Bilateral Investment Treaties: A Critique' (2013) 35:1 *Michigan Journal of International Law* 131, 187.

(ii) Other IIA Provisions as Performance Requirements

A number of less obvious features common to IIAs could impact upon the use of performance requirements by host states, depending on how broadly the concept of performance requirement is construed. Adopting a wide definition of the term which captures all types of restrictions on the foreign investor's behaviour that it has the potential to modify, the consideration of less traditional IIA provisions, meaning those not expressly labelled performance requirements, becomes apposite.

As discussed in Chapter 2, the national treatment standard found in most IIAs can operate to prevent discrimination against foreign firms on the basis of their nationality, rendering both de jure and de facto forms of discrimination illegal. As most performance requirements are inherently discriminatory (they impose conditions on foreign firms that are not imposed on local ones) the national treatment standard may prevent the imposition of a wide range of restrictive conditions placed on FDI. However, as noted in Chapter 2, problems in the interpretation and application of national treatment tests in investment arbitration, as well as its limit to the post-establishment stage in most IIAs, weakens national treatment's capacity to control performance requirements.

The definition of investment found in most IIAs could be imbued with what might be understood as a performance requirement. Most IIAs contain very broad definitions of "investment" under the heading of "any type of asset" with an illustrative list of various forms of commercial activities and entities including property, rights and interests.[22] However, arbitral case law, notably the oft-cited *Salini* decision has established that, for an activity to constitute an investment, it must have a lasting impact, or be of a long-term duration.[23] This separates FDI from one-off commercial transactions. Accordingly, there appears to be a temporal condition placed on investors' conduct; foreign firms are required to remain present and operational in the host state for an unspecified number of months or (more probably) years. More controversially, the preamble of many IIAs speak of the objective of achieving the economic development of party states,[24] a goal seen also in the preamble of the International Centre for the Settlement of Investment Disputes (ICSID)

---

[22] R. Dozer and C. Schreuer, *Principles of International Investment Law* (OUP, Oxford 2012) 63, citing the example of the Denmark–Ukraine Art. 1(1) (signed 23 October 1992).

[23] *Salini Costruttori SpA and Italstrade SpA v Kingdom of Morocco* ICSID Case No. ARB/00/4, Decision on Jurisdiction (23 July 2001).

[24] E.g. France–Ethiopia (25 June 2003).

Convention.[25] This had led some commentators to suggest that there is a duty on the part of the foreign firm to contribute to the development of the host state, or the so-called "right of development".[26] The obligation to contribute to the host state's economic development becomes the duty which balances out the assortment of rights enjoyed by the investor under the IIA. The existence of a right to development is captured also in comments made by arbitrators who have been willing to "read in" the contribution to development as part of the definition of investment.[27] The difficulty, of course, with imputing such a responsibility on an investor as a precondition for their access to the rights contained in an IIA, or dispute settlement under ICSID Convention, is the indeterminacy of the concept of development. In particular, it is not clear that this right on the part of host states, or obligation on the part of investors, is justiciable. The ambiguity of precisely what is needed for the contribution to the development of the host state criterion to be satisfied renders this understanding of "investment" highly tenuous as a performance requirement, which is normally conceived of in much more concrete if not fully quantifiable terms.

The inclusion of intellectual property in the definition of investment, a feature standard in many IIAs,[28] raises the possibility that intellectual-property-oriented conditions placed on investors could limit a host state's capacity to impose performance requirements such as those relating to the transfer of technology to the host state. Moreover, making the full recognition of intellectual property rights of foreign investors (such as the patentability of inventions and innovations and to enforcement of such rights under domestic law) conditional on the investors' conduct could constitute a derogation from various IIA-enshrined protections. Such protections include national treatment (local inventors are granted such rights where equivalent foreign ones are not), expropriation (failure to recognize or enforce a patent constitutes an unlawful taking of an

---

[25] ICSID Convention (also known as the Washington Convention) preamble: "Considering the need for international cooperation for economic development, and the role of private international investment therein".

[26] E.g. D. Desierto, 'Development as an International Right: Investment in the New Trade-Based IIAs' (2011) 3:2 *Trade Law and Development* 1–3.

[27] E.g. Salini (n 23) [52], and also *Malaysia Historical Salvors Sdn Bhd v Malaysia* ICSID Case No. ARB/05/10, Decision on the Application for Annulment (16 April 2009), Dissenting Opinion of Judge Mohamed Shahabuddeen, sec. B, [21]: '… [t]he outer limits of an ICSID investment comprise a requirement for contribution to the development of the host state …'.

[28] E.g. Canada–China Art. 1(1)I (1 October 2014).

investor's property), or even fair and equitable treatment (generally unfair treatment regarding the recognition and enforcement of various intellectual property rights by host states). As noted in the previous chapter, certain forms of preferential treatment in favour of local inventors could transgress WTO TRIPs provisions. The extent to which intellectual property protections are encapsulated by IIAs and indeed could form the basis of claims in international investment arbitration is a largely unexplored sphere of international economic law, and one that has prompted one commentator to conclude that the potential for such claims is "the sleeping giant" that is on the verge of being awakened.[29]

Some states place conditions on foreign firms in their investment legislation dictating particular business structures which must be adopted by investing firms. For example, joint ventures are mandated by a number of states with respect to investment in certain sectors. These rules are incorporated into IIAs through provisions which specify that investment must be in conformity with the laws of the host state. Linked to these types of conditions are requirements imposed by host states relating to the nationality of management or personnel of the foreign firm, which tend to be imposed in relation to investments in sectors sensitive to national security such as banking and telecommunications.[30] Such conditions may be conceived of as performance requirements because they restrict a certain aspect of the investor's behaviour, namely the nature of its ownership, and because they can in theory be satisfied by altering the ownership of the firm through closer cooperation with the host state. Management-oriented rules can represent major encroachments on foreign firms' capacity to operate in the manner it wishes and are accordingly prohibited by some IIAs. For example, the Australia–Korea FTA[31] states:

ARTICLE 11.10:

1. Neither Party shall require that an enterprise of that Party that is a covered investment appoint to senior management positions natural persons of any particular nationality.
2. A Party may require that a majority or less than a majority of the board of directors, or any committee thereof, of an enterprise of that Party that is a covered investment, be of a particular nationality, or resident in the

[29] B. Mercurio, 'Awakening the Sleeping Giant: Intellectual Property Rights in International Investment Agreements' (2012) 15:3 *Journal of International Economic Law* 871.

[30] E.g. Thailand, Foreign Business Act B.E. 2542 (1999, revised 2007).

[31] Signed 8 April 2014.

> territory of the Party, provided that the requirement does not materially impair the ability of the investor to exercise control over its investment.

Subsection 2 of this provision illustrates the need for host states to be able to enact ownership requirements for the purposes of national security. National security provisions, often framed in self-judging language, are common to IIAs.[32]

Guarantees against expropriation are among the most powerful features of IIAs, particularly given the broad scope to apply this protection to forms of indirect expropriation, effectively covering a wide range of governmental activity. The imposition of a performance requirement could be conceived as an indirect expropriation as conditions limiting the investor's use of its own assets, allowing investors to bring expropriation-based claims because of conditions placed on their conduct by host states. Put another way, some measures framed as indirect expropriation may be conceived as equivalent to performance requirements because they embody regulations which investors have the potential to satisfy through certain specified conduct.

The trend of carving out certain types of regulatory action from the definition of indirect expropriation, particularly in model IIAs,[33] has the effect of allowing host states to impose conditions on the nature of the economic activities conducted by foreign investors. With such boundaries placed upon the definition of expropriation contained in IIAs, host states would be more able to enact measures relating to legitimate public welfare objectives, such as public health, safety and the environment and not face claims.[34] A good recent example of the shrinking scope of expropriation can be seen in the draft text of the TTIP which specifies that the determination of what constitutes expropriation must be made:

> … in light of the Party's right to regulate the use of property in order to pursue legitimate public policy objectives, such as protecting society, the environment, and public health, ensuring the integrity and stability of the

---

[32] E.g. Energy Charter Treaty Art. 24 (17 December 1991).

[33] E.g. Colombia 2007 Model BIT Art. VI.

[34] See B. Mercurio, 'International Investment Agreements and Public Health: Neutralizing a Threat through Treaty Drafting' (*Bulletin of the World Health Organization*, 24 February 2014) <www.who.int/bulletin/volumes/92/7/13-130955/en/> referring to the draft text of the Trans Pacific Partnership Agreement, accessed 2 December 2014.

financial system, promoting public security and safety, and promoting and protecting cultural diversity.[35]

Given that performance requirements can serve some or all of these aims, it would be difficult in the context of this specific agreement for an investor to ground an indirect expropriation claim on the basis of a performance requirement or its equivalent.

The fair and equitable treatment (FET) standard common to most IIAs could encompass a broad understanding of performance requirements as measures used to control the behaviour of a foreign investor. In other words, a broadly construed FET clause could achieve the same effect as a performance requirement prohibition in an IIA. FET is the most frequently invoked standard of protection in international investment disputes, capturing a wide range of harmful treatment. It appears to contemplate procedural fairness in the way in which laws are applied, either judicially or administratively and it is often described as a "gap-filling" principle that embodies the concept of good faith in the interpretation of the more specific provisions of a treaty.[36] FET has been subject to a wide range of interpretations by investment tribunals and commentators.[37] The lack of precision in FET is advantageous to investors because it grants a high degree of flexibility in challenging laws, much as it acknowledges that host states are free to establish the legal procedures they wish as long as they do not fall below a minimum threshold.[38]

The vagueness of the FET standard suggests that it could encompass performance-requirement-type obligations. Indeed, the link between FET and performance requirements has been expressly made in several IIAs. France's 2006 Model BIT references a number of performance-requirement measures as examples of trade-oriented measures that will constitute violation of the FET obligation, without actually using the phrase "performance requirements". The IIA lists as examples of violations of FET treatment "any restriction on the purchase or transportation of raw and auxiliary materials, energy and combustible supplies, as

---

[35] Ch II, Art. 18(2)d), European Commission, Directorate-General for Trade, 2 July 2013.

[36] Dolzer and Schreuer (n 22) 122.

[37] See e.g. OECD, 'The Fair and Equitable Treatment Standard in International Investment Law' (OECD Working Papers on International Investment, September 2004) <www.oecd.org/dataoecd/22/53/33776498.pdf> accessed September 2011.

[38] Dolzer and Schreuer (n 22) 148.

well as on production and exploitation of any kind, any restriction on the sale and transportation of products within the country or abroad, as well as measures with an analogous effect".[39] Rather than grounding the analysis of performance requirements in the established tests for FET that have been cultivated in international investment jurisprudence, these TRIMS-oriented prohibitions are better understood as an attempt to offer greater clarity to what is a notoriously ambiguous provision, presumably so as to forestall debate as to the precise contours of FET. Inserting express performance requirement prohibitions within the FET standard in an IIA may further be seen as a strategic way of forbidding certain vital goods-based performance requirements in a context-based, case-by-case manner while avoiding an outright prohibition on such measures,[40] possibly in case France wishes to avail itself of such policy tools on occasion.

Host states could seek to impose currency-oriented performance requirements on foreign investors, for example by requiring that local currency be used, or that a certain level of foreign capital be brought into the host state. This will restrict the resources that are available to fund a foreign investor's commercial activities in the host state. Most problematically for foreign investors, host states may attempt to prevent the repatriation of profits generated by the investment back to the home state in order to ensure that it is kept within the host state economy, with the rationale that this will be used to encourage and sustain employment and guard against "capital flight". If conditions are attached to the repatriation of currency, such as waiting periods or mandatory re-investment, then these will dictate the nature of the foreign investor's operations in the host state, possibly also impairing its competitive capabilities relative to domestic firms. In this regard, provisions in IIAs typically labelled "Transfers" ensure that no undue restrictions are placed on the foreign investor's ability to return its profits home. A recent example of such a provision can be found in the Japan–Mozambique BIT, which is worth reproducing in its entirety:

> 1. Each Contracting Party shall ensure that all transfers relating to investments in its Area of an investor of the other Contracting Party may be freely made into and out of its Area without delay. Such transfers shall include, in particular, though not exclusively:

---

[39] Art. 4. Some German IIAs include similar language in the national treatment provision's definition of "less favourable treatment", e.g. Germany–Egypt Art. 3(2) (signed 16 June 2006).

[40] Legum (n 1) 53–4.

(a) the initial capital and additional amounts to maintain or increase investments;
(b) profits, interest, capital gains, dividends, royalties, fees and other current incomes accruing from investments;
(c) payments made under a contract including loan payments in connection with investments;
(d) proceeds of the total or partial sale or liquidation of investments;
(e) earnings and remuneration of personnel … ;
(f) payments made in accordance with Articles 12 [compensation for expropriation] and 13 [compensation from harm suffered during civil disturbances]; and
(g) payments arising out of the settlement of a dispute …

2. Each Contracting Party shall further ensure that such transfers may be made without delay in freely usable currencies at the market exchange rate prevailing on the date of the transfer.

IIA parties tend to retain the right to enact currency restrictions for various public policy purposes, including bankruptcy and criminal investigations, as well as exceptional circumstances such as economic crises and the general obligation to maintain balance of payments equilibrium. There are no known disputes in which the transfer obligations of IIAs were used as the basis of the investor's claim against the host states.[41]

Lastly, most-favoured-nation clauses in IIAs could be used to incorporate performance requirement prohibitions contained in other instruments if they are lacking in the treaty in question. Likewise, it is conceivable that an umbrella clause in an IIA could allow foreign investors to bring IIA-based claims through international arbitration for the application of performance requirements that were prohibited in an investment contract between the host state and the foreign firm even if such term was absent from the IIA, as the imposition of such conditions after entry could be viewed as a breach of contract, particularly if the contract contains a stabilization clause.[42]

(iii) General Exceptions and Performance Requirement-specific Exceptions

The imposition of performance requirements or equivalent obligations on foreign investors could be justified by reference to general exceptions contained in IIAs, such as those relating to environmental or social

41 *United States v Italy* [1989] ICJ Rep 15 and *Amco v Republic of Indonesia* (1983) 23 ILM 354; (1988) 27 ILM 1281; 1 ICSID Rep 509.

42 *El Paso Energy International Company v Argentine Republic*, ICSID Case No. ARB/03/15, Decision on Jurisdiction (27 April 2006) [81].

policies of critical importance to the host state. For example, host states may impose performance requirements on MNEs for the purposes of environmental protection or to ensure that employees of foreign firms are not abused, meaning that they may not be required to pay compensation for these types of actions even where they transgress substantive treaty norms. The use of general exceptions in international investment law is a subject that has attracted a great deal of academic attention, including from this author.[43] General exceptions relating to non-economic policy grounds as justifications for breach of other obligations remain uncommon in BITs; however, they can be found in some free trade agreements (FTAs) that contain investment chapters, such as NAFTA and economic partnership agreements such as the New Zealand–Taiwan Economic Cooperation Agreement as well as the ASEAN Comprehensive Agreement on Investment.[44] The language used tends to mirror that of the general exceptions in the original GATT 1947: nothing should prevent a host state from being able to enact measures necessary to protect human or animal or plant life or health as well as the conservation of exhaustible natural resources. Indeed the New Zealand–Taiwan agreement incorporates the GATT exceptions directly by reference.[45]

In some cases, treaties apply non-economic, public interest exceptions inspired by the GATT Article XX directly to provisions on performance requirements. For example, Article 11.9 of the Australia Korea FTA[46] contains the following exemption:

> 5. Provided that such measures are not applied in an arbitrary or unjustifiable manner, or do not constitute a disguised restriction on international trade or investment, paragraphs 1(b) [prohibition on domestic content requirements], 1(c) [preference for locally purchased good prohibition] and 1(f) [mandatory technology transfer prohibition] … shall not be construed to prevent a Party from adopting or maintaining measures, including environmental measures:
>
> …
>
> (b) necessary to protect human, animal or plant life or health; or
> (c) related to the conservation of living or non-living exhaustible natural resources.

---

43 Collins (n 4) ch 7.
44 Art. 17.
45 Ch 24, Art. 1.
46 Signed 8 April 2014.

More comprehensively, the New Zealand–Taiwan Economic Partnership Agreement, which includes similar exceptions to that of the Australia–Korea FTA, expressly excludes the agreement's performance requirement prohibition from any existing measures that are set out in a separate Annex.[47] Japan carves out several sectors, including transportation and agriculture, from the scope of the performance requirement prohibition in its BIT with Cambodia.[48] In its BIT with Benin, Canada excludes the application of the performance requirement prohibition from all services sectors, provided that the exemption conforms to its obligations under the GATS.[49] This carve-out effectively allows Canada to structure the nature of FDI in services from that partner country in order to meet its needs. Canada also includes in its BIT with Tanzania an express reservation to its commitment to prohibit performance requirements in relation to various polices including: the rights or preferences provided to aboriginal peoples; the rights or preferences provided to socially or economically disadvantaged minorities.[50] Such exemptions appear to illustrate one of the important purposes behind performance requirements even where they result in economic distortions, namely the more equal distribution of economic gains from FDI across all sections of the economy, especially disadvantaged groups. The logic behind prohibiting performance requirements generally, while allowing a certain group of specific requirements, appears to be that conditions imposed on foreign firms are presumptively distortive and inefficient, but there are important concerns that are worth the derivation from full liberalization. These may be conceptualized as market failures needful of regulatory interference. They also foster the very advantages resulting from FDI that may not manifest themselves as private gains to the investing firms.

3. ARBITRAL CASE LAW ON PERFORMANCE REQUIREMENTS

The limited arbitral case law on performance requirements, most of which were brought under NAFTA, will be evaluated in this section. As noted above, provisions addressing performance requirements remain relatively rare in IIAs, which may contribute to the apparent lack of understanding concerning them among investment arbitration specialists.

---

[47] Signed 10 July 2013, Annex IV.

[48] Signed 14 June 2007, Schedule of Japan.

[49] Annex II (signed 9 January 2013).

[50] Annex II (signed 13 May 2013).

Mobil Investments Canada Inc and Murphy Oil Corporation v Government of Canada[51] illustrates the potential impact of a performance requirement prohibition on a host state's attempt to impose research and training obligations on foreign investors. In this decision under ICSID's Additional Facility Rules, the tribunal determined a sub-central government's (Newfoundland and Labrador) imposition of a requirement on foreign investors to spend several million dollars per year in research and development as well as education and training to be a breach of NAFTA's prohibition on performance requirements, Article 1106(1)c. Canada argued on behalf of the provincial government that the research and education requirements did not necessarily compel the purchase of or preference for local goods or services and as such did not constitute prohibited performance requirements under the treaty. Canada further attempted to distinguish between prohibited sourcing/local content performance requirements, which would have the purpose of protecting the domestic market, and the research and education requirements, which are aimed at strengthening the host state's knowledge capacity and promoting sustainable development. The research and education requirements had been instigated because Newfoundland and Labrador had an acute dependency on the extractive sector for its economic stability. While rejecting the claim that the research and education requirements constituted a breach of NAFTA's FET guarantee because they undermined the investor's legitimate expectations in a stable regulatory framework, the *Mobil* tribunal found that Canada's measures relating to research and education were performance requirements under Article 1106(1)(c): "to purchase, use or accord a preference to goods produced or services provided in its territory, or to purchase goods or services from persons in its territory". This was because they were compulsory, constituting a legal requirement and also because the meaning of "services" within that article was held to be sufficiently broad to cover the research and development and education and training obligations. According to the tribunal, this reading was consistent with the way in which the term "services" was used in other parts of the treaty, as well as NAFTA's underlying purpose to prevent distortions in international trade and to increase investment opportunities among party countries. The US investor's spending on fulfilling these requirements was a viewed as a central feature and not an ancillary objective of the measure. In rendering this judgment in favour of the claimant, the tribunal demonstrated that the concept of performance requirements is an expensive one with the

---

[51] ICSID Case No. ARB(AF)/07/4, Decision on Liability (22 May 2012).

potential to encompass measures well beyond simple local content rules. This was despite the arguably justifiable public policy goal (the improvement of a historically economically disadvantaged region of Canada) behind the requirements. Careful to ensure that its performance requirements relating to training and education in Newfoundland and Labrador are not challenged in future disputes such as this one, Canada now routinely includes provisions in its modern IIAs which allow it to impose performance requirements for this purpose.[52]

In *Cargill v Mexico*[53] a dispute brought by a US sugar company because of alleged tax-based mistreatment at the hands of the Mexican government, the ICSID tribunal held that the respondent state breached its obligations under NAFTA through the imposition of a production tax which, by its objective and design, involved a performance requirement within the meaning of Article 1106(3). It determined that Mexico conditioned a tax advantage on the use of domestically produced cane sugar instead of corn-syrup-based sugar for the very purpose of affecting the sale of local sugar. In other words, the host state offered an investment incentive to the foreign investor that was conditional upon the operation of their investment in a manner that assisted the local economy, a classic example of a performance requirement being imposed in conjunction with an incentive. Mexico had contended that NAFTA's prohibition on performance requirements did not encompass measures "tantamount to performance requirements" meaning measures which had the equivalent effect to performance requirements. The tribunal was unpersuaded by this argument, noting that while there was limited jurisprudence under NAFTA's Article 1106, there was no need to show a direct link between the measure and the effects, as long as there was an association or relationship between them. It rendered this decision without expanding on the precise nature of that relationship that would be required for the performance requirement prohibition to be found and in failing to do so essentially conveyed a low standard of proof to satisfy the breach of the performance requirement prohibition provision in NAFTA. This conclusion was reached through reference to the Vienna Convention on the Law of Treaties principles of interpretation and its

---

[52] E.g. Canada–Cameroon Annex II 13 (signed 3 March 2014). Canada lost a dispute under NAFTA's performance requirement prohibitions in relation to research and development requirements imposed on ExxonMobil's operations in Newfoundland and was ordered to pay compensation of CDN $17.3 million (dispute unreported at the time of writing, March 2015).

[53] *Cargill Inc (Claimant) v United Mexican States (Respondent)* ICSID Case No. ARB(AF)/05/2, Award (18 September 2009).

reference to the ordinary meaning of terms in Article 31, specifically NAFTA's use of the word "connection". Following this logic, the tribunal concluded that the performance requirement relating to the use of certain sugar was integrally related to the investment of the investor. The objective of the tax incentive was precisely to put pressure on firms from the United States by restricting, if not eliminating, the opportunities for the sale of corn-syrup-based sugar in Mexico.[54] This case illustrates the inherent difficulty associated with linking an investment incentive, which are largely unregulated under international law (see further Chapter 6) and a prohibited performance requirement. Use of the latter can preclude the legitimacy of the former.

In an earlier arbitration also involving Mexico's sugar cane industry, the tribunal in *CPI v Mexico*[55] considered an excise tax imposed by Mexico on drinks using sweeteners that were not made from sugar cane, forcing suppliers to switch from foreign corn-syrup sugars to local cane-based ones. The claimant CPI, a US firm, maintained that the effect of the tax violated NAFTA's prohibition on performance requirements because it conditioned the receipt of an advantage, namely an exemption from paying the excise tax, on the use of Mexican produced cane sugar, offering an investment incentive with performance requirement strings attached. Here, however, the tribunal ruled that the corn-syrup-based tax did not constitute a performance requirement under NAFTA Article 1106. It explained that no requirement was imposed on CPI by Mexico in conjunction with the tax relief on soft drinks using corn syrup as a sweetener. Mexico made no demand on CPI for increased investment, increased local procurement or a greater level of local employees. Furthermore, neither the tax nor any other regulation cited by CPI contained a specified level of its domestic sales, imports, exports, or foreign exchange earnings undermining the claim that it constituted a legal requirement. The tribunal stated that although the challenged tax was adopted with the intent and effect of reducing the use by CPI's customers of CPI's product, the measure was placed on the soft drink manufacturers not the suppliers of the sugar, and even that was not mandatory.[56] This case reveals a close focus on both the construction and, more importantly, the effect of the performance requirement on the

---

54 [315]–[317].

55 *Corn Products International Inc (Claimant) v United Mexican States (Respondent)* ICSID Case No. ARB(AF)/04/1, Decision on Responsibility (15 January 2008).

56 [80].

investor's conduct, implicitly capturing the essence of their prohibition under NAFTA as instruments of interference with normal market activities.

The third dispute relating to the Mexican corn syrup tax engaging NAFTA's performance requirement prohibitions was *ADMC Tate & Lyle v Mexico*.[57] Here the claimant sugar companies again challenged Mexico's tax on corn syrup on various grounds, including that it was a prohibited performance requirement under NAFTA Article 1106(3), which as noted above also deals with investment incentives, and which will be explored in Chapter 6. The claimants argued that Mexico's imposition of performance requirements through advantages conferred on Mexican investors harmed their investments in corn syrup production and distribution facilities. The Mexican policy in question consisted of the requirement to use cane sugar instead of corn syrup in order to benefit from a tax exemption: effectively an investment incentive in conjunction with a performance requirement. This condition fulfilled the two requirements contained in subparagraphs (a) and (b) of Article 1106(3): "... to achieve a given level or percentage of domestic content; ... or to purchase, use or accord a preference to goods produced in its territory ..." As such, paragraph 3 of Article 1106(3) prohibits specific TRIMs-type performance requirements linked to receipt of an advantage, including a tax advantage. The tribunal reasoned that regardless of the fact that the tax relief conferred advantages on the sugar industry generally without distinguishing between domestic and foreign investors, the sugar industry in Mexico was essentially domestic with most of the sugar refineries owned and controlled by the Mexican government: evidence of de facto discrimination. The tribunal ultimately decided that both the structure of the Mexican sugar industry in Mexico and the underlying purpose behind the tax conferred advantages on the sugar industry in Mexico. These advantages were conditioned on the exclusive use of cane sugar, which was essentially domestic, discriminating against corn syrup: the industry in which the claimants were invested. As a consequence this measure was held to be a prohibited performance requirement under Article 1106(3) of NAFTA. This decision emphasizes the discriminatory nature of prohibited performance requirements and by extension the economically harmful consequences of granting investment incentives that have a discriminatory impact on competitive opportunities of foreign

---

[57] *Archer Daniels Midland Co, Tate & Lyle Ingredients Americas Inc (Claimant) v The United Mexican States (Respondent)* ICSID Case No. ARB(AF)/04/5, Award (21 November 2007).

firms. Such discrimination is separate but similar to that contemplated by NAFTA's national treatment standard and it equally operates on a de facto basis.

ADF v United States[58] was another ICSID case brought under NAFTA addressing performance requirement prohibitions, this time in the context of government procurement. In this dispute, the Canadian construction company ADF complained that the US imposition of a domestic content requirement violated Article 1106(1)(b) of NAFTA. They argued that Article 1106(1)(c) of NAFTA was also breached by the required preference given to US-produced steel materials and products, if the investor provided fabricated steel products to Federal-aid highway projects. ADF was obliged to purchase only US steel and either to fabricate that steel in the US itself, or to subcontract the fabrication to US steel fabricators rather than to its Canadian parent. The claimant argued that the respondent's measures imposed performance requirements relating to or connected with the "management, conduct or operation" of ADF within the meaning of the chapeau of Article 1106, since those measures directly impacted their daily activities, operations and sales. The US attempted to defend these claims by pointing to its listed NAFTA exceptions, which allowed performance requirements relating to construction in the waste management sector, and also the fact that the relevant performance requirements involved government procurement, which was not captured by NAFTA rules at the state level. The tribunal accepted these defences, noting that the investor knew that the relevant state authority was not subject to NAFTA's prohibition on performance requirements and as such was permitted to enact local content requirements in government construction contracts. The state and provincial governments of NAFTA members had not been brought under the treaty's procurement rules and as such there was no restriction on imposing performance requirements. As the respondent state conceded that the relevant measures were performance requirements – they were blatant local content requirements – the relevance of this decision is tied to the tribunal's interpretation of the exclusions applicable to Article 1106, in particular the scope of the term "procurement", noting that it should not cover activities where the primary responsibility for ongoing operations was within the purview of a private entity.

---

[58] *ADF Group Inc. (Claimant) v United States of America (Respondent)* ICSID Case No. ARB(AF)/00/1, Award (9 January 2003).

NAFTA's performance requirement prohibitions were contemplated in *SD Myers v Canada*,[59] a dispute relating to prohibitions placed on a US chemical treatment company operating in Canada. As discussed in Chapter 2 in the context of national treatment, the claimant US firm claimed that the Canadian law operated effectively to force it to dispose of its waste in Canada. The claimant argued that this constituted a performance requirement obliging all waste-disposal operators of the relevant chemical to accord preference to Canadian waste-disposal services and also to achieve a given level of domestic content, contrary to NAFTA Article 1106(1)(b) and (c). In its defence, Canada argued that the chemical export ban did not fall within the treaty's performance requirement rules because the export ban was not structured as an express condition: a performance requirement cannot be optional. Looking at the substance and effect of the Canadian measure as well as the literal wording of Article 1106, a majority of the tribunal ruled that no "requirements" as defined under NAFTA Article 1106(1)(b) or (c) were imposed on the investor. As such *SD Myers v Canada* was not truly a performance requirements case. A dissenting opinion by one tribunal member, Professor Schwartz, expressed the view that the export ban did constitute a performance requirement. He felt that the requirement of disposing the chemicals in Canada was "in connection with" the expansion of the operations of the specific investor and was crafted in response to SD Myers' plans to expand its business of remediating Canadian PCB wastes. If SD Myers had actually carried out the physical destruction of the chemicals in Canada, it would have had to purchase various goods or services from local suppliers and hire various local employees. As such the export ban was effectively a local content rule as under Article 1106(b), operating as a disguised restriction on international trade. The dissenting arbitrator added that the finding that the measure was a performance requirement would not have affected the damages awarded by the tribunal anyway, as these were covered by the successful expropriation claim.[60] This case illustrates the tendency of investment tribunals to consider the practical effect of the measure rather than its phrasing in determining whether or not it amounts to a performance requirement.

---

[59] First Partial Award in a NAFTA Arbitration under the UNCITRAL Arbitration Rules, *SD Myers Inc (Claimant) v Government of Canada (Respondent)*, 13 November 2000.

[60] Concurring Separate Opinion in the First Partial Award in a NAFTA Arbitration under the UNCITRAL Arbitration Rules, *SD Myers Inc (Claimant) v Government of Canada (Respondent)* [198]–[201] (opinion of Professor Bryan Schwartz, 13 November 2000).

A performance requirement prohibition-based claim was made in the NAFTA dispute brought by the lumber company Pope & Talbot against Canada,[61] also discussed in Chapter 2 in relation to national treatment. In this dispute, the investor argued that the Canadian measures required it to export a certain amount of softwood lumber each year and to restrict its sales of lumber bound for the United States, by relating such sales to the volume of exports. Canada responded that Article 1106 does not have de facto scope, and as the measures did not embody an obligation subject to enforcement by Canada, they could not be prohibited performance requirements. Canada further argued that the purpose of Article 1106 is to prohibit measures designed to require an investment to export more than it might otherwise have exported in order to raise foreign exchange earnings, which did not characterize the challenged export control regime. Lastly, Canada cautioned that the final provision of Article 1106, subsection (5) demanded that the prohibitions on performance requirements contained in the article must not be construed broadly. The Tribunal ruled that the language of that NAFTA Article 1106 is not expressly limited to the imposition or enforcement of a higher level or percentage of exports of goods and services, but could admit equally the imposition or enforcement at any given level or percentage of those exports. This broader reading of the treaty was based on Article 31 of the Vienna Convention's emphasis on the object and purpose of the treaty in which a provision is found to colour its meaning. However, as Canada had contented, Article 1106(5) must be clearly understood to restrict the scope of the rest of the article: the express provisions should not be extended beyond their stated coverage of seven categories of performance requirement. Therefore, in dismissing the claim, the tribunal concluded that the investor did not make out a valid case under Article 1106(1)(a) because the export regime did not actually impose or enforce requirements. Rather, it was a tariff-rate export-restraint regime, fixing only the level up to which covered products may be exported fee-free, then at a lower fee up to a given higher level, and thereafter in unlimited quantities at a higher fee. While Canada's export system undoubtedly deterred increased exports to the US, that deterrence was not a requirement for establishing, acquiring, expanding, managing, conducting or operating a foreign-owned business in Canada. While the export regime might have the effect of promoting similar policy goals to those achieved by

[61] Interim Merits Award in a NAFTA Arbitration under the UNCITRAL Arbitration Rules *Pope & Talbot Inc (Claimant) v Government of Canada (Respondent)* (26 June 2000).

increased exports to the US, it did not do so through one of the methods prohibited by the NAFTA. Observers have noted that this ruling indicates that the prohibition on performance requirements in NAFTA are aimed at controlling not the result but a specific means used to reach the result.[62] Perhaps more specifically, the *Pope & Talbot* dispute shows that NAFTA's concept of performance requirements should be interpreted narrowly.

In possibly the only investor–state dispute dealing with performance requirements not brought under NAFTA, *Lemire v Ukraine*,[63] the claimant argued that the host state's requirement that the investor, a radio broadcaster, play 50 per cent songs that had Ukrainian content violated the prohibition of performance requirements found in the BIT between the United States and the Ukraine. The claimant objected to the regulation because its radio broadcasts had largely comprised foreign material. The relevant provision stated:

> Neither Party shall impose performance requirements as a condition of establishment, expansion or maintenance of investments, which require or enforce commitments to export goods produced, or which specify that goods or services must be purchased locally, or which impose any other similar requirements.[64]

In rendering its decision on jurisdiction and liability in favour of the Ukrainian government, the tribunal articulated a highly deferential standard of review for nationality based performance requirements serving the goal of cultural preservation. It is worth repeating the relevant portion of the award in its entirety:

> As a sovereign State, the Ukraine has the inherent right to regulate its affairs and adopt laws in order to protect the common good of its people, as defined by its Parliament and Government. The prerogative extends to promulgating regulations which define the State's own cultural policy. The promotion of domestic music may validly reflect a State policy to preserve and strengthen cultural inheritance and national identity. The "high measure of deference in international law generally extends to the right of domestic authorities to regulate matters within their own borders" is reinforced in cases where the purpose of the legislation affects deeply felt cultural or linguistic traits of the community.[65]

---

[62] Legum (n 1) 64.
[63] ICSID Case No. ARB/06/18 (14 January 2010).
[64] Art. II.6 (signed 4 March 1996).
[65] *Lemire* [505].

The *Lemire* tribunal added, rejecting the investor's claim, that the right to safeguard national identity is not unique to the Ukraine, and indeed there was unified agreement among various European countries on the issue. The tribunal explained that performance requirement prohibition in the US–Ukraine BIT should be interpreted according to its object and purpose, which was expressly trade-related and itself tied to the overall purpose of the treaty which was to improve economic cooperation between the parties. The underlying purpose of the measure, in contrast, was to promote the Ukraine's cultural inheritance – an objective that was not incompatible with the prohibition on performance requirements. The tribunal also ruled that the local content requirement should not be seen as a violation of FET because it was imposed equally on all broadcasters, not only the individual claimant. The *Lemire* dispute illustrates the willingness of arbitral tribunals to construe performance requirement prohibitions narrowly where their purpose is one of social advancement and not economic protectionism, a clear recognition of the importance of the non-market values that FDI may often miss.

As suggested above, there may be a link between intellectual property protections and the ability of host states to use performance requirements, even where this term is not specifically used to frame claims. Intellectual-property-oriented matters have been the subject of several high-profile investor–state disputes in recent years, notably when the tobacco company Philip Morris brought claims against Uruguay and Australia under IIAs for trademark devaluation as a consequence of anti-smoking legislation.[66] With respect to performance requirement-type claims, the dispute between the pharmaceutical company Eli Lilly against Canada is worth mentioning. This claim was brought under NAFTA on the basis of Canada's failure to grant patents for pharmaceutical inventions with the claimants arguing that Canada imposed discriminatory additional disclosure requirements on American patent applicants, potentially exposing their inventions to theft, which violated both NAFTA's patent provisions as well as its general national treatment rules.[67] The extra disclosure requirement may be seen as a performance requirement

[66] *Philip Morris Asia Ltd v The Commonwealth of Australia* UNCITRAL, PCA Case No. 2012-12 and *Philip Morris Brands Sàrl, Philip Morris Products SA and Abal Hermanos SA v Oriental Republic of Uruguay* ICSID Case No. ARB/10/7 (formerly *FTR Holding SA, Philip Morris Products SA and Abal Hermanos SA v Oriental Republic of Uruguay*).

[67] *Eli Lilly and Co v Government of Canada* Notice of Intent to Submit a Claim to Arbitration under NAFTA, UNCITAL Arbitration Rules, 7 November 2012, citing NAFTA Arts 1709(1) and 1102 respectively.

(although it was not framed as such by the claimants) in that it is an adverse condition placed on the foreign investor that it has the capacity to satisfy and as such it has the ability to structure an investor's behaviour. The investor further argued that the decision of Canadian courts to invalidate the patents of Lilly's pharmaceuticals for failing to fulfil the required conditions constituted regulatory expropriation without compensation (prohibited by NAFTA Article 1110) as well as a violation of the right to fair and equitable treatment (guaranteed by NAFTA Article 1105). The investor alleged that the actions of the Canadian government, in placing these onerous conditions on it, deprived it of substantially all of the value of the asset and amounted to a sudden, arbitrary and discriminatory alteration of the framework governing Lilly's investment, in contravention of the investor's legitimate expectations of a stable business environment.[68] While again this dispute was not framed in terms of the breach of performance requirement prohibitions, this case discloses the potential for performance-requirement-related claims (essentially mandatory conditions dictating the investor's behaviour) to be brought in conjunction with intellectual property matters.

As noted earlier, some IIAs control performance requirements by express reference to the TRIMs. The enforcement of WTO obligations through the investor–state dispute settlement provisions of IIAs could be attractive to MNEs and their home states because it would provide a direct course of action against a host state for the injured company without needing to resort to home government intervention (without damages) as per the WTO dispute settlement system as well as offer financial compensation. Strengthening WTO obligations in this manner, however, could also dismantle the host state's own regulatory oversight of its economy through tools like performance requirements imposed on FDI.[69] The appearance of an umbrella clause in the treaty could reinforce the link between WTO law and investment arbitration; a clause dictating that all obligations undertaken by a party state may be subject to the dispute resolution process could incorporate WTO rules, in addition to private contractual obligations.[70] Issues of competing jurisdiction could therefore arise if performance requirements were challenged both using international trade law (through the WTO dispute settlement system) and before an arbitration tribunal empowered by an IIA.[71] General jurisdictional overlap between WTO panels and investment arbitration tribunals,

68 *Lilly* [89]–[99].
69 VanDuzer et al (n 19) 203.
70 ibid. 202.
71 Dolzer and Schreuer (n 22) 92.

the discussion of which is beyond the focus of this book, is a topic that has attracted significant academic commentary of late and remains at the forefront of ongoing debate concerning the fragmentation (or de-fragmentation) of international economic law.[72] Specific reference to the TRIMs in IIAs may represent a key manifestation of these tensions going forward.

4. OTHER INTERNATIONAL INVESTMENT-ORIENTED CONTROLS OF PERFORMANCE REQUIREMENTS

There are a number of other international legal instruments that address the use of performance requirements in conjunction with the regulation of international investment. This section will consider them by reference to the organizations through which they were established.

(i) The OECD

To begin with, the OECD Guidelines on Multinational Enterprises, which consist of recommendations for firms which operate in multiple jurisdictions regarding responsible business conduct contains some material on the use of performance requirements by host states. With 44 adhering nations, the guidelines are well regarded by the international community for their approach to sustainable FDI, although they do not establish binding obligations on firms. The guidelines contain provisions on so-called "investment dis-incentives", which are essentially performance requirements restricting foreign firms' capacity to engage in the extent or nature of the FDI that they wish. Drawing attention to the effects that performance requirements may have on home states rather than on investing firms themselves, Article IV.2 states that adhering governments "recognize the need to give due weight to the interests of (other) adhering governments affected by specific laws, regulations and administrative practices… providing official… disincentives… to international direct investment".[73] This is elaborated by Article IV.3 which, more cognizant of the harm that such measures can inflict upon firms, reads: "That

[72] E.g. B. Allen and T. Soave, 'Jurisdictional Overlap in WTO Dispute Settlement and Investment Arbitration' (2014) 30:1 *Arbitration International* 1.

[73] OECD Guidelines on Multinational Enterprises (2011) <http://mneguidelines.oecd.org/text/> accessed 2 December 2014.

adhering governments will endeavour to make such measures as transparent as possible, so that their importance and purpose can be ascertained and that information on them can be readily available". As such, the guidelines' principal contribution to the regulation of performance requirements is one of transparency: governments should minimize the harms engendered by performance requirements by creating conditions that allow foreign firms to understand and anticipate what is expected of them.

The other significant instrument instigated by the OECD that could impact upon the use of performance requirements is its Code of Liberalization of Capital Movements.[74] Adopted in 2012, the Code is binding on the adhering governments and the obligations which it imposes are extended on a non-reciprocal basis: they automatically cover all members of the IMF. Recalling the IMF's role in preventing currency restrictions as a barrier to trade discussed in the previous chapter, the basic obligations of the Code relevant to performance requirements are outlined in Article 1:

> (a) Members shall progressively abolish between one another … restrictions on movements of capital to the extent necessary for effective economic co-operation …
> (b) Members shall, in particular, endeavour:
>   (i) to treat all non-resident-owned assets in the same way irrespective of the date of their formation; and
>   (ii) to permit the liquidation of all non-resident-owned assets and the transfer of such assets or of their liquidation proceeds …
> (e) Members shall endeavour to avoid introducing any new exchange restrictions on the movements of capital or the use of non-resident-owned funds and shall endeavour to avoid making existing regulations more restrictive.

Such obligations, if observed, could curtail the use of performance requirements linked to a foreign investor's use or access to foreign or domestic currency. Most importantly for the purposes of the regulation of performance requirements, Annex A Liberalisation Lists of Capital Movements LIST A.I entitled "Direct Investment" provides that:

> The authorities of Members shall not maintain or introduce: Regulations or practices applying to the granting of licences, concessions, or similar authorisations, including conditions or requirements attaching to such authorisations and affecting the operations of enterprises, that raise special barriers or limitations with respect to non-resident (as compared to resident) investors,

---

[74] OECD, 2013 <www.oecd.org/investment/investment-policy/codes.htm> accessed 2 December 2014.

> and that have the intent or the effect of preventing or significantly impeding inward direct investment by non-residents.

Very general in scope, this provision has the potential to restrict a wide range of performance requirements, including traditional trade-related investment measures as well as requirements linked to local employment. This obligation is subject to the limitation that the above does not apply where the investor does not have a genuine commercial presence in the host state, that is, where:

> (i) an investment is of a purely financial character designed only to gain for the investor indirect access to the money or financial market of another country; or
> (ii) In view of the amount involved or of other factors a specific transaction or transfer would have an exceptionally detrimental effect on the interests of the Member concerned.

It may be inferred that the logic behind this provision is that purely financial investments of this nature do not offer the benefits associated with other types of FDI and indeed may pose systemic risks to the stability of the host state's economy. The Direct Investment provisions are further limited by Article 3, which articulates a general exception for the maintenance of public order, public health, safety and national security, capturing the many of the typical exceptions to investor-protections seen in some IIAs. Each adhering country to the OECD Code maintains a list of reservations, which typically exclude operation of the Code to FDI in the financial sector, including insurance and accounting, where restrictions on capital movement are necessary to ensure the stability of the domestic economy should it become too dependent on foreign capital. The acquisition of real estate and transportation are other spheres of economic activity where adhering states appear to have regularly specified limitations on the Code's basic commitments.

It must be recognized that while binding on adhering members, there is no mechanism specified in the OECD Code for the resolution of disputes arising under the Code between adhering states. Investors themselves have no right of action. Accordingly it is unclear how a country that felt that its right to take advantage of the stated liberalization commitments of another country had been violated would bring a claim or seek compensation. The Code's silence with respect to non-compliance is problematic and would likely frustrate any attempts by an aggrieved state (on behalf of one of its nationals) to seek legal redress, other than through informal diplomatic channels. The OECD Codes appear to have had little obvious impact on the use of performance requirements.

(ii) The United Nations

UNCTAD, which is the main organization of the United Nations dealing with trade, investment and development, maintains a list of Core Principles for Investment Policymaking, some of which could affect the use of performance requirements. These principles are highly generalized and non-binding, however, and as such could not give rise to a claim of illegal performance requirements that would be enforceable under international law. Nevertheless they are illustrative for their acknowledgement of the need for developing countries to maintain control over their own economies as they seek to attract and shape inward FDI. The principles hint at the international community's implicit recognition that performance requirements may be appropriate in some circumstances. They also evoke the need to minimize the harmful effects of such requirements on foreign investors. The relevant sections in this regard are:

> 2. Investment policies should be grounded in a country's overall development strategy. All policies that impact on investment should be coherent and synergetic at both the national and international level.
> 3. Investment policies should be developed involving all stakeholders, and embedded in an institutional framework based on the rule of law that adheres to high standards of public governance and ensures predictable, efficient and transparent procedures for investors.
> 4. Investment policies should be regularly reviewed for effectiveness and relevance and adapted to changing development dynamics … .
> 6. Each country has the sovereign right to establish entry and operational conditions for foreign investment, subject to international commitments, in the interest of the public good and to minimize potential negative effects.
> 7. In line with each country's development strategy, investment policy should establish open, stable and predictable entry conditions for investment.
> 8. Investment protection and treatment Investment policies should provide adequate protection to established investors. The treatment of established investors should be non-discriminatory in nature.[75]

Although highly generalized, UNCTAD's principles convey a careful balance between the sovereign right of investors to control their own economy, while acknowledging the right of investors to be administered by laws which are transparent and predictable.

---

[75] <http://investmentpolicyhub.unctad.org/ipfsd/core-principle> accessed 2 December 2014.

(iii) The World Bank: MIGA and the IFC

Two of the World Bank's agencies have policies which shed some light on a state's capacity to use performance requirements. The Multilateral Investment Guarantee Agency (MIGA) provides insurance against political risks in order to stimulate FDI in developing countries. MIGA's Operational Guidelines specify that, when assessing whether an investment project will contribute to the development of the host country's economy, it will consider whether support from MIGA well help host states produce exports or import substitutes and in so doing reduce their vulnerability to external economic changes. MIGA will also consider: the extent to which the investment project will diversify economic activities, expand employment opportunities and improve income distribution; the degree to which the investment project will transfer knowledge and skills to the host country; and the effects of the investment project on the social infrastructure and environment of the host country.[76] Furthermore, MIGA has a policy on Environmental and Social Standards which aim to safeguard and promote culture the environment, community health and safety and indigenous rights as well as employment and training.[77] It will not offer assistance to investors who do not address these objectives when designing their projects. Taken together, these various criteria can be described as performance requirements because they function as measurable conditions placed upon foreign investors which must be fulfilled in order to be eligible for MIGA support. In that sense, MIGA appears implicitly to condone some types of performance requirements. MIGA's political risk insurance support will be considered again in conjunction with investment incentives in Chapter 6.

Like MIGA, the International Finance Corporation (IFC), which provides financing for firms engaging in FDI in developing states, has several operational criteria which it places upon the private entities seeking its support. These may also be considered as performance requirements because they make the receipt of assistance (arguably an incentive) contingent on the investor engaging in a certain variety of conduct. The IFC maintains Performance Standards which embrace the IFC's strategic commitment to sustainable development, including safeguarding the environment and ensuring that there are no adverse social

---

[76] MIGA Operational Regulations (5 December 2012) 3.06 <www.miga.org/documents/Operational-Policies.pdf> accessed 2 December 2014.

[77] MIGA Policy on Environmental and Social Sustainability (1 October 2013) <www.miga.org/documents/Policy_Environmental_Social_Sustainability.pdf> accessed 2 December 2014.

impacts from investment projects. Recent updates to the IFC's sustainability guidelines incorporate modifications on resource efficiency, climate change, and business and human rights.[78] These policies are structured as conditions which compel investors using the IFC to behave in a manner that is responsive to the non-economic needs of the host state. As performance requirements broadly construed, the IFC Performance Standards direct investors to operate in a manner that addresses key market failures, such as those externalities that are associated with environmental damage and harm to indigenous or other vulnerable communities.

It will be interesting to see whether the New Development Bank, a development bank that will provide similar products to that of the World Bank but operated jointly by the BRICS (Brazil, Russia, India, China and South Africa) consortium of states, will mandate similar social policies when it begins lending to stimulate FDI in 2016. Given its origins in the emerging world and its recognition of the unique and often vulnerable position of many developing states, it is likely that some type of loan conditionality that addresses these market failures will feature in this organization's operational guidelines.

It has been suggested IIAs should include obligations that firms should comply with international guidelines such as those discussed in this section. Such oversight is often presented as a way to rebalance the one-sided nature of IIAs through emphasis on sustainability and transparency. Non-compliance with such norms could lead to either liability in terms of damages owed to the host state in the form of counterclaims, or else it could result in the denial of other benefits under the treaty.[79] While these types of public interest obligations are not expressly framed as performance requirements, were they to be perceived as such by arbitration tribunals then their interaction with performance requirement prohibitions in IIAs could accordingly be problematic.

---

[78] 'International Finance Corporation's Policy on Environmental and Social Sustainability' (International Finance Corporation, 1 January 2012) <www.ifc.org/wps/wcm/connect/7540778049a792dcb87efaa8c6a8312a/SP_English_2012.pdf?MOD=AJPERES> accessed 2 December 2014.

[79] D. Collins, 'Environmental Impact Statements and Public Participation in International Investment Law' (2010) 7:2 *Manchester Journal of International Economic Law* 4.

5. CONCLUSION

Although a few developed countries, such as Canada, the US and Japan, prohibit a wide range of performance requirements outright in their IIAs, most of the many thousands of IIAs in existence do not. Other states which do include performance requirements restrictions in their IIAs often do so by reference to language similar to that seen in the TRIMs Agreement (effectively prohibiting mandatory local content regulations) sometimes through express re-iteration of the TRIMs Agreement. Other provisions of IIAs could serve the same function as express prohibitions of performance requirements as broadly construed, notably FET, national treatment as well as guarantees against indirect expropriation and prohibitions on offsets for procurement purposes.

The dearth of investment arbitration on performance requirements, other than a handful of NAFTA cases, may be explained by the limited impact that performance requirement prohibitions have had on the business activities of foreign investors, just as it may disclose the preference for investors to couch these types of claims as breaches of other more traditional treaty rights such as national treatment or FET. In cases where performance requirement prohibitions were directly considered, such as *ADF Group* and *SD Myers*, these claims received scarce attention by the tribunal, in part because the implications of the provision was undisputed. Other arbitral decisions, such as *Pope & Talbot*, focus on the highly restricted nature of NAFTA's closed-list performance requirement prohibition, whereas *Lemire* emphasizes that the right to regulate in the public interest is paramount, even where it engages a performance requirement prohibition. An approach to performance requirement controls that is mindful of the overall object and purpose of the provision as well as the treaty in its entirety has been observed in arbitral practice. This is consistent with the stance taken by various instruments promulgated by a number of international organization such as the UN and the OECD, which attempt to balance the right of host states to enact laws that serve the public interest while minimizing the potential damage of performance requirements on foreign investors through weak transparency.

5. Investment incentives and international trade law

1. INTRODUCTION: TRADE-BASED INCENTIVES AND FOREIGN DIRECT INVESTMENT

Turning to the second major topic in this book, this chapter will explore the extent to which the branch of international economic law governing trade has placed impediments on host states' capacity to offer investment incentives in order to stimulate FDI. It will consider the role played by governmental assistance, otherwise known as subsidization, to foreign investors in their capacity as exporters. It will accordingly evaluate the control of export-oriented subsidies under the WTO Agreement on Subsidies and Countervailing Measures (SCM) as well as the possibility of restricting subsidies for services investors under the GATS as well as the sector specific Agreement on Agriculture. This chapter will also consider the potential for trade-based preferential treatment of foreign investors through free trade zones. Regional initiatives to regulate incentives, including notably the European Multisectoral Framework on State Aid, will be examined. Finally, some less formal mechanisms that may impair incentivisation of the trading activities of multinational firms will be discussed.

As introduced in Chapter 1, policies aimed at increasing or structuring FDI may form part of the existing economic and political landscape of the host country. This may include such factors as: the skill and price of its workforce; the availability of infrastructure; the quality of the host state's legal system, including notably the enforcement of contracts, the control of corruption and access to neutral dispute settlement, all of which reduce the risk of arbitrary government action; and finally, there may be special provisions in the state's legal framework that are structured in order to promote FDI expressly. It is this latter category that comprises the understanding of investment incentive that will be used throughout this book. Thus, incentives are benefits conferred on foreign investors that exceed those available to domestic investors for the specific purpose of encouraging either their establishment or continued operation in the host state. As noted previously, they are often provided in conjunction with performance requirements, conditioning the advantage on the foreign firm's specific behaviour. Trade-oriented incentives, which are the focus of this chapter, include exemptions on import duties for various types of fixed assets belonging to foreign investors. Such regimes tend to be granted in a country's domestic legislation covering foreign investment.[1]

Countries offer investment incentives because they assume that potential foreign investors do not find the host country sufficiently appealing for an investment project, either because the investment will not generate sufficient returns or because the risk of loss is too high. For their part, host states believe that granting potential investors certain benefits beyond those available to domestic firms will change this perception and induce them into making investments which they would not otherwise make. Investment incentives are designed not only to make the country appear more attractive in an absolute sense; they aim to render the potential host state more desirable relative to other countries that the investor might also be considering as a destination.[2] Incentives will either raise the expected rate of return of the FDI project or reduce the risk to which the foreign investors would be otherwise subjected to the point that the risk/return assessment is acceptable. As noted in Chapter 1, investment incentives are widely believed to be counter-productive because they distort international FDI flows away from the more productive regions and consume the resources of governments.

A similar logic appears to underpin the prohibitions of subsidies found in international trade law, which is focused on distortions in the markets for traded goods which ensues where governmental assistance allows producers to supply goods below their normal costs. For example, foreign investors may be granted the privilege to import capital goods and new materials at reduced tariff rates or without the payment of any customs duty. This can incentivize export, but crucially it also incentivizes FDI. Given the high customs duties that still exist in many countries, these types of exemptions may be very valuable to foreign firms.[3] Incentives

---

[1] E.g. Law on Foreign Investment in Viet Nam Art. 47. Law 18-2000-QH10 on Amendment of and Addition to a Number of Articles of the Law on Foreign Investment in Vietnam, dated 12 November 1996, was passed by Legislature X of the National Assembly of the Socialist Republic of Vietnam at its 7th Session, on 9 June 2000, and was effective as of 1 July 2000.

[2] J. Salacuse, *The Three Laws of International Investment* (OUP, Oxford 2013) 100.

[3] ibid. 101.

can enhance the exportability of the indirectly subsidized product into an importing state because the producer of the subsidized product is able to offer the product at a lower cost than would be possible in the absence of the subsidy, possibly also exporting it to external markets. This may represent a short-term welfare enhancement to consumers in the importing state, although local producers in the importing state may be unable to compete with these lower prices.[4] A further concern, at least for developing countries, is that investment incentives which are offered by sub-national governments in many developed countries, notably US states, can be very difficult to detect and therefore control, particularly where they are not regulated under national law.[5] In examining the link between trade and investment, it must be recognized that multinational firms are the primary drivers of international trade flows. Approximately 80 per cent of globally traded goods and services involve the international production networks of multinationals, with almost one-third of total trade taking place between business entities that are part of the same corporate group.[6] The chief mechanisms through which investment incentives are regulated by international trade law will now be considered.

2. WTO AGREEMENTS AND THE CONTROL OF INVESTMENT INCENTIVES

The WTO is the major international organization charged with controlling trade-oriented investment incentives, although the WTO Agreements contain no provisions that specifically address investment incentives by name. Indeed, as evident from the previous chapter, the WTO, as an organization devoted to the liberalization of international trade, has but a modest impact on FDI. Still, the WTO has a significant role to play in the control of subsidies through its SCM and subsidies in some ways have an equivalent effect to investment incentives in that they can assist the

---

[4] D. Petrov, 'Prisoners No More: State Investment Relocation Incentives and the Prisoners' Dilemma' 33:1 *Case Western Reserve Journal of International Law* 71 (2001) 74.

[5] See generally B.V.R. Subrahmanyam, 'Investment Incentives and Multilateral Disciplines' in S. Evenett and B. Hoekman (eds), *Economic Development and Multilateral Trade Cooperation* (Palgrave MacMillan and The World Bank, New York, NY 2006).

[6] UNCTAD, *World Investment Report 2013: Global Value Chains: Investment and trade for development* (United Nations, New York, NY 2013) 135.

commercial activities of foreign firms. The SCM is the only truly multilateral instrument imposing any disciplines on state assistance to private sector commercial activities. Some of the benefits conferred on foreign investors in their capacity as traders may fall under the discipline of this agreement. While the GATS currently lacks a regime for subsidies in services and as such does little to restrict FDI incentives, the WTO does maintain the Agreement on Agriculture, although it is unlikely to have an impact on FDI. These agreements and their potential to operate as limitations on the use of incentives to attract foreign investors will be evaluated in turn.

(i) Subsidy Prohibitions in the WTO Agreement on Subsidies and Countervailing Measures (SCM)

The SCM regulates the use of subsidies relating to trade in goods. As governments inevitably interact with private commercial parties with various degrees of oversight, the concept of subsidization, as in state-based assistance to a private firm, is controversial. It is typically understood by reference to the market: any measure that keeps prices for consumers below or costs for producers above the "natural" market level can be seen as a subsidy. Broadly construed, almost all form of governmental activity that is not detrimental can be seen as subsidization.[7] There are often thought to be three key components to a subsidy: public action, conferral of economic advantage and impact on the competitive process.[8]

Under the SCM, subsidy is defined the as a financial contribution, or price/income support by a government or any public body, which confers a "benefit" on the recipient.[9] Under Article 1.1(a) the SCM provides an exhaustive list of the types of financial contributions that can be considered subsides:

> … direct transfer of funds (for example, grants, loans and equity infusion), and a potential direct transfer of funds or liabilities (for example, loan guarantees); government revenue that is otherwise due is forgone or not collected (for example, fiscal incentives such as tax credits); provision of goods or services (other than general infrastructure), or government purchases

---

[7] L. Rubini, *The Definition of Subsidy and State Aid: WTO and EC Law in Comparative Perspective* (OUP, Oxford 2009) 7.

[8] ibid. 419.

[9] Art. 1.1(b).

of goods, at non-market prices; government payments to a funding mechanism, or when government entrusts or directs to a private body to carry out one or more of the three types of contributions addressed above.

Exemptions from having to comply with certain environmental or technical standards which convey an indirect benefit on firms or industries are not in that list so would therefore not be captured by the SCM's definition of a subsidy. In addition to the exhaustive list of measures that can constitute subsidies, the SCM includes in the definition of a subsidy income or price supports that directly or indirectly increase exports from or reduce imports into a WTO member state's territory. A subsidy must also confer a benefit or advantage on the recipient, as defined in relation to the normal costs and benefits occurring in the market. A benefit or advantage is conferred if the financial contribution places the recipient (for example, a foreign investor) in a more advantageous position than would have been the case but for the financial contribution. A benefit does not always need to be established under the SCM in order for a subsidy to be found. This is because the agreement contains an illustrative list of export subsidies, which if met, does not require a benefit to be established separately.

If a measure fulfils the requirements for the definition of a subsidy, it will not necessarily be prohibited under the SCM. This further depends on the measure's "specificity", a requirement that limits the impact of the SCM on a wider range of innocuous governmental policies. Specificity contemplates the lack of general availability for all enterprises and industries within a region. In other words, the advantage is extended to only a particular enterprise, industry, or group of enterprises or industries. By bringing only specific subsidies within the scope of the SCM, the WTO controls only those governmentally-conferred benefits that cause distortions and inefficiencies in international trade. In contrast to specific measures, general measures, such as the reduction of tax rates for an entire country or the creation of public infrastructure for use by all, modify the market structure in the same way for all economic operators in the market and are not restricted.

If a subsidy is viewed as "specific" it may then be subject to regulation under one of three different categories outlined in the SCM. The categorization dictates whether the subsidy can be used and when and what measures or remedies are available to other WTO members if it has been used in a manner which is harmful. These three categories, together often described as the "traffic-light approach" are: (1) prohibited subsidies, which relate to export are deemed specific and harmful; (2) actionable subsidies, meaning domestic or industrial subsidies, for which claims for relief are possible if injury can be shown to the domestic industry of another WTO Member; and (3) non-actionable subsidies, which are construed as being non-injurious because they relate to developmental initiatives.

Article 3 of the SCM states that prohibited export subsidies are: "(a) subsidies contingent, in law or in fact, whether solely or as one of several other conditions, upon export performance …; [and] (b) subsidies contingent, whether solely or as one of several other conditions, upon the use of domestic over imported goods". By encouraging this type of behaviour, beneficiary firms can damage foreign suppliers of these goods, causing inefficiencies. This method of characterizing a type of subsidy appears to contemplate performance requirements without expressly referring to them as such. The requirement to export a given quantity of production or to use locally produced goods are unquestionably performance requirements, most likely falling within the definition of prohibited trade-related investment measures under the TRIMs.

Under Article 5 specific subsidies that are not prohibited outright, but are "actionable" by other states are those that cause:

(a) injury to the domestic industry of another Member;
(b) nullification or impairment of benefits accruing directly or indirectly to other Members under GATT 1994 …; [or]
(c) serious prejudice to the interests of another Member.

Actionable subsidies therefore do not have any link to export or use of local goods and as such their harmful effects on international trade cannot be assumed. This is why injuries for these types of subsidies as suffered by other WTO Members must be demonstrated. Some specific subsidies were designated as "non-actionable" under the SCM, but these have since expired.

Remedies for prohibited or actionable subsidies can be sought at the multilateral level through the WTO's dispute settlement body, or imposed unilaterally, by a state's use of countervailing duties against the member which has applied the subsidy, which are meant to offset the benefit that was gained. There is extensive literature on the efficiency of remedies for subsidization that are beyond the scope of this discussion.[10] Importantly, unilateral action through countervailing duties will only negate the effect of the subsidy in the member state imposing the countervailing duties. It

---

10 See e.g. A. Green and M. Trebilcock, 'Enforcing WTO Obligations: What Can We Learn from Export Subsidies' (2007) 10:3 *Journal of International Economic Law* 653.

will not eliminate either the subsidy or diminish any damaging consequences on third countries. Subsidies countered via the WTO's dispute-settlement procedures, in which a panel will determine the validity of the measure under the SCM may rule that the member withdraw the subsidy. If a prohibited subsidy has been found by the WTO's dispute settlement body, it will order the member to withdraw the subsidy, and may also require repayment of the subsidy granted. If the subsidy is held to be actionable, but has caused adverse effects in another member state or states, the member granting the subsidy may either withdraw it or take action to eliminate the harmful effects, such as by providing compensation.

In order to mitigate the harmful effects of subsidies, the SCM includes the provision that all members must notify their subsidies to the WTO Secretariat. Such notifications should cover all subsidies offered within a country, at all levels of government, and include the amounts spent on such support. In the past many members had not been forthcoming in providing reports on their subsidization programmes as required under the rules;[11] however, most of the large economies within the WTO now have up-to-date and detailed subsidies notifications as of the end of 2014.[12] The SCM contained special and differential treatment obligations for developing countries but these have since expired.

WTO subsidy rules were not designed to address investment incentives and are aptly described as a "blunt tool" for dealing with them.[13] There is no express reference to FDI or investment incentives in the SCM. There is no reference to benefits constituting subsidies being made available by governments to foreign firms. In that sense, the SCM has only a limited direct impact on the control of investment incentives. Clearly, the control of subsidization under the SCM contemplates assistance provided by a government to its own firms, not to those of foreign states, although some forms of incentives for foreign firms could fall within SCM disciplines. In helping domestic firms, it is usually the foreign firms that suffer because of subsidization, often asking their governments to bring complaints through the WTO when this happens. Furthermore, while it is

[11] K. Thomas, 'Investment Incentives: Growing Use, Uncertain Benefits, Uneven Controls' (Global Subsidies Initiative, International Institute for Sustainable Development, November 2007) 44 <www.iisd.org/gsi/sites/default/files/GSI_Investment_Incentives.pdf> accessed 2 December 2014.

[12] See e.g. Semi-Annual Report under Article 25.11 – United States, G/SCM/N/274/USA (5 September 2014).

[13] Thomas (n 11) 51.

not mentioned expressly in the text of the agreement, the SCM essentially deals only with trade in goods by firms that are already present in the host state.[14] By the time production and exportation has commenced by a foreign firm entering the host state, the incentives that had been given to attract the investment in the first place have typically terminated, meaning that the SCM is useless.

The lack of reference in the SCM to the conferral of benefits (i.e. incentives) specifically on foreign firms is problematic from the standpoint of actionable subsidies which require proof of injury to the domestic industry, nullification or impairment of benefits, or serious prejudice to the interests of another Member. It is difficult to see how an incentive conferred on a foreign investor would be harmful to that firm's home country, other than possibly depriving it of economically productive activity or local employment as a consequence of the firm's shifting of commercial activities abroad. This reading is itself problematic when taking into consideration the explanation that "serious prejudice" focuses on export levels from other countries (i.e. home states) into the territory of the subsidizing state (i.e. host states), a scenario which has little to do with FDI. While the foreign firm's exports to the host state might decrease once it locates there (its domestic sales would replace what it had once exported) this can hardly be viewed as an injurious or prejudicial to an industry. If any damage were inflicted on the domestic economy of other WTO members it would be nearly impossible to demonstrate causation with respect to the incentivized internationalization of domestic firms by a foreign country.

Moreover, even were an investment incentive to fall under the scope of the SCM, most likely as a prohibited subsidy through export assistance to firms of foreign origin, compensation through WTO dispute settlement does not operate retroactively. It cannot remove a foreign investment that has already been made. While countervailing duties on goods produced by an advantaged firm can be imposed by other WTO members, this will only take place if another member has complained and been able to demonstrate that there was harm to its domestic industry as well as a link between the subsidization and that harm. In that sense, the SCM could compel a state to withdraw customs duty relief extended in order to attract FDI, but this does not contemplate repayment of these duties by

[14] The SCM does not specify to whom the benefit of the subsidy is conferred. There is no requirement that it be located in the territory of the governmental agency.

the firm which benefited from it.[15] The most common enforcement method available under the SCM, the unilateral countervailing duty, is limited. Unilateral countervailing duties are unlikely to discourage investment incentivisation systematically because they are not coordinated at a global level and they tend to apply only to a small portion of the production that actually benefits from subsidies. The other enforcement mechanism against subsidies is through a complaint by a WTO member to the WTO itself through the dispute settlement system, but has been used only a handful of times, as it is exceedingly difficult to satisfy the serious prejudice test.[16] It has been suggested that the weak enforcement of WTO obligations on trade-distorting subsidies may be the consequences of the political reality that WTO Members knew that they would eventually be compelled to depart from these obligations as a consequence of domestic interest groups.[17] Bail-outs instigated to certain industries by numerous governments during the financial crisis of 2008–09 are testament to this.

The link between subsidies and outward FDI (meaning the internationalization efforts of domestic firms) is more obvious, as home state assistance may enable domestic firms to establish or grow their foreign presence more readily, conferring a benefit or advantage relative to their international competitors. But again this type of benefit is not contemplated directly by the SCM which focuses on export-oriented assistance to firms. Still, the greater a domestic firm's profits through subsidized exports, the more resources such firms will have to devote towards their expansion to other markets. In this regard, the multi-billion dollar US–EU aircraft subsidy dispute involved allegations of various incentives offered by the US federal and many state governments to Boeing's large civil aircraft division as well as the EU's loans and other assistance to Airbus and its large civil aircraft operations.[18] While the Appellate Body ruled that many of the measures applied by both the US and the EU, including tax relocation incentives and access to research facilities totalling did constitute SCM-inconsistent subsidies, the effect of this

---

[15] Panel Report, *Australia – Subsidies Provided to Producers and Exporters of Automotive Leather* WT/DS126/R (adopted 16 June 1999).

[16] A. Sykes, 'The Questionable Case for Subsidies Regulation: A Comparative Perspective' (2010) 2 *Journal of Legal Analysis* 473.

[17] A. Nov, 'The "Bidding War" to Attract Foreign Investment: The Need for a Global Solution' (2005) 25 *Virginia Tax Review* 835, 848.

[18] Appellate Body Report, *United States – Measures Affecting Trade in Large Civil Aircraft (Second Complaint)* WT/DS53/AB/R (report circulated 18 May 2011).

assistance on either inward or outward FDI was not considered. The relocation subsidies offered by US state governments, for example, were not aimed at attracting large aircraft manufacturers from other countries but rather assisting in the relocation of a domestic firm from one region to another within the same national jurisdiction. The WTO US–EU large civil aircraft disputes[19] were focused, unsurprisingly, on their trade-effects, namely the harms suffered as a consequence of export-oriented assistance accorded to specific firms. Benefits conferred on these firms in their capacity as traders had no clear impact on their foreign investment activities, or to the extent that if it did this was not considered by the panels or Appellate Body. If the EU had subsidized Airbus' efforts to expand internationally or to sell its aircraft in the US (or if the US had done so for Boeing in Europe) then the WTO panel would have had the opportunity to consider the impact of the SCM on outward FDI incentives. As it stands, there have not been any WTO disputes concerning assistance for internationalization.

Another major difficulty in regulating investment incentives under the SCM relates to the requirement of specificity. Clearly fiscal incentives to foreign investors provide a financial contribution in the form of foregone revenue. Whether such subsidies would be viewed as specific or prohibited under the SCM would depend on the form they take. If they are aimed at particular firms or a particular industry (as in the large civil aircraft disputes), then they will likely be construed as specific and if they were expressly linked to export, then they would most likely be prohibited. The specificity of tax concessions granted to foreign firms would depend on whether there were any conditions tied to such concessions. If any conditions that were applied treat all investments (from all industries) identically, they would probably not count as specific under the SCM. In most countries, however, exemptions from various taxes are normally available only to specific investments or target export industries and as such they would therefore most likely be construed as specific. If the tax concessions were tied to a firm's export performance or local content, they would constitute prohibited subsidies.

Other non-trade incentives could raise specificity problems under the SCM. Deductions granted to foreign firms on their taxable earnings based for example on the number of employees are normally given to firms as general tax concessions and therefore would probably not be

---

[19] See also the EU's request for consultations in respect to Washington State's relocation tax incentives for large civil aircraft manufacturers: *United States – Conditional Tax Incentives for Large Civil Aircraft* WT/DS487/1 (23 December 2014).

viewed as specific under the SCM. Exemptions from employee-based taxes would probably be both specific and actionable if they are extended only to foreign investors or only to investors from specific sectors or specific countries. If exemptions are based only on the number of employees then such exemptions would not be specific. A direct tax reduction or credit based on local content of output would be a violation of the TRIMs as a prohibited local content rule. As a domestic content subsidy, it would probably also constitute a prohibited subsidy under the SCM. A similar credit or deduction based on net value earned would not be directly based on local content and would not likely be specific, nor a TRIMs violation. Likewise, tax reduction incentives with conditions such as volume of sales or employee training would probably be viewed as a general tax concession and would only be specific if provided only to certain firms or industries, although it would not engage the TRIMs rules.

Linking fiscal incentives to trade-based ones, direct tax deductions based on other expenditures would be seen as general tax rules applicable to all firms and would therefore not be construed as specific or actionable. However, any additional deductions in tax offered for export promotion expenditures would constitute prohibited subsidies because they would represent trade distortions. Exemptions from local taxes and duties are often extended on an individually negotiated basis to specific investments or to specific sectors. Accordingly they would likely be seen as specific and actionable. If such assistance was aimed at export industries, they would be considered prohibited subsidies. As these exemptions are often provided by sub-national governments they would be difficult to detect. They also tend not to be notified as a subsidy to the WTO, compounding this problem.[20]

More clearly aimed at trade, exemptions from import duties and value added taxes on capital goods tend to be given to a few industries or to particular firms. Accordingly, these incentives would most probably count as specific and actionable. Exemptions from import duties on raw materials would typically be extended only to a handful of firms and may therefore be specific under the SCM. If the exemption was extended to all raw inputs used by a firm and only a portion of the firm's production is exported, this would be a prohibited subsidy, as the remission of duty is in excess of that levied on imported inputs used in export-oriented production. An exemption from export duties is most likely to be concentrated on a few industries and therefore be specific and actionable.

---

[20] Subrahmanyam (n 5) 333–6.

Since by definition such an incentive is linked to exports, it would also be a prohibited subsidy.[21]

Financial incentives in the form of direct government grants, investment-based tax concessions, subsidized infrastructure and training allowances are likely not to be construed as actionable under the SCM. This is because they are often one-time concessions and this makes it difficult to isolate their effects (for example, on the price of the goods and services the firm offers) than it is to ascertain the effect of indirect tax concessions or profit-based tax concessions. Grants provided to foreign firms are among the most commonly used instrument for attracting FDI by developed countries. Such policies would most likely be actionable under the SCM because they are specific in that they are normally offered to individual firms. If they are extended for the purpose of export, they will also be prohibited. Relatedly, direct subsidies to foreign firms for employment or reimbursement of salaries tend to be based on objective criteria and as such they would most likely not be captured by SCM rules. Subsidized loans for foreign investors are frequently directed at particular firms or industries and would therefore be specific and actionable. If they are linked to export targets, they will also be prohibited. Loan guarantees should be construed as subsidies if they are offered to foreign investors at below market rates. Similarly, guaranteed export credits would be assessed against market rates to determine whether they confer a benefit to investors. If they are tied to export targets, then they would be prohibited. Loans offered for job creation tend to be viewed as a form of subsidized loan. They are not likely to be specific since they are usually extended on the basis of objective criteria.[22]

Although not strictly trade-related, exchange based incentives offered in conjunction with FDI could engage WTO subsidies disciplines. Favourable exchange rates and debt equity conversion rates tend to be given to a few firms or industries and as such would count as specific subsidies, potentially helping firms to augment exports as well as compete with domestic equivalents. Special exchange rates are also often attached to export requirements and are therefore prohibited subsidies. Likewise, the elimination of exchange risk on foreign exchange loans could also be an actionable subsidy because it likely confers a benefit, depending on whether or not a fee is charged for it and if that fee is at the market rate. Concessions on foreign exchange credits for export earnings

---

[21] ibid. 333–8.

[22] ibid.

and free foreign exchange management and transfer would be viewed as prohibited subsidies because they are offered in conjunction with export targets. Other advantages relating to foreign exchange, such as the repatriation of earnings and capital, the release of foreign exchange in lieu of domestic contribution to a joint venture, and permissions to take foreign exchange loans, would not likely be construed as subsidies because there is no direct financial contribution from the government. These types of FDI incentives compensate for an adverse regulatory environment in the host state and are difficult to classify as subsidies because there is no financial contribution or there is a lack of specificity.[23]

Recent WTO jurisprudence has demonstrated the possibility that governmental support offered to firms which engage in environmentally protective behaviour may escape illegality under WTO subsidies disciplines.[24] It has been suggested that setting aside emission allowances for new firms, including both foreign and domestic, could be considered as an FDI incentive where such regimes target foreign firms. This is because such assistance (allowing firms to depart from emissions obligations) would render recipient firms better placed to invest in research and development as well as increase their productive output generally. This could adversely affect competitor firms for whom such benefits are not offered and as such could represent a market distortion.[25]

Generally speaking, although some incentives offered to foreign firms to instigate or prolong FDI could be captured by the SCM, host states can evade these rules without difficulty by structuring their incentives packages to be nonspecific. Indeed, the concept of specificity may be inappropriate as a means of establishing illegality for types of governmental assistance in the context of investment incentives.[26] The industry-by-industry targeting contemplated by specificity has accordingly attracted criticism as an inappropriate proxy for inefficient government support because governments can achieve identical economic results with programs that pass the specificity test simply by altering their form and not their substance.[27]

---

[23] ibid. 339–43.

[24] E.g. Appellate Body Report, *Canada – Measures Relating to the Feed in Tariff Program* WT/DS426/AB/R (report circulated 6 May 2013).

[25] L. Rubini and I. Jegou, 'Who'll Stop the Rain: Allocating Emissions Allowances for Free: Environmental Policy, Economics and WTO Subsidy Law' (2012) 1:2 *Transnational Environmental Law* 325.

[26] Subrahmanyam (n 5) 343.

[27] Sykes (n 16).

(ii) The Agreement on Agriculture

There has been a rapid increase in the level of FDI in agriculture, although this is associated primarily with developing countries, especially those in Africa.[28] As such, subsidies for firms engaging in agriculture are a variety of investment incentive that could fall under the sphere of influence of the WTO. Since many provisions of the SCM are not applicable to trade in agricultural commodities, subsidies relating to this sector are governed instead by the WTO Agreement on Agriculture (AOA). The AOA establishes a regime controlling export subsidies as well as assistance for domestic production, both of which can be harmful to international trade because of their capacity to distort markets for agricultural products. Because of the critical importance of agriculture to the economies of many developing countries as well as the political influence of farming organizations, agricultural subsidies remain one of the most contentious issues in world trade negotiations. Still, their effect on FDI patterns is probably limited because governmental assistance to agricultural production tends to be granted to domestic rather than foreign firms. As with the SCM, the AOA was not designed to address incentives aimed at FDI.

Still, some types of incentives offered to foreign firms operating in the agricultural sector could constitute export subsidies and be captured by the AOA. Under Article 9, export subsidies consist of the provision by governments of direct subsidies of various different kinds. These include: payments to firms that are contingent on their export performance (meaning that a certain quantity of agricultural products are exported in a given time period); the sale or disposal for export by governments of non-commercial stocks of agricultural products at a price lower than the comparable price charged for the like product to buyers in the domestic market; reductions in the cost of marketing exports of agricultural products (other than widely available export promotion and advisory services, capturing the concept of specificity); and subsidies contingent on the incorporation of agricultural products in exported products.[29] Those export subsidies that are listed in each member's schedule of commitments under the AOA are subject to reduction commitments requiring decreases in both the amount of subsidy granted and amount of

---

[28] D. Hallam, 'Foreign Investment in Developing Country Agriculture – Issues, Policy Implications and International Response' OECD, Global Forum on International Investment VIII (9 December 2009) <www.oecd.org/investment/globalforum/44231828.pdf> accessed 31 July 2015.

[29] Art. 9(1).

products subsidized. Commitments for reduction are more onerous for developed than for developing countries, and they do not apply at all to least developed countries. Export subsidies that have not been scheduled are prohibited outright. It had been the intention of WTO members to phase out all agricultural export subsidies by 2013; however, this has not yet occurred.

The AOA also regulates domestic subsidies, meaning those that do not have an export-oriented purpose, by categorizing them according to their deemed trade-distorting impact.[30] So-called "amber box" agricultural subsidies (using a loose traffic-light categorization system) are forms of assistance by governments that are deemed to be highly trade distorting. These include price supports or subsidization that is directly related to quantity of agricultural commodities produced. Reduction commitments by developed states have been applied to amber box subsidies, although some less restrictive commitments have also been imposed on developing countries. There are no controls on amber box subsidies for developed states in the AOA. Applying conditions to the assistance may be viewed as a performance requirement, although this variety would not be captured by the TRIMs.

The least harmful agricultural subsidies as assessed by their effects on international trade are known as blue box. Such measures include price support for agricultural commodities that would otherwise be deemed as amber box, but have been made contingent on agricultural producers limiting production instead of increasing production or export. Controlling the quantity of production, while still economically distortive, is not believed to be as harmful as measures which encourage unnatural increases or artificial levels of export because they do not suppress prices as drastically. Accordingly these types of subsidies do not require reduction commitments. As with amber box subsidies, this type of assistance would constitute a performance requirement but not of the kind controlled by the TRIMs.

The final variety of domestic support regulated by the AOA is green box subsidies, which are considered to have little or no impact on international trade. There are several conditions attached to the classification as a green box subsidy. First, this type of assistance contemplates those measures which are provided through a publicly-funded government programme not involving transfers from consumers, meaning that consumers are not charged higher prices. Such programmes can include policies where governmental revenue is foregone. Blue box subsidies

---

30 Art. 6.

must also not have the effect of providing price support to producers and they must meet criteria regarding specific policy purposes or objectives, which include the promotion of food security, the provision of food aid or support for services such as research and development, extension and advisory services and infrastructure services. Such conditions may comprise performance requirements as broadly defined. If these conditions are satisfied, then the subsidy will fall within the green box category and as such it will not be subject to the disciplines of the AOA.

(iii) The General Agreement on Trade in Services (GATS)

Despite its purview over FDI through the commercial presence mode of services delivery, the GATS does not contain any provisions on investment incentives. GATS' national treatment obligation, which is tied to the sectors and modes of delivery listed in each Members schedule of specific commitments, speaks of treatment that is "no less favourable" than that accorded to like domestic services and service suppliers (in other words, investments and investors under Mode 3).[31] As noted in Chapter 2, this language arguably preserves the capacity for Members to accord better than national treatment to foreign investors in order to attract FDI. Moreover, the GATS does not contain any rules on subsidies in relation to services. The SCM has been criticized for this latter omission, notably because disciplines on services subsidies may have prevented what some view as the excessive support provided to the financial sectors of many countries during the global financial crisis of 2008–09.[32] The absence of specific rules in the GATS on subsidies may be partly explained by the difficulties experienced in defining, identifying and measuring subsidies, as well as assessing their effects. Such issues are particularly problematic because regulatory forms of subsidization are more pervasive in the provision of services than they are in goods. This is compounded by the fact that there is a lack of adequate data, not only on subsidies but on the categorization of services themselves and in the quantification of prices per unit of output.[33]

Article XV of GATS does state that WTO members "recognize that, in certain circumstances, subsidies may have distortive effects on trade in services". If one Member considers that it is adversely affected by a

---

[31] Art. XVII.1.

[32] G. Horlick and P. Clarke, 'WTO Subsidies Discipline During and After the Crisis' (2010) 13:3 *Journal of International Economic Law* 859.

[33] M. Daly, 'Investment Incentives and the Multilateral Agreement on Investment' (1998) 38:2 *Journal of World Trade* 5, 18.

subsidy of another Member, it may request consultations with a view to resolving the matter. Importantly Article XV also compels Members to share information on services subsidies and "enter into negotiations with a view to developing the necessary multilateral disciplines to avoid such trade-distortive effects". Such rules have yet to be developed and it is unlikely that there will be comprehensive multilateral rules on services-oriented subsidies in the near future. The lack of progress in GATS subsidies negotiations may be explained by the need, especially among the wealthiest countries, to preserve their capacity to provide assistance packages to sectors like financial services in light of financial crises.[34] The main points of contention that likely slowed the negotiation of a services-oriented subsidy discipline were the unsettled definition of subsidy, its application to various modes of services delivery, and the lack of political will, possibly due to governments' recognition that services sectors might well be needful of assistance because of their highly volatile nature.

Shortcomings in the Doha Round of trade negotiations at the WTO has shifted the emphasis of many countries to bilateral and regional FTAs to advance their trade and investment agendas. In addition to investment chapters, which will be discussed further in the next chapter, some of these instruments contain provisions on trade in services. As with GATS, none of these contains comprehensive disciplines on the use of subsidies, although some envision that subsidization of services could lead to tension between signatory states. In this regard, the Australia-Japan Economic Partnership Agreement's chapter on trade in services states which recalls that of GATS Article XV, above: "In the event that either Party considers that its interests have been adversely affected by a subsidy of the other Party, the Parties shall, on request of the former Party, enter into consultations with a view to resolving the matter."[35] This article also includes provisions on the mandatory sharing of information relating to the nature and extent of the subsidy. Such requirements reflect the understanding that while it may be difficult to regulate subsidies in services, some of the damaging effects of these measures can be mitigated through enhanced availability of information.

---

[34] P. Delimatsis and P. Sauve, 'Financial Services Trade after the Crisis: Policy and Legal Conjectures' (2010) 13:3 *Journal of International Economic Law* 837.

[35] Art. 9.11(2) (signed 8 July 2014). A similar provision can be found in the China–Australia FTA Art. 8.12(1) (signed 6 July 2012).

3. FREE TRADE ZONES AS INVESTMENT INCENTIVES

Free trade zones (FTZ)s are special areas within individual states where imported materials undergo some degree of processing before being transported outside the zone. Designated by law and supported by infrastructure, FTZs are designed to attract foreign investors (as well as assist local ones) by allowing approved firms to import goods through these zones without the payment of duties. Beneficiary firms may then process them and export the finished goods duty free and without the intervention of customs authorities. FTZs are typically located at seaports and airports along major transportation routes (maritime, rail and road) and/or in border regions. At these locations firms are able to unload imported goods without paying customs duties or taxes and with minimal formalities, pending re-export to a third country usually after some period of time in storage or release for sale in the domestic market with payment of customs duties. FTZs also encompass export-processing zones, which are specialised in manufacturing production areas for goods such as textiles, consumer electronics and light industrial components. Export-processing zones can also include call centres and facilities for the processing of digital data.

There are believed to be more than 1700 FTZs in more than 133 countries around the world.[36] Generally speaking, countries establish them in order to secure foreign exchange earnings through the development of non-traditional exports, to create employment and raise the income of local workers. Most importantly for the purposes of this book, FTZs are used to attract FDI and its associated benefits including raising employment and transferring technology.[37] For example, China has begun experimenting heavily with FTZs in order to stimulate market reforms and shift towards higher technology manufacturing.[38] The advantages of such zones to foreign investors are clear; eliminating customs charges can result in significant cost savings.

FTZs are regulated by the International Convention on the Simplification and Harmonization of Customs Procedures (known as the Kyoto Convention, but not to be confused with its more famous climate-oriented

---

[36] F. Bost, 'Are Economic Free Zones Good for Development?' (West African Challenges, OECD, November 2011) 4 <www.oecd.org/swac/publications/49814045.pdf> accessed 31 July 2015.

[37] J. Salacuse (n 2) 101–2.

[38] J. Anderlini, 'New China Free Trade Zones to Lift Growth' *Financial Times* (London, 14 December 2014).

namesake),[39] which contains harmonized rules on the operation of FTZs. The convention defines the legal status of FTZs in the context of customs procedures and outlines basic requirements for governments which have FTZs in their territory with a view to achieving procedural efficiency. As of 2015, 102 countries have signed the convention. Broadly speaking, the convention provides that goods shipped from a FTZ into the rest of the country's territory or vice-versa are to be considered as if they were respectively imported to or exported from the national customs territory. Goods in FTZs should be subject to flexible customs control so as not to unduly restrict or delay the movement of goods. Goods entering FTZs should also enjoy exclusive tax and customs benefits.[40] Not only imported but also domestic goods must be authorized to be admitted to the zone. Any restriction of admission of imported goods should be based only on public morality, national security or health reasons or for the sake of protection of intellectual property rights: not a disguised restriction on international trade, incorporating concepts familiar to WTO law.[41] The Kyoto Convention additionally contains rules on transparency, requiring that party states' national legislation must clarify how customs procedures for the admission and processing of goods in FTZs will be handled, including time frames.

As of 2015, more than 100 of the WTO's 161 members operate FTZs. Consequently, a consideration of the extent to which FTZs are compatible with WTO law is apposite. New Members of the WTO have tended in their accession protocols to recognize explicitly that FTZs are an integral part of their territories and subject to the full range of their WTO commitments.[42] In this regard, it should be noted that Article II:2 of the WTO Agreement states that annexed multilateral trade agreements and legal instruments are "binding on all Members". Accordingly, WTO rules apply, in principle, to the whole territory of member countries, including any FTZs, unless otherwise specified. Additionally, Article XVI:4 of the WTO Agreement further requires each member to "ensure the conformity of its laws, regulations and administrative procedures with its obligations as provided in the annexed Agreements". As such, FTZs must comply with non-discrimination rules (both national treatment and most favoured nation) found in the GATT and GATS, as well as rules on subsidies and trade-related investment measures and intellectual property, as discussed

---

39 Done at Kyoto, Japan on 18 May 1973 and revised on 26 June 1999.

40 Convention Ch 2.

41 ibid.

42 See e.g. Accession of the People's Republic of China WT/L/432 (23 November 2001) Art. V.

earlier in this book. In addition to ensuring that FTZs conform to its substantive rules, each WTO member has an obligation to publish and notify its trade measures so that they can be readily accessed by other members.[43]

It is possible that, as a kind of trade-oriented FDI incentive, a FTZ could transgress one or more of a WTO Member's substantive WTO obligations because the legal regime inside and outside the zone is different. It is important to recognize that some of the benefits of FTZs are available only to the foreign firms and not the equivalent local ones; indeed, this is part of what makes them function as tools to increase FDI. FTZ incentives must equally be available to all firms in the zone that meet the eligibility criteria under WTO law. If access to the benefits associated with a FTZ were offered only to investors from certain countries, or only to locally incorporated investors, then WTO rules on non-discrimination could be engaged. An origin-specific exemption or reduction of duties or indirect taxes would violate Article I and III:2 of the GATT, just as discriminatory taxes based on the nationality of the enterprise could be challenged under GATT Article III:4, or GATS Articles II and XVII (if such a commitment is made with respect to service suppliers). Furthermore, there may be an illegality associated with the lack of FTZ benefits in other parts of the host state which may be more desirable as a location of operations to foreign firms. Clearly WTO rules are intended to apply uniformly throughout each member's geographical territory, including their FTZ, with domestic remedies available in situations of non-uniform application.

It may further be possible that FTZ-oriented investment incentives could be viewed as illegal subsidies under the SCM. While the concept of "general infrastructure" as a benefit was not defined in the SCM, it can be understood to include railways, roads, ports as well as telecommunications. Most FTZs are located near airports, ports, or major roads so that goods that are manufactured in these zones can be readily transported. As access to these types of facilities is usually not limited to those firms that are using the FTZ, the provision of infrastructure of this nature is unlikely to constitute a subsidy under the SCM because of the specificity requirement. However, the provision of FTZ firms with electricity, water and other public utilities at below market rates would likely not fall within the meaning of "general infrastructure" and as such they may well

[43] Ministerial Decision on Notification Procedures annexed to the Final Act Embodying the Results of the Uruguay Round of Multilateral Trade Negotiations (Marrakesh, 15 April 1994).

be considered a subsidy. Moreover, any governmental loans or other financial incentives offered in conjunction with a FTZ provided on non-commercial conditions would confer a benefit and would therefore also likely be viewed as subsidies. This would likely include customs or tax benefits granted to capital goods offered in conjunction with free zones.[44]

Most FTZ incentives would likely be deemed to be of regional specificity under the SCM. Article 2.2 of the SCM states that a subsidy limited to certain enterprises within a designated geographical region under the jurisdiction of the granting authority is specific. So preferences for FTZ enterprises would be viewed as regionally specific if they are generally available within the territorial jurisdiction of the granting authority. In other words, if the government limits certain incentives to FTZs only while not extending these privileges to outside firms under their respective jurisdictions, the incentives will have regional specificity under the SCM. But if the FTZ is the only geographical area for which the granting authority has responsibility (for example, the local authority is in charge of the whole city which is itself a FTZ) then this arrangement would likely be deemed non-specific. Furthermore, in countries where FTZ treatment is granted to companies regardless of where they are located, then the regional specificity test would not be applicable. If a single firm or group of firms within the same industry (such as automobiles or textiles) are themselves designated as a FTZ, then this would satisfy the industry-specificity requirement under the SCM.[45] It must be recognized that some countries have taken the position that the special treatment applicable to FTZs is not a subsidy specifically provided to an enterprise or industry or group of enterprises or industries, and is therefore not controlled by Article 25 of the SCM.[46]

In some FTZs, especially export-processing zones, the government may provide tax relief or duty exemptions/reductions on condition that the beneficiary firm exports its goods or uses some domestic materials in the production, effectively investment incentives being offered in conjunction with a TRIMs-illegal performance requirement. Since host states create FTZs mainly with a view to attracting investment and not to restrict it, they tend not to impose restrictive TRIMs. Still, it is believed

---

44 S. Shadikhodjaev, 'International Regulation of Free Zones: An Analysis of Multilateral Customs and Trade Rules' (2011) 10:2 *World Trade Review* 189, 204–5.

45 ibid.

46 Trade Policy Review, Report by the Secretariat, Republic of Korea, Revision WT/TPR/S/204/Rev.1 (4 December 2008).

that a number of countries impose local content-oriented TRIMs in conjunction with their FTZs but choose not to notify these to the WTO.[47] The special and differential treatment provisions of the TRIMs have not been widely used in relation to free zones. Few member countries notified their inconsistent FTZ trade-related performance requirements to which transition periods applied. This could suggest that WTO members have been reluctant to use prohibited trade-related performance requirements in free zones or else they were unwilling to notify them to the WTO. WTO members actively use the WTO Trade Policy Review Mechanism as well as the Council for Trade in Goods and the SCM Committee in order to monitor FTZs. Additionally FTZ of countries seeking to accede to the WTO are thoroughly reviewed by the existing members as part of the accession negotiations. Newly acceded countries have typically guaranteed that their trade-related performance requirements, including those linked to FTZs would conform to WTO rules by the date of their accession.[48]

Despite the large number of FTZs in existence around the world, there has not yet been one dispute in which one has been formally challenged through the WTO Dispute settlement system for any of the potential transgressions discussed above. This may be explained by the fact that virtually all WTO Members operate FTZs and no one wants to risk having their own investment incentives challenged. Indeed, most WTO members appear to be willing to "turn a blind eye" to the discriminatory nature of such arrangements.[49] Additionally, it should be noted that some FTZs actually offer very little in the way of meaningful benefits as distinct from those which are available elsewhere in the country and as such may be accurately characterized as publicity stunts.[50] Accordingly they are likely low on the priority list of most member states' WTO trade representatives.

The *Colombia – Ports of Entry* dispute[51] sheds some light on how an FTZ may be accommodated within WTO law. This dispute concerned three types of Colombian customs measures which affected textiles, apparel, and footwear originating from Panama and from Panama's FTZ, the Colon Free Zone (CFZ). The first measure that the panel examined

---

[47] Shadikhodjaev (n 44) 207.

[48] P. Williams, *A Handbook on Accession to the WTO* (CUP, Cambridge 2008) 97–8.

[49] Shadikhodjaev (n 44) 199–200.

[50] E.g. China's Shanghai FTZ: Anderlini (n 38).

[51] Panel Report, *Colombia – Indicative Prices and Restrictions on Points of Entry* WT/DS366/R (27 April 2009).

was the Colombian customs authorities' indicative pricing system in which the values of subject goods shown in import declarations were priced relative to the product-specific reference prices, or indicative prices. If the former was lower than the latter, the customs authorities permitted the goods to be released on condition that the importer corrected the declared value on the basis of the indicative price and paid duties and taxes accordingly. The second measure concerned Columbia's policy to allow entry of textiles, apparel and footwear, from both Panama and the CFZ, through only two ports of an available 26. Under the third measure at issue, the products arriving from Panama and the CFZ were subject to stricter requirements of advance import declaration and advance payment of customs duties and taxes than like products from other countries. With respect to the indicative prices, the panel found that the Colombian measure mandated the use of "minimum prices" as the customs value of subject goods which was not permitted under the WTO Customs Valuation Agreement.[52] As for the ports of entry restriction, the panel ruled that the limited access to the Colombian ports constituted a prohibited restriction on imports in violation of Article XI:1 of the GATT. In particular, the panel found that measures subject to elimination under Article XI were not confined only to quantitative measures, meaning restrictions placed on the quantity or value of imports or exports, but had to be construed broadly to include other types of trade-restrictive measures, such as access to ports of entry. Finally, with respect to the advance measures, the panel held that, by subjecting goods from Panama and the CFZ to the discriminatory requirements of advance declaration and payment, Colombia conferred advantages to like products from other countries that were not extended to the Panamanian textile, apparel, and footwear imports. This was a clear violation of GATT Article I:1. The panel went on to consider Colombia's invocation of GATT Article XX(d) – exception for securing compliance with domestic law as a justification for its ports of entry restriction. Colombia had argued that this measure was necessary to counteract fraudulent practices such as under-invoicing, smuggling and other criminal activities, such as money laundering and drug trafficking. The panel recognized that combating illicit activities at issue was legitimately important to Colombia but that Colombia failed to show that the ports of entry measure had contributed to its goals as the least trade-restrictive measure available. Colombia had not established that the measure at issue was necessary to ensure compliance with Colombian customs laws and regulations.

---

[52] Art. 7(f).

The *Colombia – Ports of Entry* case demonstrates most obviously that any restrictions that WTO members impose on goods from other members' FTZs will be subject to WTO rules, just as goods from normal customs zones. For countries that export from FTZs, the panel's ruling clarifies that benefits available under the WTO agreements are as applicable to their FTZ as to the rest of their territories, irrespective of whether national laws consider them to be inside or outside of the customs territory.

4. REGIONAL CONTROL OF INVESTMENT INCENTIVES

Many developed countries maintain rules on the use of primarily trade-focused subsidies as investment incentives, including most notably the European Union. Australia and Canada also have regimes aimed at reducing incentive competition among their regional governments. None of these regimes should be seen as truly international in as much as they are aimed at controlling the use of incentives offered to firms from within the jurisdiction, rather than as instruments regulating measures used for the encouragement of FDI. Still, the approach taken by these regimes illustrates some of the key regulatory challenges that arise in conjunction with governmental assistance to foreign firms in their capacity as traders.

(i) The EU Multisectoral Framework on State Aid

The most comprehensive regime for the control of subsidization for investment (including by extension FDI) is embodied in EU regional aid policy, which sets a maximum level of subsidy for every region in the EU. Established in 1997, the European rules on subsidies, which it refers to as state aid, are outlined in Articles 107 through 109 of the Treaty on the Functioning of the European Union (TFEU). The type of measures regulated by the EU's state-aid regime are specified in Article 107(1):

(1) aid, in any form whatsoever, which confers an advantage or benefit for the recipient;
(2) granted by a Member State or through State resources;
(3) that distorts or threatens to distort competition by favouring certain undertakings or the production of certain goods; and
(4) affects trade between Member States.

All four of these elements must be satisfied in order for government assistance to count as state aid. This understanding of governmental assistance demonstrates the trade focus of the EU multi-sectoral rules: they are aimed at preventing obstructions to the flow of traded goods within the European common market. They do not deal expressly with investment, either domestic or foreign. Clearly though, benefits conferred on private firms that enhance their competitive advantage as traders may influence their decisions on where to locate their operations.

Since these provisions offer limited guidance on their application, the communications, guidelines and decisions by the European Commission, as well as judgments of the Court of Justice of the European Union (CJEU) are essential to understanding the practical effect of the rules. There is now a well-established body of official material governing the use of state aid which clarifies in large part the circumstances under which it will be permitted. Decisions of the CJEU have held in order for aid to fall within these rules it must involve a direct or indirect transfer of state resources, or a charge on the public account.[53] This means that price and income supports not funded by the government would not constitute state aid, nor would any assistance initiated by the government directing a private body to make a payment or forgo income that was otherwise due – a narrower concept than that envisioned by the SCM. However, the European Court of First Instance explained that state aid is a broader concept than is understood by subsidies under the WTO regime. It covers not just subsidies and direct assistance, but also indirect forms of aid such as fiscal and social measures, which may be equally damaging to the competitiveness of markets.[54] Unlike the WTO subsidies rules, there is no serious injury test in the EU state aid regime. The CJEU cases suggest that a threat to competition is generally presumed if the aid package confers a material advantage on the firms that receive it, subject to a *de minimis* test.[55]

As under the WTO SCM, the assessment of the granting of a benefit of advantage under the EU regime contemplates the application of a market test. This means a court will examine whether the same advantage would have been available under normal market conditions. The types of advantages contemplated by the rules can include many types of measure, including through government ownership of a company's capital, the

---

[53] Case C–303/88 *Italy v Commission* [1991] ECR I-1433.

[54] Case T–55/99 *CETM v Commission* [2000] ECR II-3207 [50]: "the reference to the concept of subsidy within the meaning of the WTO Agreement on Subsidies and Countervailing Measures has no relevance whatsoever to the classification of the measure in question as state aid within the meaning of Community law."

[55] Sykes (n 16).

granting of loans or guarantees, tax relief, exemptions from social welfare charges, provision of goods or services, and payment for goods and services. The advantage must favour certain undertakings or the production of certain goods or services. An undertaking is any entity (this includes legal persons, such as a company, and individuals acting as sole traders) which is engaged in an economic activity.[56] An economic activity is any activity consisting of offering goods and services on a given market. When an entity carries out an activity for which it is capable of being remunerated and competing against other organisations within a market, it will be an undertaking for the purposes of state aid. The undertakings test tends to be applied quite narrowly by the EU Commission. Given the above definition, subsidies which are granted to individuals, or general measures open to all firms are not prohibited and do not constitute state aid. Still, a measure that is open to all sectors may be selective and therefore constitute state aid if there is an element of discretion by the awarding authorities, and if the scheme applies to only part of the territory of a member State.

Granting certain forms of state aid, including investment incentives, is incompatible with the EU's common market because it distorts competition. The firms which receive governmental assistance have an unfair advantage over competing firms which do not.[57] While state aid is generally considered to violate the principles of the common market, it can be permitted if it is aimed at one of several Community objectives or corrects certain identified market failures. In this regard, Article 107(2) of the TFEU lists three categories of state aid that are always allowed in order to achieve certain policy goals of the Community. Among the most important of these are: aid with a "social character" granted directly to individual consumers, provided that it is granted without discrimination relating to the origin of relevant products (for example, tax deductions for low-income or disabled persons, or tax benefits for purchase of environmentally sustainable products); and aid to repair damage caused by natural disasters or other exceptional occurrences.

Article 107(3) proceeds to mention other objectives that may, in certain cases, also justify the use of state aid. Under this provision, the Commission has discretion regarding whether to authorize state aid aimed at addressing any one of these policy goals. This includes: furthering economic development of areas where the standard of living is abnormally low or where there is serious underemployment as compared

---

56 *Italy v Commission* (n 53).

57 Treaty Establishing the European Community (25 March 1957) Art. 87(1).

to EU averages; promoting important projects of common European interest (for example, construction of a power plant to provide energy to other EU members, construction of infrastructure that helps link Member states); remedying a serious upheaval in the economy of a member state that affects the state as a whole; facilitating the development of certain economic activities or certain economic areas (regions that are economically disadvantaged relative to the state in which they are located), provided that such aid does not adversely affect trading conditions to an extent contrary to the common market; promoting conservation of culture and heritage; and achieving other goals specified by decision of the Council acting on a proposal by the Commission.

The Commission has issued guidelines outlining the criteria that must be satisfied in order for aid under Article 107(3) to be permitted. These guidelines, issued in 2013, cover the period from 2014 to 2020.[58] The criteria consist of: a contribution to a well-defined objective of common interest; need for state intervention, meaning a situation where aid can bring about a material improvement that the market cannot deliver itself; appropriateness of the aid measure, meaning that the proposed aid measure must be an appropriate policy instrument to address the objective of common interest; incentive effect, meaning that the aid must change the behaviour of the undertaking(s) concerned in such a way that it engages in additional activity which it would not carry out without the aid or it would carry out in a restricted or different manner or location; proportionality of the aid, meaning the amount of aid must be limited to the minimum needed to induce the additional investment or activity in the area concerned; avoidance of undue negative effects on competition and trade between Member States, meaning the negative effects of aid must be sufficiently limited, so that the overall balance of the measure is positive; and lastly, transparency of aid, meaning that EU member states, the Commission, economic operators, and the public, must have easy access to all relevant acts and to pertinent information about the aid that has been awarded.

The Commission and the ECJ have developed more specific guidance regarding the scope and nature of support that may be allowed for each category of potentially permissible state aid. In order to ascertain whether a regional package will be authorized, the Commission applies detailed rules that specify acceptable levels of aid intensity. Aid intensity, a concept that is not found in WTO subsidies rules, is a measurement that

---

[58] European Commission, Guidelines on Regional State Aid for 2014–20 [2013] OJ C209/01 (23 July 2013).

encompasses the amount of the aid relative to the size of the project to which it is applied. EU rules require calculation of aid intensity in terms of gross grant equivalents, which means the value of the aid expressed as a percentage of the value of specified eligible investment costs, including discount rates. Under EU rules, the permissible level of aid intensity is dependent upon the economic conditions in the jurisdiction granting incentive. More economically disadvantaged states as well as sub-national regions are permitted to offer incentives with higher aid intensity than the less disadvantaged states, the logic being that the more prosperous states should not need incentives as much. If an incentive is aimed at supporting SMEs for example, the permissible aid intensity will rise, the rationale being that such firms are more needful of non-market assistance than larger ones. If the incentive is used to assist a large investment project, the permissible aid intensity decreases accordingly. The concept of intensity, while numerically quantifiable, facilitates a degree of discretion among authorizing authorities that is somewhat more nuanced that the SCM's more rigid traffic-light approach.

Regional aid is generally only permitted to support establishment of a new enterprise or the expansion, diversification or upgrading of an existing one. The granting of regional aid is permitted to promote the economic development of disadvantaged regions within the EU. The amount of aid that is allowed under EU rules depends on the degree to which the region is disadvantaged relative to other areas of the EU, or in the case of sub-national grants, relative to the national average.[59] It is uncommon for regional aid to be permitted if it is designed to cover operating expenses of an existing investment. Application of these rules has led to the removal of a number of investment incentives programmes.[60] EU state-aid rules distinguish between investment aid that is awarded for investment relating to the setting up of a new establishment, and operational aid, which contemplates assistance in the extension of an existing establishment, diversification of the output of an establishment into new, additional products, or a fundamental change in the overall production process of an existing establishment. Since operating aid is not considered to assist in the development of new investment, job creation, or general development, it is very rarely allowed. The distinction between establishment and operational aid thus does not capture the

---

[59] Report from the Commission: State Aid Scorecard: Report on State Aid Granted by the EU Member States, Autumn 2012 Update COM(2012) 778 final (21 December 2012).

[60] K.P. Thomas, *Investment Incentives and the Global Competition for Capital* (Palgrave Macmillan, London 2011) 7–8.

difference between distortive or non-distortive assistance (as both can lead to market distortions) but rather addresses the availability of beneficial spillovers associated with one form of aid and not with another.

Member states must notify the European Commission and seek prior approval of a new state aid package that they intend to offer or amendments to existing state aid. The notification must consist of information relating to the relevant government authority that grants the subsidy, the intended beneficiaries, and their location and economic sectors of activity. The government must also indicate the nature and the source of the aid, as well as its policy objectives. There are some exceptions to the notification requirements, such as where the state aid is covered by a block exemption, such as those that have been set aside for SMEs and which support research and development and environmental protection.[61] The Council adopted new rules for block exemptions for social purposes including culture, natural disasters as well as internet connectivity.[62] There are also notification and approval exemptions for *de minimis* state aid, which is defined as aid to a single recipient that does not exceed the value of €200 000 over a three-year fiscal term. The Commission is currently reviewing the *de minimis* block exemption regulation.[63]

In addition to the notification rules concerning new aid packages and amendments to existing aid, member states must provide annual reports to the Commission on existing aid schemes. Subsidies must be notified in advance to the Commission with the Commission having wide discretion to approve, prohibit or modify a proposed subsidy. The Commission is further empowered to monitor compliance of the state aid rules. It can conduct on-site surveillance relating to existing aid programs as well as evaluate whether existing package schemes maintain ongoing compliance

---

[61] Commission Regulation EC No 800/2008 of 6 August 2008 declaring certain categories of aid compatible with the common market in application of Articles 87 and 88 of the Treaty (General block exemption Regulation) [2008] OJ L 214/3.

[62] Council Regulation EU No. 733/2013 of 22 July 2013 amending Regulation (EC) No. 994/98 on the application of Articles 92 and 93 of the Treaty Establishing the European Community to certain categories of horizontal State aid [2013] OJ L 204/11.

[63] Vale Columbia Center, 'Background Paper for the Eighth Columbia International Investment Conference on Investment Incentives: The Good, the Bad and the Ugly' (Columbia University, Draft 8 November 2013) <http://ccsi.columbia.edu/files/2014/01/VCC_conference_paper_-_Draft_Nov_12.pdf> accessed 2 December 2014.

with relevant rules. In situations where a member state has either failed to notified the Commission of the existence of a state-aid package and that aid is later determined to be incompatible with the common market, or the member has fulfilled its notification commitments and obtained approval but it has implemented the aid in a manner contrary to the terms of that approval, the Commission may order the member to terminate the aid package. It may also take all steps necessary to recover the aid that was already granted.

The use of state aid appears to be declining in the EU, most likely as a consequence of the implementation and enforcement of disciplines on state aid. There has been a significant decline in the usage of state aid across the EU, dropping from an average of approximately 2 per cent of GDP in the 1980s to less than 0.5 per cent of GDP by the 2010s. The EU regime for controlling FDI-incentives is generally believed to have saved a number of countries from the damaging "prisoner's dilemma"-type bidding wars associated with incentives and mentioned in Chapter 1.[64] Recent high-profile examples of the impact of the EU's rules include Ireland's eventual cancellation of its tax incentive program for foreign investors, widely viewed as causing harmful tax competition. This incentive regime had allowed Ireland to attract large US technology companies, fuelling the country's economic boom in the early 2000s.[65] Similarly, under pressure from Germany the UK abandoned its "patent box" scheme which encouraged high-tech businesses to commercialise their intellectual property in the UK by charging just 10 per cent tax on the resulting income, even where there was little economic activity in the jurisdiction.[66] Under the EU state aid framework, EU countries tend to grant much smaller subsidies for example than US state governments for similar investments.[67] Perhaps most encouragingly, studies have shown that the EU's robust regime for the control of investment incentives relative to those of other regions has not hindered the EU's capacity to

---

64 J. Witkowska, 'Foreign Direct Investment in the Changing Business Environment of the European Union's New Member States' (2007) 7:4 *Global Economy Journal* 1, 4–5, noting also that some new states had difficulty adapting their existing incentive packages to conform to EU rules. The intellectual value of the prisoner's dilemma model to investment incentives has been criticized by other commentators because of its excessive malleability: Petrov (n 4).

65 V. Boland, 'Dublin to Shut Double Irish Corporate Tax Loophole Next Year' *Financial Times* (London, 14 October 2014).

66 V. Houlder, 'UK and Germany Reach Compromise Over Patent Box Tax Break' *Financial Times* (London, 12 November 2014).

67 K. Thomas, 'Investment Incentives and the Global Competition for Capital' Columbia FDI Perspective no 54 30 December 2011.

attract FDI. Indeed the EU has actually seen a relative growth in FDI since the rules on state aid were implemented. This can be explained by the fact that locational bidding wars to attract foreign firms focus on regional differences rather than global ones – meaning that firms tend not to be persuaded to locate to a different continent if they have already settled on one, whereas they might be quite willing to locate to a different region within that continent.[68] The observed relaxation in the enforcement of Europe's state aid rules in recent years, partially due to the global financial crisis of 2008–09, has been condemned by some commentators, along with the recommendation that greater emphasis should be placed on the economic scrutiny of measures for their distortive effects on competition. Under this theory, only aid which is clearly non-distortive should be allowed.[69] As will be explored further in the next chapter, the revocation of incentive packages may lead to claims by foreign investors based on breaches of IIAs.

(ii) Other Regional Initiatives on Incentive Control

The terminology regional is used here to describe legal regimes that are more accurately characterized as federal rather than international, meaning that there are several sub-central regions within a single country which are subject collectively to a second layer of national jurisdiction. In the context of investment incentives, the aim of the federal rules is to prevent wasteful competition between sub-central governments for investment. In other words, such rules prevent firms from extracting costlier incentive packages by playing regional governments against each other, the so-called "prisoner's dilemma". It has been suggested that it may be more difficult to impose rules on investment incentives in countries with a federal structure because of the importance of sub-central government policy in the extension of incentives to foreign investors, often on a highly competitive basis. The development of disciplines at the federal level is often seen as a vital starting point for this type of regime.[70] Like the EU rules, these regimes have a trade

---

[68] K. Thomas, 'EU Control of State Aid to Mobile Investment in Comparative Perspective' (2012) 34:6 *European Journal of Integration* 567, 578–9.

[69] A. Heimler and F. Jenny, 'The Limitations of European Control of State Aid' (2012) 28:2 *Oxford Review of Economic Policy* 347.

[70] S. Amarasinha and J. Kokott, 'Multilateral Investment Rules Revisited' in P. Muchlinksi, F. Ortino and C. Schreuer (eds), *The Oxford Handbook of International Investment Law* (OUP, Oxford 2008) 145.

focus: they contemplate the control of incentives which are aimed at improving a firm's trading performance.

Australia's now defunct Interstate Investment Cooperation Agreement (IICA) aimed to control competitive bidding for investments between Australia's states for foreign investments that appear definitely to intend to enter the country, and to prevent the situation where one Australian state is attempting to wrest investment from another Australian state through incentives – seen as being counterproductive to the country's economy as a whole. Unfortunately the IICA was voluntary and not all states signed it, significantly impairing the agreement's utility, as investors could simply target one of the states that was not bound by it. One of the key features of the IICA were provisions on transparency and information sharing – the idea being that the states should cooperate with one another to determine which one can achieve the greatest efficiencies when offering an incentive package to a foreign investor.[71]

Canada instigated its Code of Conduct on Incentives as an annex to its 1994 Agreement on Internal Trade (AIT) governing trade and investment between Canada's provinces. The Code, which is still in effect, prohibits incentives that are contingent on a company that is already located in one Canadian province to re-locate to another province.[72] Less effectively, other provisions require provincial governments to take into account the economic interests of other provinces when offering incentives to attract firms and endeavour to provide incentives that are harmful in that regard.[73] It also includes a provision on information sharing and consultations between provinces.[74] Commentators have criticized Canada's Code of Conduct because of the non-binding nature of its central commitment, as well as the complicated nature of dispute resolution under the AIT, which led to several disputes being abandoned because of systemic delays.[75] The AIT contained a provision which prohibited investment incentives in conjunction with trade-oriented performance requirements:

> 1. No Party shall impose or enforce, in relation to an investor of a Party or an enterprise in its territory, or condition the receipt of an incentive by an enterprise on compliance with, any requirement to:

---

[71] M. Novak, 'Dropping the Lure' (Institute for Public Affairs, Australia, 11 February 2011) <http://ipa.org.au/news/2286/dropping-the-lure-> accessed March 2015.

[72] Code of Conduct on Incentives, Art. 4 (September 1994).

[73] ibid. Art. 8.

[74] ibid. Arts 10–13.

[75] Thomas (n 68).

> (a) achieve a specific level or percentage of local content of goods or services;
> (b) purchase or use goods or services produced locally;
> (c) purchase goods or services from a local source; or
> (d) achieve a certain level of sales in the territory of another Party.
>
> 2. For greater certainty, nothing in paragraph 1 shall be construed to prevent a Party from conditioning the receipt of an incentive on any requirement to carry out economic activities in its territory or to create or maintain employment.

Importantly, however, the AIT allowed incentives which served a developmental purpose:

> 3. A Party may, under exceptional circumstances, adopt or maintain a measure inconsistent with paragraph 1 for regional economic development purposes, provided that:
> (a) the measure does not operate to impair unduly the access of persons, goods, services or investors of another Party;
> (b) the measure is not more trade restrictive than necessary to achieve its specific objective; and
> (c) the Party promptly notifies the other Parties of the details of the measure.[76]

Such conditions appear to contemplate incentives which do not cause market distortions. The AIT also prohibits the discriminatory granting of incentives to investors on the basis of their location of origin (ownership or control or location of head office).[77]

Finally, as the largest economy in the world (depending on how China's GDP is measured) and as a country with 50 sub-central governments under a federal umbrella, the US is remarkable for lacking an investment incentive framework. This omission is thought to have created a problematically unregulated environment in which bidding wars abound just as the amount of inward FDI has not increased.[78] Such an initiative had been pursued at one point through a non-binding state governor's resolution among several states, but it never matured into a formal agreement as a consequence of lobbying by private firms against it.[79] The

---

[76] ibid. Art. 607.

[77] AIT Art. 608.1.

[78] Thomas (n 68).

[79] M. Schaefer, 'State Investment Attraction Subsidy Wars Resulting from a Prisoner's Dilemma' in C.D. Ehlermann and M. Everson (eds), *European Competition Law Annual 1999: Selected Issue in the Field of State Aid* (Hart Publishing, Oxford 2001) 625.

regulation of state aid is considered by some to be an essential component of effective competition law, and the absence of such a regime in the US has been the source of much criticism by commentators.[80] Incentive packages in the US have been described as "out of control" with billions of dollars spent every year, especially in relation to manufacturing firms.[81]

5. CONCLUSION

Heightened competition for FDI that has come with globalization has increased pressure on governments to offer assistance to those investors who have the capacity to move between jurisdictions and as such can be more selective in their target locations. Much more prevalent than performance requirements, investment incentives which help foreign investors in their capacity as traders are largely unregulated under international law. The WTO SCM and the European multilateral framework on state aid were initially designed to address the impact of governmental assistance on cross-border trade, not to address the use of incentives as a means of attracting inward or supporting outward FDI. For their part, WTO rules on subsidies focus on a narrow range of export-oriented incentives offered to local firms and can be easily bypassed through specificity rules. There are no rules on services subsidies at all. This has led commentators to suggesting that improved regulation of the trade-oriented aspect of investment incentives is needed.[82] As an attractive alternative mode for regulating trade-oriented subsidies, the EU's state aid rules appear to have helped the EU to cope with competitive pressures among FDI-eager jurisdictions without lowering the overall level of inward FDI to the region. It is a testimony to the effectiveness of the rules that the EU has actually seen its inward flows of FDI increase since the incentive controls were introduced.[83] The EU regime is remarkably comprehensive and flexible, facilitating case by case ex ante scrutiny by a centralized agency based on a range of factors which contemplate social as well as economic benefits. Still, at a general level there remains much uncertainty associated with evaluating the

---

80 E.g. A. Collins, 'Is The Regulation of State-Aid a Necessary Component of an Effective Competition Law Framework?' (2005) 16 *European Business Law Review* 379.

81 Thomas (n 68) 568.

82 Subrahmanyam (n 5) 301.

83 Thomas (n 68).

legality of subsidies or state aid for FDI through the lens of economic or non-economic activity, the latter of which tends to be permissible under both WTO and EU rules. Authorization of incentives based upon a distinction between private and public goods or distortive and non-distortive effects (in other words financial assistance that is ultimately in the broader interest of society) is fraught with difficulties because of the inherent ambiguity of these concepts.[84] Until such indicia can be more objectively quantified, both the SCM and the EU regime on state aid remain imperfect instruments to regulate the trade-distorting aspect of FDI incentives.

---

84 E.g. Rubini (n 7) 318–19.

6. Investment incentives and international investment law

This chapter will explore the extent to which policies that have been implemented by host and home states to attract and export FDI have been regulated by bilateral investment treaties and FTAs with investment chapters, collectively referred to as international investment agreements (IIA)s. It will then consider how the revocation of such investment incentives by host states may be actionable under IIA dispute settlement provisions through protections such as fair and equitable treatment (FET) and the guarantee of compensation in the event of expropriation. This chapter will conclude by considering guidelines issued by international organizations, mostly advocating against the use of investment incentives, including those of the OECD, the IMF and the World Bank. Before beginning, it must be clarified that this chapter will not consider double taxation treaties, concentrating instead on traditional international vestment instruments. While some forms of tax concessions may operate as investment incentives and tend to be set out in domestic legislation governing foreign investment,[1] the availability of these schemes is usually controlled by tax-specific treaties, which are beyond the scope of this book. Many IIAs expressly confirm that they in no way affect tax obligations or preferences granted between signatory parties or to any third parties.[2] Furthermore, it must be recalled that the actual effectiveness of IIAs on FDI flows remains a matter of much debate.[3] This fallacy is mirrored by the economic studies, discussed in Chapter 1, which question the utility of conventional investment incentives as FDI attractors.

[1] E.g. Foreign Investment Law of Mongolia Art. 20 (came into force 1 July 1993).

[2] Art. 18 Japan–Myanmar (30 April 2013).

[3] See e.g. J. Salacuse and N. Sullivan, 'Do BITs Really Work?: An Evaluation of Bilateral Investment Treaties and their Grand Bargain' in K. Sauvant and L. Sachs (eds), *The Effect of Treaties on Foreign Direct Investment* (OUP, Oxford 2009).

1. THE CONTROL OF INVESTMENT INCENTIVES THROUGH INTERNATIONAL INVESTMENT AGREEMENTS (IIAs)

(i) General Provisions

Given that IIAs support the international mobility of capital, as this capital is scarce relative to the domestic markets which can absorb it, IIAs also contribute to the intensification of competition among states to attract mobile capital through incentive regimes. States may therefore be pressured into entering IIAs so as not to risk losing out on FDI to their neighbours. With this situation in mind, the mere existence of IIAs between an investor's home state and a host state may itself be viewed as a form of investment incentive, much like tax relief or the provision of subsidized services in that these treaties grant foreign investors highly attractive types of legal protection that may not exist under domestic law.

As a consequence of their role in encouraging investors to locate in high-risk countries by reducing the probability of harmful political intervention with their commercial activities, IIAs are sometimes referred to as investment incentive agreements. Indeed, this function is reflected in the language used by many IIAs. For example, the ASEAN Comprehensive Agreement on Investment states that its purpose is to provide "enhanced protection for investors" and to "create favourable conditions for investment by investors".[4] Since they offer a wide range of protections to foreign investors that are unavailable under domestic law and in so doing reduce some of the political risks associated with FDI, IIAs are believed to have increased FDI flows beyond a level which would have taken place in their absence. FDI increases commensurate with IIA signage are thought to be particularly evident with respect to high-risk developing states.[5]

IIAs tend to grant protections only to investments that are already located within a state's territory. This is seen most obviously in the post-establishment guarantee of national treatment. Some IIAs, however, such as those of the US and Canada, offer foreign investors pre-establishment rights, allowing them to enter host states under the same conditions as local firms, which subject to conformity with the host states laws. One established, IIAs extend various protections, such as FET, as well as the guarantee of compensation in the event of expropriation and

---

4 Art. I(b), (e).

5 Salacuse and Sullivan (n 3).

the right to repatriate their profits back to the home state. In order to avail themselves of the guarantees contained in IIAs, the activities of foreign firms must meet the relevant treaty's definition of investment. Broad definitions, such as those encompassing "any type of asset", have allowed a wide range of international commercial activity to satisfy this definition, often where there are limited genuine links to the host state.[6] Such an all-encompassing understanding of investment can result in a situation where foreign firms are able to enjoy the benefits of IIAs just as host states suffer the potential liabilities associated without significant tangible gains like as long-term employment, technological advancement and a reliable tax base.

One of the chief protections contained in IIAs is the promise to treat established investors the same as local ones, normally meaning no adverse nationality-based treatment against foreign firms which undermines their competitiveness, as noted in Chapter 2. The national treatment obligation found in IIAs tends to guarantee treatment to foreign investors that is "no less favourable" than that provided to nationals, potentially allowing foreign firms to receive more favourable treatment than the equivalent local one. Such protection could be particularly conducive to FDI in situations where host states suffer from chronic regulatory and political instability and which lack institutions such as the rule of law – in other words, treatment imposed upon citizens that falls below the international minimum standards. While the interpretation of the phrase "no less favourable" to include better-than-national treatment has been supported by UNCTAD[7], there have been no investment arbitration decisions which have confirmed this interpretation. It is doubtful whether it would validate incentives favourable to foreign firms where domestic firms enjoyed treatment that was in conformity with international minimum standards. Its effect on legitimizing investment incentives which might otherwise be prohibited under a treaty (see further below) is therefore uncertain.

To the extent that in some respects IIAs do offer "better-than-national treatment", meaning that foreign firms enjoy preferable regulatory treatment than local ones, the global IIA regime has been the target of led to accusations of one-sidedness in favour of foreign investors and for its undue encroachment on state sovereignty over economic governance.

---

[6] R. Dolzer and S. Schreuer, *Principles of International Investment Law* (OUP, Oxford 2012) 62–5.

[7] National Treatment, UNCTAD Series on International Investment Agreements (New York and Geneva, 1999) 37.

These criticisms are particularly associated with capital importing developing states which have had limited control over the contents of IIAs as a consequence of international pressures.[8] The unequal treatment granted by states in favour of foreign firms is further thought to have the potential to trigger a revival of the Calvo Doctrine as a backlash. Under this doctrine, discussed in Chapter 2, foreign investors are assured treatment that is no better than that of locals, including with respect to the measure of compensation for expropriations, placing investors of all origins on an even footing.[9]

If the national treatment standard in IIAs is understood to offer nothing more than equal treatment between foreign and local investors, then derogations from this standard would be essential to justify favourable treatment granted to foreign firms through incentive packages. A number of developed countries have specifically exempted subsidies and grants from the coverage of the non-discrimination obligations in their IIAs. For example, Canada's bilateral investment treaty (BIT) with Cameroon excludes from the scope of its national treatment obligation "the rights or preferences granted to socially or economically disadvantaged minorities".[10] Modern US IIAs contain similar reservations, facilitating a wide range of subsidies aimed at disadvantaged groups and regions, in some cases explicitly permitting tax benefits.[11] Sector-specific carve-outs for non-discrimination can be found in many IIAs concluded by developed states. In Canada's BIT with Barbados, for example, Canada excludes from the coverage of its national treatment guarantee measures relating to all services sectors.[12] Japan carves out a number of sectors from the scope of its national treatment obligations, including transportation and agriculture.[13] The US has taken this approach in several of its IIAs as well.[14] These states have also excluded measures in force at the time of the treaty's conclusion which might have been inconsistent with the non-discrimination obligations.[15] Of course, these types of limitations on

---

[8] E.g. S. Montt, *State Liability in Investment Treaty Arbitration* (Hart, Oxford 2009).

[9] E.g. M. Sornarajah, *The International Law on Foreign Investment* (CUP, Cambridge 2010).

[10] Annex II (3 March 2014).

[11] E.g. US–Rwanda, Annex II: US (signed 19 February 2008).

[12] Annex (signed 29 May 1996).

[13] E.g. Japan–Cambodia (14 June 2007) Schedule of Japan.

[14] E.g. US–Rwanda, Annex I: US (signed 19 February 2008).

[15] E.g. Canada–Armenia Art. IV(2)(a)I (signed 8 May 1997).

non-discrimination are aimed at assisting local firms rather than attracting foreign ones. Indeed, it is the conventional protectionist form of discrimination based on national origin that they intend to preserve.

In addition to the provisions on equal (or better than equal treatment) one of the most important but less obvious mechanisms through which IIAs could potentially control the use of investment incentives is through provisions on transparency. The need for transparency in the regulation of investment incentives, as with performance requirements, will be considered in more detail in the final chapter. Transparency guarantees in IIAs may mandate that signatory parties must ensure that all levels of government must disclose all relevant laws, including judicial decisions, relating to foreign investment. This can include disclosure of regulations or procedures that are anticipated in the near future or under active consideration by the government. It could also include complete or more complete information relating to available investment incentive schemes or other promotional activities that are available to foreign firms. Obligations on regulatory transparency are included in many modern IIAs yet few are enforceable through the treaty's dispute settlement procedures because they tend to be framed in hortatory or optional language. Since the FET standard found in most IIAs is often thought to embrace the concept of transparency in governmental behaviour, fulfilling the FET obligation could address some of the concerns that investment incentives are often extended in a secretive and discretionary manner.[16]

(ii) Investor–State Dispute Settlement

Incentives offered to foreign firms may be procedural in nature. Access to neutral, confidential international arbitration for the resolution of disputes directly against host states is among the most valuable investment incentives available to investors in IIAs. Investor–state dispute settlement provisions are found in many thousands of IIAs.[17] Investor–state dispute settlement provisions are perhaps the best example of disguised "better than national treatment" in international investment law. Affording foreign investors the opportunity to bring claims directly against the host government through international arbitration in confidential, specialized fora like ICSID, often without the need to exhaust local remedies, are a

---

[16] S. Picciotto, *Regulating Global Corporate Capitalism* (CUP, Cambridge 2011) 163.

[17] Investor–State Dispute Settlement, UNCTAD Series on International Investment Agreements II (United Nations, New York and Geneva, 2014) 18.

procedural advantage available only to foreign firms. Local firms must use local courts, even if they lack independence or expertise.

Some of the difficulties associated with investor–state dispute settlement as an investment incentive become apparent in situations where it is offered in IIAs between two developed states. Clearly, foreign investors would want this type of assurance when engaging in an FDI project in a developing country that lacks a stable legal infrastructure or independent courts. Indeed, this is one of the reasons that investor–state arbitration exists in the first place. It is less clear that such a procedure is needful where the signatory states of an IIA are highly developed, democratic governments with impartial and independent courts. This puzzle is one of the reasons that investor–state dispute-settlement provisions in TTIP under negotiation between the United States and Europe, and the CETA between the EU and Canada have drawn so much criticism.[18] It is far from evident why investor–state dispute settlement, which grants foreign investors the capacity to preclude the very domestic judicial processes which local investors are relegated to use, must be included in such arrangements, other than as an investment incentive. It is fairly obvious that the intentions of parties to these agreements is to give foreign investors access to a preferential (cheaper and confidential) regime for dispute settlement in order to stimulate FDI.

One of the chief problems associated with extending the incentive of international arbitration to foreign investors is that the availability of this procedure is believed to erode the development of more sophisticated and fairer domestic judicial systems within the host states of countries that badly need it – extra-territorial substitute for domestic inadequacies. A plausible example of this scenario can be found in China, where the China International Economic Trade Arbitration Commission (CIETAC) is highly respected and widely used by investors (although in this case both national and foreign) whereas China's domestic courts are still relatively corrupt and low quality.[19] Once the needs of foreign firms bringing lucrative FDI have been met, there may be little motivation on the part of host states to implement vital changes to their domestic legal infrastructure, because domestic firms are not free to use alternatives.

[18] See e.g. 'Statement of Concern about Planned Provisions on Investment Protection and Investor–State Dispute Settlement (ISDS) in the Transatlantic Trade and Investment Partnership (TTIP)' <www.kent.ac.uk/law/isds_treaty_consultation.html> accessed July 2014.

[19] T. Ginsburg, 'International Substitutes for Domestic Institutions: Bilateral Investment Treaties and Governance' (2005) 25:1 *International Review of Law and Economics* 107.

Studies have shown that IIA signage often has a negative effect on domestic institutional quality,[20] quite possibly for this reason.

In order to take advantage of dispute-settlement incentives in IIAs, investors must satisfy any jurisdictional requirements mandated by the relevant tribunal, such as meeting the definition of investment contained in the relevant IIA, including the often problematic need for long-term duration. As arbitration is based on consent, host states may further delimit such procedural advantages as they see fit, confining its availability to certain sectors or types of claim, for example China's early IIAs only allowed investor–state arbitration to determine the amount of compensation owed, not whether an expropriation had occurred.[21] These restrictions may limit the effectiveness of such provisions as genuine incentives aimed at augmenting FDI. Still, the status of access to international arbitration as a subsidy to foreign firms, and such potentially illegal under international economic law, is highly doubtful. It would not fit as such under the WTO SCM because IIAs do not link it to the investor's export output, nor would it satisfy the requirement of specificity because this procedural advantage tends to be granted generally across sectors, not to specific firms.

(iii) Investment Incentive Specific Provisions

IIAs tend to say very little about investment incentives directly. Perhaps the strongest express controls of investment incentives found in these instruments relate to prohibitions on the reduction of regulatory standards for the specific purpose of attracting FDI, although such provisions provide relatively weak enforcement mechanisms. For example, a small number of IIAs contain terms which state that parties should not or must not reduce or fail to enforce environmental or labour regulations in order to attract FDI. These provisions aim to prevent the so-called "race to the bottom" predicament, where foreign firms are drawn to the jurisdictions with the weakest regulations, allowing the firm to cut costs as it either pollutes or mistreats workers without fear of reprisal. Such treaties appear to imply both an absolute reduction in standards as well as a relative one (relative to local investors). In this regard, the 2012 US Model BIT contains a provision that restricts signatory states' capacity to diminish their regulatory standards in order to attract FDI. First, with respect to the environment:

---

20 ibid.

21 E.g. China–Singapore Art. 13(3) (21 November 1985).

> The Parties recognize that it is inappropriate to encourage investment by weakening or reducing the protections afforded in domestic environmental laws. Accordingly, each Party shall ensure that it does not waive or otherwise derogate from or offer to waive or otherwise derogate from its environmental laws in a manner that weakens or reduces the protections afforded in those laws, or fail to effectively enforce those laws through a sustained or recurring course of action or inaction, as an encouragement for the establishment, acquisition, expansion, or retention of an investment in its territory.[22]

And with respect to labour:

> The Parties recognize that it is inappropriate to encourage investment by weakening or reducing the protections afforded in domestic labour laws. Accordingly, each Party shall ensure that it does not waive or otherwise derogate from or offer to waive or otherwise derogate from its labour laws where the waiver or derogation would be inconsistent with … labour rights …, or fail to effectively enforce its labour laws through a sustained or recurring course of action or inaction, as an encouragement for the establishment, acquisition, expansion, or retention of an investment in its territory.[23]

Unlike the model treaty's substantive obligations, such as the guarantee against expropriation without compensation, these provisions lack effective enforcement mechanisms, i.e. they are not subjected to the agreement's dispute settlement provisions. The treaty simply requires that signatory states consult with each other regarding any issues that may arise under these provisions. It adds that signatory states may, should they wish to, create opportunities for public participation regarding relevant matters. While offering little in the way of formal redress for transgression of these provisions through the imposition of environmental or labour-oriented investment incentives, this is an intriguing recognition of the impact that investment incentives may have on the general public and how their concerns may often fail to be appreciated by either firms or governments during the construction or negotiation of investment packages.

Similarly, although NAFTA does not contain any express rules on investment incentives or subsidies, it does state that signatory parties must not lower health, safety or environmental regulations for the purposes of attracting FDI. Article 1114 states:

> Parties recognize that it is inappropriate to encourage investment by relaxing domestic health, safety or environmental measures. Accordingly, a Party

[22] Art. 12.2.
[23] Art. 13.2.

> should not waive or otherwise derogate from, or offer to waive or otherwise derogate from, such measures as encouragement for the establishment, acquisition, expansion, retention in its territory of an investment or an investor.

These types of controls are also seen outside North American IIAs entered into by other developed states, capturing the sensitivity of many states to principles of sustainability. For example, Article 21 of the Japan–Myanmar BIT states:

> The Contracting Parties recognize that it is inappropriate to encourage investment by investors of the other Contracting Party by relaxing environmental measures. To this effect each Contracting Party should not waive or otherwise derogate from such environmental measures as an encouragement for the establishment, acquisition or expansion of investments by investors of the other Contracting Party.[24]

The Austria–Nigeria BIT includes labour as well as the environment in its prohibition on lowering regulatory standards:

> ARTICLE 4
>
> (1) The Contracting Parties recognise that it is inappropriate to encourage an investment by weakening domestic environmental laws. …
>
> ARTICLE 5
>
> (1) The Contracting Parties recognise that it is inappropriate to encourage an investment by weakening domestic labour laws.[25]

The language of "appropriateness" seen in each of these instruments is interesting as this qualifier lacks a clear definition or even systemic analysis under international law, unlike for example, terms such as unreasonable or illegitimate, which have an established jurisprudence. It may allude to informal social norms such as those associated with custom. Accordingly, failing to fulfil the standard of appropriateness could be difficult to challenge in international arbitration, or even to raise in consultations as envisioned by a number of these types of provisions. In contrast, the distinction between "weakening" and "relaxing" appears to be a simple semantic choice, with the latter perhaps conveying somewhat more euphemistic assertiveness on the part of the state.

---

[24] Signed 13 April 2013.
[25] Signed 8 April 2013.

As noted above in relation to the US Model BIT, these provisions tend to contemplate complaints (or consultations at least) brought by treaty parties, that is, the governments themselves, not local investors who feel they have suffered as a consequence or citizens. As such they have limited effect and have never been the subject of any arbitration claims. It is difficult to envision how a claim based on one of these provisions would operate, not simply because of the indeterminacy of the phrase "inappropriate", but also because it would seem to infringe too closely on a state's right to lower regulations for legitimate purposes, for example if an environmental assessment determined that a particular environmental regulation was too strict, or if an economic study ascertained that a minimum wage or other labour provision was unnecessarily burdensome. These provisions appear to contemplate intentionality – the very purpose of the weakening was to attract FDI. Accordingly it is unclear what the consequences would be if FDI enhancement was but one of many motivations. There is also the notorious problem of ever proving the intent behind a regulation without comprehensive records of legislative debate, which are unavailable in many jurisdictions.

It is important to recognize also that the impetus towards weaker regulations in spheres such as the environment or labour in order to entice and extract long-term commitments from mobile foreign investors are but one variety of mechanism through which host states can make themselves more appealing relative to other jurisdictions which are more sensitive to sustainability issues. States may also cover any additional costs that the foreign investors incur as a result of onerous environmental or labour regulations. This type of incentive should be viewed in a more positive light in that it fulfils the public policy behind the relevant laws while also attracting FDI. Of course it can also risk depleting the host state's limited resources, rendering the economic purpose behind attracting the FDI futile. It is important to recognize that despite numerous high-profile environmental catastrophes and extensive populist criticisms of the "pollution haven" theory of FDI location strategy, there is actually very little evidence that industries that cause pollution, such as those in manufacturing or extractive sectors, do choose to locate to jurisdictions with weaker environmental laws.[26] Likewise, the view that MNEs tend to seek out locations where the labour standards are poor in order to operate exploitative "sweat shops" appears to be untrue, as foreign firms tend to

---

[26] See e.g. A. Harrison, 'Do Polluters Head Overseas? Testing the Pollution Haven Hypothesis' (Giannini Foundation, Berkeley, CA 2002).

pay on average higher wages than local firms and typically offer greater job stability and training.[27]

In addition to encouraging host states not to lower regulatory standards to make themselves more attractive to foreign firms, IIAs curtail the use of investment incentives directly via their prohibition of performance requirements, which are typically forbidden (along with their conventional prohibitions discussed in Chapter 4) when they are imposed in conjunction with an incentive. For example, NAFTA Article 1106(3), the same provision which deals with performance requirements, states:

> 3. No Party may condition the receipt or continued receipt of an advantage, in connection with an investment in its territory of an investor of a Party or of a non-Party, on compliance with any of the following requirements:
> (a) to achieve a given level or percentage of domestic content;
> (b) to purchase, use or accord a preference to goods produced in its territory, or to purchase goods from producers in its territory;
> (c) to relate in any way the volume or value of imports to the volume or value of exports or to the amount of foreign exchange inflows associated with such investment; or
> (d) to restrict sales of goods or services in its territory that such investment produces or provides by relating such sales in any way to the volume or value of its exports or foreign exchange earnings.

Importantly, as discussed in Chapter 4, Article 1106(5) further states that this provision does not apply to any requirement other than the requirements set out in those paragraphs (trade-based investment measures), effectively allowing NAFTA parties to impose other types of performance requirements as part of an incentive package, such as those relating to training or knowledge exchange.

Echoing NAFTA, the Canadian Model BIT of 2004 contains the following restriction on the use of incentives to attract FDI:

> 7(3). Neither Party may condition the receipt or continued receipt of an advantage, in connection with an investment in its territory of an investor of a Party or of a non-Party, on compliance with any of the following requirements:
> (a) to achieve a given level or percentage of domestic content;
> (b) to purchase, use or accord a preference to goods produced in its territory, or to purchase goods from producers in its territory;

[27] See e.g. H. Gorg, E. Strobl and F. Walsh, 'Why Do Foreign-Owned Firms Pay More? The Role of On-the-Job Training' IZA Discussion Paper No. 590 (October 2004) <http://ftp.iza.org/dp590.pdf> accessed 1 August 2015.

(c) to relate in any way the volume or value of imports to the volume or value of exports or to the amount of foreign exchange inflows associated with such investment; or
(d) to restrict sales of goods or services in its territory that such investment produces or provides by relating such sales in any way to the volume or value of its exports or foreign exchange earnings.

Interestingly, however, this treaty goes on to state:

> 7(4). Nothing in paragraph 3 shall be construed to prevent a Party from conditioning the receipt or continued receipt of an advantage, in connection with an investment in its territory of an investor of a Party, on compliance with a requirement to locate production, provide a service, train or employ workers, construct or expand particular facilities, or carry out research and development, in its territory.

Again, this clause appears to draw a distinction between traditional local content or TRIMs-type performance requirements, which are presumptively harmful to international trade and which may be instigated in conjunction with an incentive, and the less traditional, non-economically distortive performance requirements that might simply serve social worthy goals. Recall that this distinction was at the root of the *Mobil v Canada* dispute examined in Chapter 4.

Similar provisions appear almost verbatim in Article 11.9 of the Australia–Korea FTA, with an express additional exception for various types of preferences accorded under certain circumstances.

> 3. Nothing in paragraph 2 [the prohibition on preferences linked to performance requirements] shall be construed to prevent a Party from conditioning the receipt or continued receipt of an advantage, in connection with an investment in its territory of an investor of a Party or of a non-Party, on compliance with a requirement to locate production, supply a service, train or employ workers, construct or expand particular facilities, or carry out research and development, in its territory.

The interpretive footnote to this article adds:

> For greater certainty, nothing in paragraph 1 [the prohibition on performance requirements] shall be construed to prevent a Party, in connection with the establishment, acquisition, expansion, management, conduct, operation or sale or other disposition of an investment of an investor of a Party or of a non-Party in its territory, from imposing or enforcing a requirement or enforcing a commitment or undertaking to locate production, supply a service, train or employ workers, construct or expand particular facilities, or carry out research and development, in its territory …

Again, these IIAs establish two categories of performance requirements linked to incentives: those that are traditionally seen to be harmful to global markets for goods and services; and those which expressly contemplate a developmental or social purpose and therefore implicitly should not operate as distortions to international markets for goods and services, or to the extent that they do these effects should be tolerated. It would seem as though international economic law's greatest concern with respect to investment incentives is that they do not result in distortions to international trade.

General exceptions relating to public policies are established in order to allow incentive based use of performance requirements. In this regard, the Australia–Korea FTA goes on to state, recalling the familiar language of GATT Article XX:

> 5. Provided that such measures are not applied in an arbitrary or unjustifiable manner, or do not constitute a disguised restriction on international trade or investment, paragraphs … and 2(a) [preferences linked to domestic content] and 2(b) [preferences linked to domestic purchasing], shall not be construed to prevent a Party from adopting or maintaining measures, including environmental measures
>   (a) necessary to secure compliance with laws and regulations that are not inconsistent with this Agreement
>   (b) necessary to protect human, animal or plant life or health; or
>   (c) related to the conservation of living or non-living exhaustible natural resources

This IIA also establishes two further carve-outs for investment incentives which have performance requirement conditions attached:

> 6. [Prohibitions on preferences] shall not apply to qualification requirements for goods or services with respect to export promotion and foreign aid programs.
> 7. [Prohibitions on preferences] shall not apply to government procurement.

Similar provisions can be found in US IIAs, such as that with Jordan, which expressly provides that performance requirements, which would otherwise be prohibited, may be imposed where they are offered in conjunction with an incentive.[28] This method reveals an interesting logic: while performance requirements should be generally be prohibited because they are harmful to international trade in goods and services, this harm can be tolerated where protectionist trade distortions can act as an

[28] US–Jordan Art. IV (2 July 1997).

incentive for FDI. In other words, to the extent that there are trade distortions as a consequence of performance requirements, these are more than compensated for in terms of efficiency gains resulting from increased FDI. It is not clear that this logic is supported by economic evidence.

Finally, given the absence of global rules on subsidies in services as well as the widespread practice of instigating reservations for subsidies and incentives in various services sectors, some IIAs have embodied the practice of GATS to include provisions where signatory parties which feel they have suffered as a consequence of incentives offered in services may request consultations to achieve redress. For example, the Australia–Japan Economic Partnership agreement outlines the need for parties to share information in relation to the subsidization of services in the event that a disagreement arises and consultations are initiated:

> During the consultations [on the use of subsidies in services] …, the Party granting a subsidy shall, if it deems fit, consider a request of the other Party for information relating to the subsidy program such as:
>
> (a) laws and regulations under which the subsidy is granted;
> (b) form of the subsidy (for example, grant, loan, tax concession);
> (c) policy objective or purpose of the subsidy;
> (d) dates and duration of the subsidy and any other time limits attached to it; and
> (e) eligibility requirements of the subsidy.[29]

While this provision falls short of a prohibition on services-oriented subsidies, it does recognize the reality that such forms of assistance can have damaging consequences on treaty parties and that open discussion of these issues and resulting harms can be advantageous. It also reveals the importance of more complete information regarding the nature and extent of an incentive, which, as noted earlier, tends to be severely lacking.

(iv) Investment-promotion Provisions

Perhaps the most obvious feature of IIAs that relates to investment incentives are the provisions for investment-promotion. The weak links that have been found between IIAs and FDI flows may at least partially be explained by the fact that few IIAs contain such investment-promotion

[29] Art. 9.11(3).

provisions.[30] Proactively creating arrangements between signatory states that encourage FDI, such as through the exchange of information on available opportunities, countries attempt to achieve greater levels of FDI than they would be able to in the absence of these efforts. Generally speaking, investment-promotion provisions in IIAs tend to involve a combination of measures aimed at improving the host state's regulatory framework by making it more transparent and efficient in order to reduce the costs borne by foreign investors, and assisting the investment process by providing formal information dissemination and facilitating partnerships with local firms. Together, these two strategies have been described as one of removing barriers (often the first stage of FDI promotion) and putting down red carpets (often seen as the second or mature stage).[31] The type of investment-promotion strategy undertaken by a host state tends to depend on its own approach to economic governance. States that embrace a more market-oriented economy will be more likely to seek to improve their internal legal institutional framework in order to become more attractive to FDI, whereas countries that operate a more statist economic structure will be motivated to promote foreign investment that is directed at specific sectors, often in conjunction with targeted subsidization.[32] It is widely believed that placing a legally binding commitment to promote investment in the text of an IIA will increase the likelihood that party states will actually engage in FDI promotion activities,[33] although it is not clear how such a provision would be enforceable.

Investment-promotion provisions in IIAs may take the form of requirements placed upon home states. Indeed, most IIA investment-promotion obligations embody initiatives that will be performed by the host state. Home state efforts to increase outward FDI have been the subject of only a handful of studies and are widely viewed as less transparent and less clearly defined than those instigated by host states seeking to attract

---

[30] UNCTAD, 'Investment Promotion Provisions in International Investment Agreements' (United Nations, New York and Geneva, 2007).

[31] J. VanDuzer, P. Simons and G. Mayeda, *Integrating Sustainable Development into International Investment Agreements: A Guide for Developing Countries* (Commonwealth Secretariat, New York, NY 2012) 493, and T. Harding and B. Javorcik, 'Roll Out the Red Carpet and They Will Come' (72 *Columbia FDI Perspectives*, 18 June 2012) <http://ccsi.columbia.edu/files/2014/01/FDI_72.pdf> accessed 2 December 2014.

[32] VanDuzer et al., ibid. 496.

[33] ibid. 495.

FDI.[34] Investment-promotion provisions in IIAs may be mandatory, voluntary or best efforts. Still relatively rare in IIAs, such provisions tend to be vague and non-binding, consisting of little more than aspirations in favour of FDI-oriented policies between the signatory parties, or even simply the continuation of existing programmes.[35]

IIAs that form part of regional economic integration programmes contain more detailed provisions in this regard. For example, Article 24 of the ASEAN Comprehensive Investment Agreement reads:

> Member States shall cooperate in increasing awareness of ASEAN as an integrated investment area in order to increase foreign investment into ASEAN and intra-ASEAN investments through, among others:
>
> (a) encouraging the growth and development of ASEAN small and medium sized enterprises and multinational enterprises
> (b) enhancing industrial complementation and production networks among multi-national enterprises in ASEAN
> (c) organising investment missions that focus on developing regional clusters and production networks
> (d) organising and supporting the organisation of various briefings and seminars on investment opportunities and on investment laws, regulations and policies and
> (e) conducting exchanges on other issues of mutual concern relating to investment promotion

Again though, it is difficult to imagine how the requirement to "cooperate in increasing awareness" could possibly be enforceable, especially when placed alongside incredibly vague obligations such as organizing missions and exchanges, seemingly empty government-speak that, while well meaning, adds very little to the treaty's overall purpose of increasing FDI flows. To this is added in Article 25:

> Member states shall endeavour to cooperate in the facilitation of investments into and within ASEAN through among others:
>
> (a) creating the necessary environment for all forms of investments;
> (b) streamlining and simplifying procedures for investment applications and approvals;
> (c) promoting dissemination of investment information, including investment rules, regulations, policies and procedures

---

[34] See e.g. P. Buckley, J. Clegg, A. Cross and H. Voss, 'What Can Emerging Markets Learn from the Outward Direct Investment Policies of Advanced Economies?' in K. Sauvant, G. McAllister and W. Maschek (eds), *Foreign Direct Investment From Emerging Markets* (Palgrave MacMillan, New York, NY 2010).

[35] VanDuzer et al. (n 31) 494.

(d) establishing one-stop investment centres
(e) strengthening databases on all forms of investment for policy formulation to improve ASEAN's investment environment;
(f) undertaking consultation with the business community on investment matters and
(g) providing advisory services to the business community of the other member states.

Clearly, this second provision cannot impose a binding obligation on members, because it is framed in best-efforts language: "endeavour to". However, it seems to contemplate somewhat more substantial initiatives, such as the establishment of investment centres, the improvement of databases and the provision of advisory services. Despite their ambiguity, a number of ASEAN countries have fulfilled this provision, suggesting that the aspirational investment-promotion features of IIAs can have some value. The Common Market for Eastern and Southern Africa (COMESA) Agreement has similar provisions, including commitments regarding the establishment of a regional database of investment opportunities available to firms from within the region.[36] Provisions that contain non-binding intentions that parties will endeavour to promote FDI may extend less tangible benefits to signatory states. Negotiation of such provisions grant the opportunity of the states to discuss their economic needs and how these may be addressed by FDI, allowing parties to deliver investment-promotion policies that are consistent with their needs. In theory of course, if the investment-promotion provisions in an IIA are binding and a state party does not fulfil them, then this will mean that the treaty's dispute-settlement provisions can be engaged in response.[37]

The value of investment-promotion provisions in incentivizing FDI can be seen in situations where they are absent. For example, many African states have been deficient in providing business development services to foreign investors as well as their own firms, particularly SMEs. African firms, which tend to lack the resources of firms from emerging or developing states require more information about trade and investment opportunities to help better access foreign markets. Stronger investment-promotion clauses in IIAs with African states have been advocated to address these needs.[38] Commentators have suggested that governments in developing countries generally must be more proactive in providing

[36] COMESA Investment Agreement (2007) Schs I, II.
[37] VanDuzer et al (n 31) 496.
[38] U. Ofodile, 'Africa–China Bilateral Investment Treaties: A Critique' (2013) 35:1 *Michigan Journal of International Law* 131, 180.

business development services for SMEs in particular and must consider appropriate financial and fiscal incentives to support smaller firms, especially those which operate in distressed priority sectors and in rural areas.[39] More thorough information dissemination about investment incentives is key.

Investment-promotion provisions that are conditional on investors performing certain kinds of activities, such as transferring technology or using local goods, will likely be inconsistent with prohibitions on performance requirements found elsewhere in the IIA, unless there is a relevant exception to the performance requirement prohibition for such initiatives. Implementation of incentives that discriminate against investors from a particular state may also be inconsistent with an MFN obligation in an IIA with another state, unless that MFN clause is also subject to an exception concerning investment-promotion obligations offered to other states in other instruments.[40]

Many developed and emerging countries have taken the investment-promotion provisions in IIAs seriously and established agencies for that purpose. Investment-promotion agencies seek to provide relevant information as well as feedback to governments regarding the investment climate within the jurisdiction in order to facilitate inward FDI through reductions in information barriers suffered by foreign firms. More advanced, well-resourced investment-promotion agencies can be more responsive to the precise needs of foreign investors. It has been suggested that the longer an investment-promotion agency has been operating, the more likely that it will be successful in attracting foreign investors and achieving FDI goals. Such agencies may also be better skilled at targeting sustainable FDI that contributes to the host state's economy in a productive manner.[41] Promotion agencies tend to offer incentives based on the economic developmental potential of the proposed investment. This will include its capacity to generate employment and training, as well as the establishment of research and development facilities, particularly in disadvantaged regions. As noted above, such objectives tend to be excluded from the prohibition on performance requirements seen in many IIAs. The provision of general infrastructure may be high on the list of goals sought by investment-promotion agencies.

---

[39] U. Ewelukwa, 'South-South Trade and Investment: The Good, the Bad and the Ugly' (2011) 20:2 *Minnesota Journal of International Law* 513, 581.

[40] VanDuzer et al. (n 31) 497.

[41] 'Investment Promotion Agencies and Sustainable Development' (Vale Columbia Center on Sustainable International Investment, New York, NY 25 June 2010) 30.

With economic goals in mind, investment-promotion agencies often construct their promotion programs and incentive packages in order to achieve FDI in certain sectors of greatest priority to the national economy. Given the limited budgets of many governments, it is not surprising that investment-promotion agencies would prioritize economic considerations over environmental or social ones when seeking FDI. Few such bodies implement incentive regimes to attract investors on the basis of environmental and social sustainability in isolation.[42] While the dominant objective has traditionally been that of economic advancement, some observers are calling for investment-promotion agencies to direct their attention towards the social or environmental aspects of FDI. This may necessitate special government training for investment-promotion agencies in order to identify target priorities, to tailor incentive regimes to achieve these ends, and finally to monitor the implementation of the investment project to verify whether policy goals are met. This could be coupled with a regime of bonus incentives for firms that achieve targets, or ideally, exceed them.

One of the chief burdens associated with investment-promotion obligations in IIAs is that they can inhibit the flexibility of party states in designing and operating FDI promotion strategies. For example, the obligation found in an incentive package to grant tax relief to foreign investors can limit the funds available to a host state to adopt subsidization programmes aimed at augmenting FDI in particular sectors or regions.[43] In this sense, two investment-incentive schemes may conflict with each other, possibly neutralizing any overall economic advantage.

(v) Removal of Investment Incentives as Breaches of IIAs

If traditional investment incentives like tax relief are granted by host states in order to entice or retain foreign firms, IIAs may compel signatory states to extend the promised benefits to the investors over a longer time-frame than the host state wishes. Indeed, the removal of the incentive may itself be construed as an IIA breach. This is problematic from a government's standpoint because it may wish to curtail its incentive program due to budget restraints or changing economic conditions, or simply because it observes that the incentives offered have not resulted in the benefits that were expected. From the perspective of the investor, any attempt to renege on promised incentives, even where there

---

[42] ibid. 27.

[43] 'Development Implications of International Investment Agreements' UNCTAD IIA Monitor no. 2, (United Nations, New York and Geneva, 2007) 2.

are policy or budgetary justifications, may be viewed as an illegitimate interference. More specifically, orders for firms to repay subsidies or to relinquish various advantages offered to foreign firms in order to stimulate FDI could be deemed to breach various protections enshrined in an IIA, including most notably the guarantee against expropriation without compensation and the FET guarantee. The potential scope of such claims is likely one of the reasons that most IIAs have carve-outs for tax-oriented measures that are captured by other agreements such as double taxation treaties, as noted above. The provision of investment incentives can be fraught with risks on the part of host states: what had intended to be an initial or short term inducement could be framed as a long-term commitment for support. Investors' legitimate expectations can be formed through the provision of assistance that was not transparently identified as a one-off inducement. Fear of claims based on the removal of incentive packages, in some cases in order to conform to other international rules[44] could render governments overly cautious about pursuing IIAs in the future.

The highly ambiguous FET standard, common to most IIAs, is perhaps the most promising feature of an IIA that an aggrieved investor which has experienced a withdrawal of an incentive could use to base its claim. UNCTAD has stated that FET means that the host state "act consistently, transparently, reasonably, without ambiguity, arbitrariness or discrimination, in an even-handed manner, to ensure due process in decision-making and respect investors' legitimate expectation".[45] Even more expansively, tribunals have reiterated that FET compels the contracting parties to refrain from any actions towards foreign investors that affects their initial expectations upon which the foreign investor makes its investment.[46] The emphasis here appears to be on predictability: investors do not want to be surprised by governmental action. In an effort to achieve greater clarity in the FET standard, the US draft proposal of the Trade in Services, Investment and E-Commerce Annex of the TTIP under negotiation with the EU provides a non-exhaustive list of actions which would constitute breach of the FET obligation, one of which is: "A

---

[44] See *Micula v Romania* (n 56).

[45] 'State Contracts', UNCTAD Series on Issues in International Investment Agreements, (United Nations, New York and Geneva, 2004).

[46] *Tecmed v Mexico* ICSID Case No. ARB (AF)/00/2, Award (29 May 2003) [154].

breach of legitimate expectations of investors arising from a government's specific representations or investment-inducing measures".[47] Still, the legitimacy of such expectations in light of any promises or inducements tendered to investors by host state representatives must be assessed in accordance with the political, socio-economic, cultural and historic conditions prevailing in the host state as well as their role in causing the investor to decide to invest.[48]

IIAs could further be used to bring claims for the revocation of investment incentives that were offered in an investment contract between the investor and the host state. Umbrella clauses, now common to many IIAs, may be used to incorporate provisions contained in contracts between the host state and the foreign investor. For example, a stabilization clause in a contract between a host state and an investor could be seen as a form of inducement to attract a foreign investor. Such clauses tend to be captured by umbrella clauses in investment treaties.[49] As such, the failure of a host state to observe the obligations encompassed by a stabilization clause would empower an international investment tribunal to take jurisdiction over the removal of this form of investment incentive, particularly if the withdrawal is done in a manner that is not in keeping with due process, in which case it could also represent a violation of FET.[50] The idea behind such claims is that the investor chose to locate in a particular jurisdiction because of special regulatory arrangements that were in place on the understanding that these would remain in place over time, ensuring a more predictable stream of profits.

Since the removal of promised investment incentives may operate as a breach of contract, there could also be remedies against host states under national legal systems. Breach of contract claims could arise in the context of incentive guarantees where unrealistic deadlines or price stipulations are established. Of course, such issues could equally lead to claims (under domestic contract law) against the investor where the

---

[47] Ch II, Art. 12(2)f), European Commission, Directorate-General for Trade, 2 July 2013.

[48] *Duke Energy International Peru Investments Ltd No 1 v Peru* ICSID Case No. ARB/03/28, Award (18 August 2008) [320].

[49] *El Paso Energy International Company v Argentine Republic* ICSID Case No. ARB/03/15, Decision on Jurisdiction (27 April 2006) [81].

[50] As in *Burlington Resources v Ecuador* ICSID Case No. ARB/08/5, Decision on Jurisdiction (2 June 2010) [24].

investor discovers that it cannot establish or continue the commercial activity upon which the incentives were contingent.[51]

A final way that IIAs could control investment incentives is through the inclusion of international guidelines on the conduct of MNEs, as developed by organizations such as the OECD and the UN. No known IIAs make adherence to these guidelines mandatory, although they could be embraced through best efforts clauses. The potential impact of these instruments on investment incentives will be explored further below.

2. INVESTMENT ARBITRATION CASE LAW RELATING TO INCENTIVES

As in Chapter 4, given the high degree of overlap among many of the issues noted above, as well as the custom of investor–state arbitration claims to be based on numerous provisions within a given IIA, the limited arbitral case law addressing the use of investment incentives will be considered together in this section.

The withdrawal of investment incentives that have been offered to foreign investors has been the subject of investor–state dispute settlement. Such claims bring into question the capacity of a state to revoke undertakings in a manner that fulfils its sovereign right to control its own economy. As indicated above, these types of claims are typically tied to the investor's legitimate expectations, captured in part by the FET standard, as well as the principle of estoppel under international law.[52] The importance of such issues becomes evident when, as suggested earlier, a more expansive notion of investment incentive is contemplated in which beneficial contractual terms, such as stabilization clauses, can be used as inducements to foreign investors and which constrain considerably the host state's capacity to regulate its economy in the longer term. The cases discussed below give a flavour of the type of claims that could be framed as injurious revocations of investment incentives. Depending on which provisions of IIAs and investment contracts one considers to be incentives, there are dozens of cases that could be characterized as claims based on the revocation or non-fulfilment of such schemes. The series of

---

[51] H. Markova and M. Zajickova, 'Budgetary Legal Consequences of Breaching the Terms of Investment Incentives' (2011) 157 *Czech Yearbook of International Law* 165.

[52] E.g. *Texaco Overseas Petroleum Co v the Government of the Libyan Arab Republic* Ad Hoc YCA 1979 (19 January 1977).

NAFTA disputes discussed in Chapter 4 on the imposition of performance requirements in conjunction with incentive regimes will not be explored again because of their primary focus on the legality of performance requirements.

David Minnotte & Robert Lewis v Republic of Poland[53] concerned the activities of a US blood plasma facility in Poland owned by an investor which claimed it had suffered detrimental effects as a consequence of the revocation of a business permit to operate within the host state in a special economic zone which granted favourable tariff and customs treatment. The investor argued that this revocation constituted a violation of the US–Poland BIT's FET clause. Deciding in favour of Poland, the tribunal ruled that the investor had not been given formal assurances that there would be an extension of their permission to operate within a special economic zone. While the permit to operate in the zone was determined to be an inducement to engage in FDI, it had not been intended by the government to operate permanently. Moreover, while there had been some long delays by governmental representatives in responding to the investor's letters in which it queried the revocation, this was not sufficient to constitute a denial of fundamental justice. This case illustrates that inducements cannot be inferred to be permanent if they are not specifically promoted as such, and that the manner of their revocation (rather than the simple revocation itself) will be instrumental in dictating whether the FET guarantee has been breached.

In a similar vein, *Rumeli Telekom and Teslim Mobil v Kazakhstan*[54] was a claim based on a breach of an investment contract as a consequence of the host state's failure to fulfil promised investment incentive guarantees and to renew a licence granted to the investor so that it could operate a mobile phone network. The government of Kazakhstan had granted the investor tax concessions, including a five year exemption from corporate income tax, in order to induce them to locate their investment in their territory. The ICSID tribunal decided that the respondent's wrongful termination of the investment contract without offering the possibility of re-negotiation amounted to a breach of the FET standard as well as an indirect expropriation, contrary to the BIT between Turkey and Kazakhstan. The tribunal ruled that the host state had a duty to act in a manner which conformed to the investor's reasonable and legitimate expectations, which included the fulfilment of the host state's contractual

[53] ICSID Case No. ARB (AF)/10/1 (16 May 2014).

[54] *Rumeli Telekom AS, Telsim Mobil Telekomikasyon Hizmetleri AS (Claimants) v Republic of Kazakhstan (Respondent)* ICSID Case No. ARB/05/16, Award (28 July 2008).

promises, even in the absence of an umbrella clause. The decision to terminate the contract, particularly given that there had been no prior notification that such termination was pending, was arbitrary, unfair, unjust, and lacking in due process. It also resulted in a substantial deprivation of the investor's asset which had been given to it by the host state as an inducement, namely the licence to operate a mobile telephone company in the host state.[55] This decision again emphasizes that the manner of removal of incentives (in this case indirectly as a consequence of the termination of the investment contract) will affect the validity of the host state's actions.

The revocation of investment incentives was framed as a breach of the Sweden–Romania FET provision in *Micula Bros v Romania*.[56] Here the tribunal considered various claims brought by a Swedish-based food and soft drinks company including those in connection with the treaty's umbrella clause and its FET provision. These were asserted in relation to regulatory changes that took place during Romania's accession to the EU during which period Romania was compelled to revoke some of its existing regional investment incentives (including tax and duty exemptions) five years early as a consequence of EU rules on state aid (which were explored in the previous chapter). These actions harmed the claimant's operations by forcing it to raise prices beyond a level that was sustainable in the established market. The tribunal upheld the claim based on breach of the FET standard by imposing what were determined to be discriminatory measures on the company's investment through fiscal incentive revocation. This led to increased costs of materials, including sugar, which also amounted to the expropriation of assets without the payment of appropriate compensation. Without the generous incentive system that had attracted the soft-drink company to Romania, the Swedish firm drastically lost market share. The tribunal focused again on the manner in which the host state withdrew the incentives which it held to be arbitrary and discriminatory. In particular, the Romanian government had required the investors to maintain their obligations under the incentive regime despite abolishing its advantages to them. Romania also failed to inform the investors of the premature termination of its incentive regime in a timely fashion, exacerbating the resulting injury. Moreover it terminated the incentives entirely at once, rather than phase them out

---

[55] [615].

[56] *Ioan Micula, Viorel Micula, SC European Food SA, SC Starmill SRL and SC Multipack SRL v Romania* ICSID Case No. ARB/05/20, Award [672]–[679].

incrementally, which it could have done under EU rules.[57] This case confirms that the removal of investment incentives may be viewed as a breach of international investment law even if those incentives are incompatible with another regime, namely that of the EU state aid rules. It is interesting to observe that the European Commission later asserted that any attempt by Romania to pay compensation to the investors under the tribunal's award would be considered by it a further violation of EU state aid rules and at the time of writing this matter remains unresolved.[58]

In *Lao Holdings v Laos*[59] the investor, a gaming and tourism firm incorporated in the Netherlands brought a complaint against the Laos Government for the wrongful termination of its fiscal investment incentive program, which included a flat tax arrangement. The claimant argued that it had been promised that when the original flat tax arrangement expired it would be replaced by another similar agreement most likely for the remainder of the 50-year concession. The terms (and in particular the tax rate) of the new agreement were to depend on negotiations arising out of the experience of the initial five year period. However, the Laos Government declined to enter into a renewal of agreement, including the favourable tax arrangement, leading to allegations of breach of contract. According to the claimant investor, government officials induced them to believe that the tax incentive arrangement would be renewed, despite changes to the country's tax code. This dispute was eventually settled in June 2014 with the reinstatement of the original agreement, including the flat-tax-rate incentive, for a period of 50 years.[60] While the tribunal did not reach a decision on the legitimacy of the host state's revocation of its tax incentives, it is evident that there was a potential for such action to constitute a breach of the investor's contractual expectations capable of compensation.

Lastly, *Ruby Roz Agricol v Kazakhstan*[61] concerned a contract-based claim brought by an agricultural production company. In this dispute, the revocation of investment incentives was used to ground a claim against

---

[57] ibid. [1019].

[58] European Commission Letter to Romania on State Aid Investigation (1 October 2014) C(2014) 6848 final.

[59] *Lao Holdings NV (Claimant) v Lao People's Democratic Republic (Respondent)* ICSID Case No. ARB(AF)/12/6, Decision on Jurisdiction (21 February 2014).

[60] Settlement Agreement (15 June 2014).

[61] *Ruby Roz Agricol LLP (Claimant) v Republic of Kazakhstan (Respondent)*, Award on Jurisdiction in the Matter of an UNCITRAL Arbitration (1 August 2013).

the host state for breach of contract as well as breach of the national legislation covering foreign investments, which contained an obligation to ensure a stable legal environment. The incentives that had been offered by Kazakhstan included various tax privileges, the revocation of which allegedly contributed to the investor's ultimate bankruptcy. In a decision that unfortunately sheds no light on the status of investment incentives as legal entitlements held by investors, the United Nations Commission on International Trade Law (UNCITRAL) tribunal ultimately declined to take jurisdiction over the dispute because there had not been a valid agreement to arbitrate the dispute. Still, the fact that this claim was brought at all illustrates that investors are aware of the strategic potential to ground legal obligations in incentive packages which may have been intended simply to affect a location decision rather than to support ongoing operations.

In conceptualizing these cases in somewhat of an opening salvo of what may end up being a trend in investment claims tied to incentive revocation, it is worth mentioning that Spain, the Czech Republic and other European countries have faced a number of claims under the Energy Charter Treaty (ECT) for reductions in the incentives that had been offered to investors in order to promote development of renewable wind and solar energy projects.[62] Canada faced a similar claim under NAFTA.[63] In these disputes, which remain pending and unreported at the time of writing, the investors in question claim that they relied on the subsidies and feed-in tariffs offered by these governments to fund new green energy projects that have now become either financially unviable or less profitable than expected. Initially offered in 2007, the incentive schemes were removed in 2010 pursuant to changes in governmental policy in the various host states in the wake of the global recession. Other harmful changes in such policies, including Spain's plan to impose an additional tax, went into effect in late 2014. The Czech Republic has instigated similar reforms, including a retroactive tax on renewable energy generators. These regulatory actions are based on illegal expropriation as well as breach of FET in that the governments' actions were

---

[62] Much of the information relating to this dispute has not been made publicly available: 'Spain Round-UP: Twin Energy Charter Claims Moving at Different Speeds; Arbitrator in Third Case Agrees to Hear Jurisdictional Objections First' *Investment Arbitration Reporter* (18 June 2013) <www.iareporter.com/articles/spain-round-up-twin-energy-charter-claims-moving-at-different-speeds-arbitrator-in-third-case-agrees-to-hear-jurisdictional-objections-first/> accessed 1 August 2015.

[63] *Mesa Power Group LLC v Government of Canada* UNCITRAL, PCA Case No. 2012-17, Notice of Intent to Arbitrate (filed 4 October 2011).

unreasonable and did not respect the investors' legitimate expectations. The number of claims against Spain, the Czech Republic and other European countries is expected to grow as the full impact of the changes in regulatory and fiscal policy towards renewable energy investment is felt.[64]

This flurry of cases appears to illustrate that the revocation of investment incentives can be construed by arbitration tribunals as breaches of ordinary contractual terms as well as IIAs and as such they are capable of supporting a broad range of claims of compensation to aggrieved investors. None of these cases offers any indication that incentives should be seen as a special category of entitlement that rests upon the implied capacity of the host state to maintain them irrespective of changes in circumstance, including legislative as well as economic. Although there is no arbitration case law yet on point, it seems plausible to suggest that the revocation of incentives, to the extent that this is actionable under international law, could however be defensible (as any breach of obligation whether contract or treaty based) on grounds of necessity or economic emergency, given that the circumstances are sufficiently grave. The removal of incentives linked to environmental protection has the further potential to bring the expansive field of the international law relating to climate change into the sphere of investor–state arbitration, which represents a compelling counterpoint to the alleged fragmentation of international investment law as legal regime isolated from other aspects of public international law.

3. DEVELOPMENT-ORIENTED INVESTMENT INCENTIVE REGIMES

In addition to the disciplines found in the text of IIAs, there are a number of "soft law" instruments in place that have been promulgated by international institutions that have attempted to impose restrictions on the use of investment incentives at the international level. These have primarily served the purpose of achieving developmental goals through the encouragement of FDI that is sensitive to the needs of host states.

[64] R. Thorn, 'Renewable Energy Policy Changes Lead to Damages Claims – Investment Treaties, European Feed-In Tariffs, Arbitration, Political Risk, Expropriation' *Project Finance Newswire* (June 2014) <www.chadbourne.com/renewable_energy_policy_changes_june2014_projectfinance/> accessed 1 August 2015.

(i) National FDI Support Regimes

To begin with, some mention should be made of the incentives offered to foreign investors through national governments of home, rather than host states, in order to stimulate developmentally-minded outward FDI. The Overseas Private Investment Corporation (OPIC) is a branch of the US government established to encourage socially and environmentally sustainable investment into developing countries by providing support to private-sector US investors. Its intervention in incentivizing the direction and extent of outward FDI by US firms should not be viewed as a market distortion in as much as its objective is development. Whether or not organizations such as OPIC actually achieve their developmental aims by assisting firms in their foreign investment activities is another question. Still, it may be asserted that given the high risks associated with investments in many lesser developed regions, it is often the case that firms would choose not to enter into commercial activities in these areas without this type of governmental support, which includes political risk insurance, loans or equity investment. OPIC enters into investment incentive agreements with capital-importing countries in order to stimulate FDI into that foreign country. International investment agreements may be seen as incentives in that they grant OPIC the right to operate in the country. Such treaties, of which there are now several hundred, are different from conventional IIAs because they are designed to protect the home government (or more specifically OPIC) rather than the private investor which ultimately benefits from OPIC's services. They resemble IIAs in that the host state is the party that incurs the principle obligations. Generally speaking such investment incentive agreements recognize OPIC's rights as transferee, assignee, and subrogee in conjunction with the investment support that it offers. Such agreements also specify that OPIC is not liable to pay any tax in the host state and typically contain provisions on dispute settlement between the state parties through arbitration.[65] Because of their fairly limited scope, investment incentive agreements should not be viewed as a means of regulating the use of investment incentives. Rather, as with most IIAs, they are methods of protecting against political risks in unstable host states.[66] In addition to OPIC, which is perhaps the most high profile of the national overseas

---

[65] See e.g. US–People's Republic of Laos (signed 8 March 1996).

[66] K. Thomas, 'Investment Incentives: Growing Use, Uncertain Benefits, Uneven Controls' (Global Studies Initiative, Geneva November 2007) 49 <www.iisd.org/gsi/sites/default/files/GSI_Investment_Incentives.pdf> accessed March 2015.

development organizations, there are a number of agencies maintained by governments around the world that aim to offer support to private firms in order to increase their exports (notably the Exim Bank of China and Export Development Canada). OPIC is significant not only because of its size but because it has a specific focus on FDI rather than on trade.

(ii) The OECD

Several international organizations impose controls on the investment incentives that they themselves offer, such as political risk insurance or loans for foreign developmentally-focused investors, either through non-binding recommendations or through mandatory conditions attached to such products. Although the OECD's Export Credit Arrangement's focus is on assisting firms in increasing their exports rather than promoting internationalization or FDI, its approach to regulating governmental assistance is apposite. The OECD's Export Credit Arrangement is best described as a "gentleman's agreement" which provides the institutional framework for an orderly export credit market. The arrangement seeks to prevent competition in the granting of export credit on the basis of which country grants the most favourable incentives, rather than on the basis of which country offers the highest quality service at a reasonable price. In applying the agreement, the term "official support" means any support that is provided by or on behalf of governments in the sphere of export credits. This can take the form of direct financing from governmental institutions, refinancing, interest rate support, aid financing, export credit insurance provided directly or on behalf of governments, and guarantees issued by governments. The Arrangement is relevant for all official support for exports of goods or services, regardless of whether the official support for export credits is given by means of direct credit or any indirect means, such as interest support. The Arrangement also applies to official support in the form of tied aid, meaning funds that must be spent in either the country that provides the aid or in various listed countries.

The OECD had attempted to control the use of investment incentives more directly. Aimed at influencing the extent and nature of FDI, the proposed OECD Instrument on Investment Incentives and Disincentives, which was part of the Multilateral Agreement on Investment negotiations that took place between 1995 and 1998 but ultimately failed, was aimed specifically at regulating the use of investment incentives that affect FDI. The draft instrument was designed with the simple objective of enhancing transparency and encouraging consultations between OECD Member Countries' use of incentives, as well as performance requirements.

There was no attempt in this instrument to eliminate or modify incentives, nor was there any contemplation of an enforcement mechanism against prohibited incentives through some kind of sanction. While the Instrument on Incentives and Disincentives never came to fruition due to negotiation difficulties, one of the positive outcomes from this project was the inclusion of the topic of investment incentives in the OECD's regular FDI reviews. This project also drew greater attention to the issue of investment incentives within the international community.[67]

Perhaps most well-known of the international guidelines attempting to modify the regulatory approach of host states towards FDI, the OECD Guidelines on Multinational Enterprises, discussed in Chapter 4, also contains provisions on investment incentives. In particular, declaration IV.2 states that adhering governments: "recognize the need to give due weight to the interests of (other) adhering governments affected by specific laws, regulations and administrative practices … providing official incentives … to international direct investment".[68] This optional instrument goes on to specify, somewhat weakly: "that adhering governments will endeavour to make such measures as transparent as possible, so that their importance and purpose can be ascertained and that information on them can be readily available".[69] An earlier iteration of the OECD Guidelines also included a provision that any state which considered that its interests were adversely affected by another state adopting an incentive program would be able to request consultations to examine the possibility of reducing the adverse impacts to a minimum.[70]

As outlined in Chapter 4, the OECD Guidelines take the form of recommendations provided by governments to firms operating in or from adhering countries, of which there are now more than 40, including both developed and developing states. While the Guidelines are voluntary and therefore not legally enforceable, adhering countries have made a binding commitment to implement them. They have also created mechanisms such as the system of National Contact Points, essentially governmental offices which can receive complaints for the transgression of the guidelines, as a way to encourage their implementation. The Guidelines are seen as indicative of "good practice" applicable to both foreign and domestic firms. With respect to their impact on the use of incentives as tools to increase FDI, the Guidelines state that MNEs should "[r]efrain

---

[67] M. Daly, 'Investment Incentives and the Multilateral Agreement on Investment' (1998) 38:2 *Journal of World Trade* 5, 21.

[68] OECD Guidelines on Multinational Enterprises, 2011.

[69] Art. IV.3.

[70] Picciotto (n 16) 164 fn 11.

from seeking or accepting exemptions not contemplated in the statutory or regulatory framework related to human rights, environmental, health, safety, labour, taxation, financial incentives, or other issues". This rationale is similar to that seen in the text of some IIAs, notably NAFTA, as discussed above. Crucially, the Guidelines advise against firms making requests for certain financial, fiscal, and regulatory incentives, and discourage passive receipt of those benefits if they are offered by host governments.

(iii) UNCTAD

Recognizing the value in actively promoting FDI through formal cooperation initiatives as well as the cost associated for developing countries in drafting such arrangements, UNCTAD offers model precedents for investment-promotion commitments.[71] UNCTAD further operates an international investment facilitation program in order to liaise with national investment-promotion agencies as well as various other institutions that aim to facilitate FDI. Part of this service includes the publication and distribution of materials that assist host states in identifying and attracting beneficial foreign investment. UNCTAD also offers advisory services on investment-promotion and retention strategies. This encompasses capacity-building workshops, offered in conjunction with partner organizations such as the World Association of Investment Promotion Agencies, which provide training and other practical assistance to host states and operate as networking events.[72] It is interesting to note that at one point UNCTAD specifically recommended that countries should refrain from granting tax-oriented investment incentives at all because they are more harmful in the long run.[73]

As discussed in Chapter 4, UNCTAD maintains a list of Core Principles for Investment Policymaking. It is worth reviewing policies 2–4, which hint at the organization's approach towards investment incentives (in addition to FDI policies generally):

---

[71] 'Home Country Measures' UNCTAD, (United Nations, New York and Geneva, 2001).

[72] <www.unctad.org> accessed March 2015.

[73] UNCTAD sponsored a study by G. Hanson on tax incentives and FDI in 2001: G. Hanson, 'Should Countries Promote Foreign Direct Investment?' (G-24 Discussion Paper Series, Discussion No. 9, February 2001) <http://213.154.74.164/invenio/record/17103/files/gordon.pdf> accessed 1 August 2015.

2. Policy coherence

Investment policies should be grounded in a country's overall development strategy. All policies that impact on investment should be coherent and synergetic at both the national and international level.

3. Public governance and institutions

Investment policies should be developed involving all stakeholders, and embedded in an institutional framework based on the rule of law that adheres to high standards of public governance and ensures predictable, efficient and transparent procedures for investors.

4. Dynamic policymaking

Investment policies should be regularly reviewed for effectiveness and relevance and adapted to changing development dynamics

And most importantly:

9. Investment promotion and facilitation

Policies for investment promotion and facilitation should be aligned with sustainable development goals and designed to minimize the risk of harmful competition for investment.[74]

The reference in policy number 9 to "sustainable development" embodies the need for host states to be mindful of the long term social and economic impacts of FDI, including any initiatives used to attract it.

In addition to its investment incentive operations pursued through UNCTAD, the UN established its Principles for Responsible Contracting. Like the OECD Guidelines, the UN Principles provide non-binding recommendations to ensure that contracts between investors and states are consistent with the state's duty to protect human rights as well as the firm's responsibility to respect them. These recommendations are important for investment incentives because incentive packages often take the form of private contracts between the host state and the foreign investor. Principle 4 applies to incentives that grant investors exemptions from changes to the legal regime within the host state, or which offers them compensation in the event that they are harmed as a consequence of regulatory changes, known as stabilization clauses. The principle provides that states and investors should ensure that: contractual stabilization clauses are carefully drafted so that any protections for investors against future changes in law do not interfere with the state's legitimate efforts to

---

[74] <http://investmentpolicyhub.unctad.org/ipfsd/core-principle> accessed 2 December 2014.

implement laws, regulations or policies in a non-discriminatory manner in order to meet its human rights obligations. According to the principles, stabilization clauses that have the potential to frustrate human rights (and should therefore be approached with caution) include those that freeze fiscal terms, and those that restrict, or requiring compensation for, changes in laws relating to health, protection of the environment, labour and safety. More careful use of these clauses could prevent many of the types of claims brought by investors against host states discussed above.

(iv) The World Bank – The Multilateral Investment Guarantee Agency (MIGA) and the International Finance Corporation (IFC)

Examined briefly in Chapter 4, MIGA is a branch of the World Bank that provides insurance to foreign investors for political risks in host states. Given that MIGA helps investors deal with some of the political risks associated with FDI into unstable countries, support by MIGA may be viewed as a kind of subsidy for FDI that has a developmental objective. MIGA provides insurance for a wide range of investment projects in developing countries against losses relating to actions undertaken by host states, such as: currency inconvertibility and transfer restrictions; expropriation; war and other civil disturbances; breach of contract; and non-honouring of financial obligations. Support from MIGA can assist investors in obtaining project finance from private banks and also lower the borrowing costs. Moreover, along with its guarantees, MIGA offers extensive background knowledge support through its expertise on developing countries. In 2014 MIGA issued US $3.2 billion in investment guarantees.[75] While take-up of political risk insurance by MNEs remains sporadic and its effectiveness in augmenting FDI is debatable,[76] there is little doubt that many FDI projects in the developing world would not proceed without the assistance of political-risk-insurance providers such as MIGA. As such, MIGA's PRI initiatives can accurately be described as a form of investment incentive offered by the World Bank. To the extent that this type of investment incentive operates as a distortive force for global FDI, it may be justified on non-economic grounds because it facilitates the movement of capital into regions that would otherwise not receive it, and much of it may help to achieve development in some of

---

[75] <www.miga.org/documents/Annual_Report_MIGA_Highlights_2014.pdf> accessed 1 August 2015.

[76] K. Nadakuvkauran-Schefer, *International Investment Law* (Edward Elgar, Cheltenham 2013) ch 7.

the world's poorest regions. As noted in Chapter 4, MIGA places a number of conditions on its insurance packages, which may be likened to performance requirements linked to investment incentives.

Support from the International Finance Corporation of the World Bank may be characterized as an investment incentive which has facilitated some FDI projects in the developing world. As mentioned in Chapter 4, the IFC provides direct financial support to private sector organizations for engaging in FDI in the developing world. It also provides informational support and assists its clients in finding additional sources of capital as well as improving their business operations by identifying new investment opportunities in developing host states. The IFC's focus is on the establishment and expansion of productive private enterprises through the provision of loans on reasonable repayment terms where sufficient private capital is not available.[77] In 2014 the IFC loaned a total of US $65 billion.[78] As with MIGA, there are a number of FDI projects that would most likely not have taken place in the absence of IFC support. While IFC assistance could in the strictest sense represent a market distortion, because it gives advantages to firms that are not able to function under normal conditions (accessing private financing from banks), the IFC's investment incentivisation serves the public goal of stimulating development where there is not always a clear business case because of the weak risk-to-reward ratio and information deficiencies. As with MIGA, the IFC places a number of operational conditions on the firms to which it lends, which were proposed as performance requirements in Chapter 4.

(v) The IMF

Lastly, the work of the IMF in relation to the control of investment incentives has been limited. It has mostly taken the form of surveillance and recommendation, notably in relation to the implication of trade policies in assessing the appropriateness of a country's exchange-rate regime. In this regard, the essentially passive role of the IMF's Surveillance Decisions can be seen in the 2007 Decision on Bilateral Surveillance over Members' Policies (which replaced a decision from 1977). This report stated that the IMF should consider with a view to thoroughly

---

77 As amended through 27 June 2012.

78 IFC Annual Report 2014, 7.

reviewing not only restrictions on, but also incentives for current transactions or payments.[79] The IMF's most obvious role in relation to the control of investment incentives is the regulation of those which may impact upon free transfer of currency (for example, by conditioning incentives on capital movement) and on a host state's capacity to meet its balance of payments obligations (for example, if a host state offers more in the way of incentives than it can genuinely afford).

The purpose of the discussion of the investment incentive/promotion policies instigated by these international organizations was not intended to critique their effectiveness as instruments of FDI nor to characterize their activities as beneficial or detrimental from a social or economic perspective. Rather, this section aimed to illustrate the reasonably sharp distinction between measures which have a discriminatory and competition-impairing intent and effect and those which have a more benign impact, namely the soft support for development-oriented projects among host states or regions that are needful of FDI in order to address long-term structural deficiencies. While the former type of incentive may merit some degree of enforceable regulation at the international level, the latter arguably does not, as it is more closely analogous to the special and differential treatment exceptions for developing states seen in various WTO and regional trade agreements than it is to classic, competition-distorting subsidization.

4. CONCLUSION

Despite the fact that investment incentives can lead to inefficient market distortions for the flow of FDI as well as goods and services, and can represent a key means through which mobile firms pressure states to outcompete one another, often to their own economic detriment, investment incentives remain largely unregulated under international investment law. While some IIAs contain provisions that prevent state parties from lowering some kinds of standards in order to attract FDI, IIAs do not contain provisions that restrict states from engaging in competition with one another in order to attract FDI through incentivisation. Moreover, the prohibition of some varieties performance requirements seen in most IIAs is often suspended when they are imposed in conjunction with incentives, as if incentives are so vital that they justify what would

79 Independent Evaluation Office of the International Monetary Fund, 'IMF Involvement in International Trade Policy Issues' (International Monetary Fund, Washington DC 2009) 56.

otherwise be considered unlawful. This lacuna appears to be exacerbated by the fact that the removal of incentive packages is readily enforceable under investor–state arbitration as a breach of various protections enshrined in IIAs. The extent to which host states may escape liability for the removal of such measures based on social policy grounds remains untested, however, and it is feasible that such actions may be permissible where there is sufficient justification, particularly in the event of an emergency. At the time of writing, ongoing negotiations over the TTIP between the US and the EU could have presented an excellent opportunity to revisit some of these issues, however there is no indication that investment incentives were ever part of the agenda of this agreement or any other currently under negotiation worldwide. Although they are not cast in the form of binding laws, it is encouraging that international organizations have cautioned states against the use of investment incentives that are not compatible with sustainability principles, just as developmental organizations have attached various conditions on the granting of assistance to firms engaging in FDI in developing host states.

7. Conclusions and recommendations

1. OVERVIEW OF THE REGULATION OF PERFORMANCE REQUIREMENTS AND INVESTMENT INCENTIVES UNDER INTERNATIONAL ECONOMIC LAW

The use of performance requirements and investment incentives as instruments for controlling the nature and extent of FDI is problematic from a regulatory standpoint, because in their simplest form they represent departures from the principle of non-discrimination – one of the central pillars of international economic law. Performance requirements tend to discriminate against foreign investors while investment incentives discriminate in favour of them, arguably violating national treatment as well as encroaching on more specific standards contained in both international trade and investment law. While both performance requirements and investment incentives can in some circumstances engender positive outcomes for host states both economically (for example, helping disadvantaged regions) and socially (for example, encouraging environmentally protective behaviour), economists are for the most part severely critical of both policy tools. Since they establish artificial commercial circumstances (either negative or positive) for foreign investors relative to equivalent local firms, both performance requirements and investment incentives are accurately described as forces of market distortion which can result in the misallocation of resources, ultimately leading to welfare losses. The highly variable consequences of the use of these policies, which are often implemented in conjunction with one another, requires a cautious, well-informed, case-by-case consideration that is not seen in either international trade or investment law as it currently stands.

A further problem with the regulation of performance requirements and investment incentives under international economic law is the apparent selective prohibition of these policy tools in a manner that disadvantages developing states. Performance requirements are a traditional tool of protectionism wherein the activities of foreign firms are structured in a manner that suits the needs of the host state rather than based on principles of a truly liberalized market, a strategy that many now-developed countries employed in the past during their industrialization and which now, by virtue of their prohibition, represent lost opportunities for emerging and developing states. In contrast, trade and tax-investment incentives continue to operate as tactics through which predominately developed state governments, as well as regions within them, seek to attract firms, often for both economic and political aims and with questionable social benefits. Unable to afford generous incentive packages, developing states offer less formal incentives including IIA protections in order to reduce the perception of political risk by foreign firms. Yet while a wide variety of performance requirements are now banned by international treaties, investment incentives, other than a narrow range of export-oriented subsidies, remain essentially unregulated. Moreover, to the extent that performance requirements restricting foreign firms' actions are on occasion allowed under international treaties, it is usually only when they are offered in conjunction with advantageous incentives. Consequently the internationally mobile firm faces few unwanted conditions at the hands of host states and even when it does, this tends to be compensated through benefits. It as if the potential harmful distortions in the international markets of goods, services and capital that are associated with performance requirements are somehow neutralized rather than exacerbated by the inherent efficiencies of subsidies and incentives packages. If this is true, which it may be in some circumstances, then it is up to economists to instruct when and to what degree these packages should be used and for this analysis to inform international law. And if there are non-economic reasons for either disallowing or permitting one or both of performance requirements and investment incentives, then this must also be established with clarity, objectivity and ideally with meaningful public participation. Likewise, when harm is suffered by a firm, government or other stakeholder as a consequence of the implementation of these measures, either in isolation or together, then there must be robust processes in place in international law for the neutral assessment of both their content as well as the manner of their application.

Adopting a very wide definition of performance requirement to encompass any type of measure that controls a foreign investor's conduct which can be fulfilled by the investor through a modification of its conduct, this book has demonstrated that performance requirements are heavily controlled under both international trade and international investment law. The TRIMs of the WTO prohibits performance requirements from being imposed on foreign investors that have an explicit trade-distorting focus, namely those which are linked to the discriminatory use of local over foreign goods. IIAs tend to provide a much more comprehensive ban on performance requirements, prohibiting a variety of measures including those relating to preference for local services and the insistence on local ownership or use of local currency. Some forms of performance requirements are often expressly allowed, such as those which mandate training or knowledge exchange. Thus it can be concluded that international economic law has imposed disciplines on the use of performance requirements which appears to capture the concerns of economic inefficiencies voiced by economists while allowing those measures which are less harmful and may serve valid social as well as developmental purposes. International organizations, like the World Bank and the OECD continue to advocate the application of conditions on foreign investors to ensure that such goals are supported along with investment projects.

By contrast, this book has also shown that investment incentives, which it has also deliberately construed broadly, are glaringly underregulated by international trade and investment law. International organizations such as the EU and the WTO have addressed some of the market-distorting concerns associated with the use of trade-oriented subsidies to attract FDI that can have damaging effects on international markets. These regulatory efforts, notably the WTO's SCM and the EU's Multisectoral Framework on State Aid, have thus far been relatively minor either in scope (only covering the EU in the case of state aid rules) or only controlling assistance that modifies export-oriented trade in goods (in the case of the WTO subsidies disciplines). The incentive control agreements of both Australia and Canada, which prohibit policies aimed at moving FDI from one region to another within the same country, appear to have enjoyed some success, particularly when compared with decentralized attempts at cooperation in the United States, which have not been fruitful. The control of incentives under IIAs similarly is circumscribed, typically only prohibiting incentives when they constitute derogations from existing regulatory standards in fields such as environmental protection and labour rights. These instruments appear moreover to establish that failure to fulfil investment incentive promises will be actionable as a claim in investor–state arbitration, possibly under standards such as FET or guarantees against indirect expropriation. International organizations like the OECD have been somewhat more progressive in their attempts to restrain the use of harmful incentives, although these policies have not crystallized into formal legal obligations.

2. RECOMMENDATIONS

Taking into consideration the incomplete or unbalanced control of investment incentives and performance requirements under international economic law, some recommendations for improving the current situation will now be considered. The first two contemplate changes to existing investment and trade regimes. The third considers the development of an entirely new multilateral regime for both incentives and disincentives, whereas the fourth suggests improvements that can be made at the national level, obviating the need for such instruments. The final section takes a somewhat more modest yet innovative and holistic approach to the dilemma addressed above, proposing improvements in transparency coupled with enhanced civic engagement. These recommendations are not intended to be comprehensive; rather, they are meant to convey ideas for the purposes of future discussion.

(i) Modifications to IIAs

Performance requirements and investment incentives could be regulated more effectively through more comprehensive treatment in IIAs. Both varieties of measure could be variously prohibited or allowed based on more careful categorization of the disincentive or incentive. For example, local content requirements could be banned because of their economically distortive effects, whereas training and education-oriented requirements may be permissible where worthwhile goals are evidenced. Similarly, the provision of infrastructure for foreign investors may be allowed whereas fiscal incentives are not, again because of the generally beneficial and economically distortive effects of these measures respectively. Alternatively, measures of either kind could be permitted so long as they do not lead to unfair advantages for certain firms relative to others, the existence of which could be determined by designated national agencies to be reviewed through international arbitration in the event of a dispute. It may be useful for IIAs to draw a distinction between greenfield- and mergers-and-acquisition-based investments when imposing disciplines on the use of performance requirements and investment incentives. As greenfield investment is widely thought to be more economically beneficial to host states because it creates entirely new economic activity from nothing – unlike mergers and acquisitions, which often result in reductions of existing economic activities – it may be appropriate to forbid a wider range of performance requirements for greenfield investments, much as it may be sensible to allow more incentives for this type of FDI.

Somewhat more specifically, IIAs could be modified in order to prevent the abuse of performance requirements by host states in order to favour their own firms or suppliers. This could be achieved by restricting the definition of indirect expropriation found in IIAs to allow for legitimate performance requirement type measures that serve the public interest, such as those relating to health, the environment or economic crisis. The definition of indirect expropriation contained in the IIA could exclude conditions placed upon foreign investors aimed at proactively supporting the above aims. The timely removal of investment incentives could also be expressly excluded from the definition of indirect expropriation. The definition of FET could be similarly circumscribed, with an indicative list of the types of measures that should not constitute a violation of the FET standard. Such modifications would help prevent vexatious litigation brought by investors when host states are compelled to terminate investment incentive packages as economic circumstances changed in unforeseen ways. Finally, greater use of general exceptions in IIAs, such as those contained in GATT Article XX and GATS Article XIV could give host states some leeway in imposing performance requirements on FDI that have genuine public welfare goals, as distinct from those that are economically damaging attempts to advantage poorly performing local firms. To the extent that arbitration tribunals are not yet appropriately skilled at interpreting general exceptions (which remain rare in IIAs), arbitrators may be able to draw upon the extensive WTO jurisprudence on these issues, much as they have done in the past relating to the national treatment standard. With a wider range of general exceptions in mind, possibly including culture, human rights and the environment, signatories of IIAs should consider adopting prohibitions on the reduction of existing regulatory standards in a wide range of spheres for the purpose of attracting foreign firms, as some RTAs have done.

The decision whether to include express rules on performance requirements and investment incentives in individual IIAs must be considered carefully. State parties must be cognizant of the fact that they may take the role of both capital importer and capital exporter, particularly when dealing with developed and emerging markets. If negotiators are willing to accept controls on the use of performance requirements and investment incentives, it is important that they ensure that whatever disciplines they accept must conform to their economic needs as sources of as well as destinations for capital. Judicious use of reservations, as seen in a number of IIAs especially relating to services, may help simplify this procedure.

(ii) Improvements to WTO Agreements: TRIMs and the SCM

This book has shown that the WTO's two main instruments for regulating performance requirements (the TRIMs Agreement) and investment incentives (the SCM Agreement) have failed to address the use of these policy tools in a sufficiently comprehensive manner. Yet given the broad global membership and institutional weight of the WTO as a forum for negotiation (as well as a respected an efficient system of dispute resolution), the potential for improved control over these measures through the WTO should not be overlooked. With respect to the TRIMs, the main debate appears to be whether the TRIMs prohibitions should be maintained or reduced so that developing countries have more control over FDI, or whether this agreement should be strengthened to prevent an even broader range of performance requirements, such as envisioned by many IIAs. If the latter, the TRIMs would arguably reach beyond its WTO trade-focused mandate, venturing into other forms of economic governance. There is also the question as to whether the control of performance requirements should be linked to those affecting investment incentives, given the regulatory imbalance in IIAs between provisions that address performance requirements (now primarily used by developing countries), while at the same time neglecting provisions on investment incentives (which are mostly used by developed countries).[1] Commentators have urged that the TRIMs agreements should have created two categories of TRIMs, either incentives or disincentives (much as in the structure of this book) in order to achieve greater clarity.[2]

In light of the above, it may be worth considering whether the TRIMs should adopt some of the features of the SCM, including its categories of subsidy, an enlargement of which may itself be used to restrict the use of investment incentives. Clearly, trade-related investment measures and subsidies have similar purposes. Governments use both as tools of industrial policy to promote economic growth and to achieve other social objectives. Yet there is no parallel between the TRIMs in terms of the "conferral of benefit" analysis seen in the subsidies agreement. The word "advantage" used in the TRIMs to mean government assistance granted to producers for their compliance with the local content requirements is

---

[1] P. Muchlinski, 'Policy Issues' in P. Muchlinski, F. Ortino and C. Schreuer (eds), *Oxford Handbook of International Investment Law* (OUP, Oxford 2008) 33.

[2] R. Edwards and S. Lester, 'Towards a More Comprehensive World Trade Organization Agreement on Trade-Related Investment Measures' (1997) 33 *Stanford International Law Journal* 169, 203.

different from the word "benefit" under the SCM, despite the superficial similarity between these terms. "Advantage" is a contingent term that contemplates a superior position relative to other firms within a given market, whereas "benefit" is an absolute quality which may assist the firm in its operations even if this does not correspond to a disadvantage suffered by its competitors. It may therefore be sensible to reform the TRIMs regime in line with the SCM, most crucially by instigating some kind of an injury test for measures that do not have clearly internationally harmful export-oriented aims. Alternatively, some commentators have suggested adapting the WTO's subsidy rules under the SCM to cover TRIMs and other performance requirements in a more systemic, effects-based regime than is contemplated by the narrow TRIMs Agreement.[3]

In this regard, the prohibited or "red light" category of performance requirement under an enhanced SCM would cover those investment-oriented measures that have a definite effect on international trade flows. Such measures may either increase the implementing country's exports or reduce its imports, both of which can be viewed as distortive of international markets. Since these performance requirements would be inherently damaging to the natural flow of traded goods across international borders, no domestic social or economic benefits justify their use, and they should therefore be prohibited. Performance requirements that would fall into this category would include: export performance requirements; product-mandating requirements; trade-balancing requirements; local content requirements; and manufacturing requirements and restrictions. Actionable or "yellow light" performance requirements would be those which have a less clearly defined impact on trade flows. It is sometimes impossible to determine beforehand whether certain laws which apply to foreign firms will reduce, increase, or have no effect on trade flows. Such measures should therefore be considered "actionable" as this term is understood in the SCM, and accordingly subject to the "adverse effects" test. If another WTO member believes that it has suffered damaging effects as a consequence of such performance requirements, for example by experiencing a reduction in outward FDI to the relevant host state as a consequence of the measure, then the performance requirement will be prohibited. Performance requirements fitting into this category would include local equity requirements, licensing requirements, and technology transfer requirements. The final classification of permitted "green light" performance requirements would correspond to those subsidies that the SCM allowed in connection with regional aid,

---

[3] ibid.

environmental matters and research initiatives. As with the SCM, performance requirements that fall into the red-light category in this proposed framework should be prohibited regardless of their purpose.[4] Although according a wider exception for developing countries may be contrary to the goal of limiting the use of performance requirements, it may be the only way to achieve a globally equitable agreement. Since many developing countries use performance requirements extensively and likely wish to continue doing so it may be necessary to include transition periods and exemptions granted to developing countries under the GATT in general and SCM in particular.[5]

The objective of this categorization scheme, so the recommendation goes, would be to prohibit those performance requirements with particularly damaging trade-distorting effects, while permitting other performance requirements that provide legitimate broader social or economic benefits. Under the proposed framework, prohibition of a given performance requirement does not depend only on whether it violates existing GATT articles on national treatment or quantitative restrictions. Rather, certain performance requirements will be banned based on the assessment that they are inherently trade distorting. Other types of performance requirements with less clear effects will be allowed only if they do not adversely affect the economies of other WTO members.[6] Admittedly, this proposal adds another layer of scrutiny through the application of artificial and highly arbitrary categories. Unfortunately also, modifications of the nature described above do not capture investment incentives such as those which may be engaged by the SCM. The only link between the two varieties of measure is a conceptual one, in that the regulation of an incentive-oriented, trade-based concept – the subsidy – is used to control performance requirement – an investment-based disincentive.

Reform of the SCM may also more effectively address the use of incentives in conjunction with performance requirements. SCM in its current form fails to control many indirect but critical forms of incentives, such as general infrastructure development as well as labour market

---

4 During the Uruguay Round negotiations, Switzerland devised a traffic-light based approach to TRIMS: T. Stewart, *The GATT Uruguay Round: A Negotiating History (1986–1992)* (Kluwer, The Hague 1999) 2094.

5 Edwards and Lester (n 3) 212–13.

6 ibid.

liberalization.[7] The SCM has been extensively criticized by commentators, notably in relation to the inadequacy of the specificity test to control distorting subsidies which can be structured to escape its coverage, as well as the narrowness of the benefit test, which does not capture the wide array of government programs which can confer net competitive advantages on firms.[8] It is not the place to explore these criticisms in detail here. Still, it must be re-emphasized that the SCM's lack of disciplines on incentives that have been offered in relation to services is highly problematic. This omission is exacerbated by the fact that the GATS has weak commitments in many service sectors, and many IIAs carve out services from the scope of their national treatment commitments. In this regard, commentators have encouraged the creation of permissive subsidies for certain key service sectors that are crucial to the establishment of economic infrastructure. This approach has been linked to the use of carve-outs for subsidies that aim to address certain policy goals as opposed to ones that afford an artificial competitive advantage, which of course is one of the main purposes behind performance requirements.[9] Some commentators have advocated that certain subsidies should be actively encouraged, including those aimed at promoting entrepreneurial programs in new activities, possibly through aspirational language in the SCM. This should be non-discriminatory (foreign and domestic firms) because the nationality of innovating firms is irrelevant for the purposes of knowledge transfer.[10] It is noteworthy in this regard that the TRIPS imposes an obligation on developed countries to find ways to increase technology transfer to least-developing countries.[11] One potential area that such carve-outs could be established would be for services aimed at advancing the economic development of the least developed countries. For example, it may be that certain service sectors are critical to the development of an economic infrastructure. In these

---

[7] E. Blanchard, 'What Global Fragmentation Means for the WTO' (World Trade Organization, Economic Research and Statistics Division, Geneva 19 December 2013) 27.

[8] A. Sykes, 'The Limited Economic Case for Subsidies Regulation' The E15 Initiative (World Economic Forum, March 2015) 4 <http://e15initiative.org/wp-content/uploads/2015/03/E15_Subsidies_Sykes_final.pdf> accessed 1 August 2015.

[9] G. Horlick and P. Clarke, 'WTO Subsidies Disciplines During and After the Crisis' (2010) 13:3 *Journal of International Economic Law* 859.

[10] B. Hoekman, K. Maskus and K. Saggi, 'Transfer of Technology to Developing Countries: Unilateral and Multilateral Policy Options' (2005) 33:10 *World Development* 1587.

[11] Art. 66.2.

cases, support in the form of investment incentives would enlarge, rather than distort trade. Such sectors could include logistics services, capital markets and communication. Carve-outs of this nature must be carefully crafted to avoid discriminating against potential investors based on their nationality.[12] Research and development is a sphere where FDI incentives could be more useful than harmful. This because research and development can be prohibitively expensive for a firm, meaning that it cannot be expected to recover its costs in the short term. Accordingly companies tend to invest less on new technology than is socially desirable. Some form of exemption within the SCM for a limited level of research-and-development subsidy may be worth pursuing. Carve-outs for regional development subsidies, possibly limited to developing country Members could serve developmental goals through increased trade flows might be similarly advisable. There could be an exemption for investment subsidies relating to natural disaster recovery. In crafting such a provision, the WTO members would need to find a way of ascertaining which disasters are sufficiently large to merit assistance of this nature. Environmental subsidies also could be effective in encouraging beneficial forms of investment without distorting trade. With this approach in mind, any provision for such subsidies must conform to the widely accepted "polluter pays" principle that liability for environmental harm should rest with the party that caused the harm. Additional incentives for investment in environmental improvement could possibly be tied to actions agreed upon by a supermajority of all WTO members. The WTO Appellate Body has already demonstrated a willingness to tolerate subsidies that have environmental objectives even though this category does not appear as a designated exemption in the text of the SCM.[13] The importance of climate-change prevention subsidies in particular has increased significantly, suggesting that clearer guidance with respect to how these types of initiatives can be used to control inward FDI either as an incentive or as a performance requirement, is crucial.[14] A *de minimis* rule could allow for subsidies to foreign investors that fall below a certain threshold, as these should not inflict a detrimental effect on world trade. This method is line with *de minimis* levels seen in the EU state aid rules as well as the WTO GPA. Lastly, as noted in Chapter 5, host states can evade potential

---

[12] Horlick and Clarke (n 9).

[13] Appellate Body Reports, *Canada – Certain Measures Affecting the Renewable Energy Generation Sector* and *Canada – Measures Relating to the Feed in Tariff Program* WT/DS412/AB/R, WT/DS426/AB/R (6 May 2013).

[14] S. Shadikhodjaev, 'First WTO Judicial Review of Climate Change Subsidy Issues' (2013) 107 AJIL 864.

conflicts with the WTO subsidies rules by structuring their incentives packages to be nonspecific. While the concept of specificity can be helpful for controlling subsidies, it may be inappropriate as a limiting instrument in the context of investment incentives. One way of resolving the issue could be to place certain prohibited investments incentives on a designated list as an appendix to the SCM, irrespective of whether the specificity criterion is satisfied.[15]

More generally speaking, an enlarged role for the WTO as an institution in the regulation of investment incentives or FDI competition has been recommended by several commentators.[16] In particular, it has been suggested that the rapid increase in complex global supply chains and fragmented production sharing has created a new urgency for the WTO to establish multilateral disciplines on investment incentives as well as other "behind the border" policies.[17] Less ambitiously but still crucially important, WTO notification requirements for investment incentives should be strengthened. Incomplete notifications should be identified and countries involved must be urged to give cost estimates for subsidies at all levels of government. The International Institute for Sustainable Development has established a template to assist countries in notifying their subsidies including investment incentives to the WTO, which includes many of these indicia.[18] Still, it is difficult to envision the introduction of sanctions for breach of such rules. If the WTO is to have a role in this sphere of governance, it may be better to pursue the combined regulation of performance requirements and investment incentives through the WTO via a plurilateral regime rather than a mandatory multilateral one. The incremental success that has been observed with the revised GPA (as well as the ongoing difficulties associated with multilateral negotiations in the Doha Round) suggest that this approach may represent the way forward in international economic law.

---

[15] See generally B.V.R. Subrahmanyam, 'Investment Incentives and Multilateral Disciplines' in S. Evenett and B. Hoekman (eds), *Economic Development and Multilateral Trade Cooperation* (Palgrave Macmillan and The World Bank, New York, NY 2006).

[16] E.g. C. van Beers and A. de Moor, *Public Subsidies and Policy Failure: How Subsidies Distort the Natural Environment, Equity and Trade and How to Reform Them* (Edward Elgar, 2001) 96.

[17] Blanchard (n 7).

[18] <www.iisd.org/gsi/trade-and-investment-related-subsidies> accessed 2 December 2014.

(iii) A Multilateral Agreement on Performance Requirements and/or Investment Incentives

Following on from recommendation (i) and (ii) above, rather than instigating changes to existing IIAs or WTO agreements, it may be more effective to establish a performance requirement / investment incentive-specific multilateral agreement, possibly through a new multilateral treaty with this specific purpose. As a starting point to this analysis it is worth considering the previous efforts to construct a multilateral treaty with investment disciplines. The draft Multilateral Agreement on Investment (MAI) from the late 1990s included provisions on performance requirements which largely duplicated those found in the TRIMS, essentially banning local content requirements and other requirements imposed on trading firms that would have violated the national treatment standard of GATT or placed conditions on the entry or continued existence of foreign firms. The MAI did not address investment incentives, although a number of observers argued in favour of including disciplines on both performance requirements and investment incentives during the negotiations for the MAI.[19] This was framed in terms of the need to ensure that countries did not discriminate against FDI generally, either as conventional discrimination (favouring domestic firms over foreign ones) or via positive discrimination (favouring foreign investors over local ones).[20]

This book has illustrated the strong linkages between performance requirements and investment incentives, both in terms of their pairing as policy tools as well as the manner in which they are dealt with in IIAs (less so in the WTO agreements). Given the almost inseparable nature of these instruments, it would be both unhelpful and probably impossible to effectively regulate either in isolation, even if this would mean adding an additional topic of negotiation into an already difficult arena at the multilateral level (161 states in the case of WTO membership were such a treaty to be embraced by the WTO). A future multilateral investment agreement should probably also address rules relating to taxation and investment incentives.[21] The lack of coverage of tax-oriented incentives

---

[19] E.g. 'Investment Incentives in Commonwealth Developed Countries and the WTO Investment Negotiations' Economic Paper No. 58 (Commonwealth Secretariat, London 1 January 2003).

[20] M. Daly, 'Investment Incentives and the Multilateral Agreement on Investment' (1998) 38:2 *Journal of World Trade* 5.

[21] S. Amarasinha and J. Kokott, 'Multilateral Investment Rules Revisited' in P. Muchlinksi, F. Ortino and C. Schreuer (eds), *Oxford Handbook of International Investment Law* (OUP, Oxford 2008) 145.

in a multilateral treaty could simply cause states to substitute tax- for non-tax incentives, curtailing any meaningful control of their harmful effects. Coverage of both performance requirements and investment incentives in one instrument could possibly make it more appealing to a greater number of countries in a manner that the MAI was not, in part because it did not adequately address the concerns of developing states. This is because limits on the use of investment incentives are more likely to be of interest to potential capital importing states, many of which will be developing countries seeking to improve their economies through FDI and as such will wish to be as attractive as possible relative to other states which may have greater financial ability to offer incentive packages. Likewise, rules controlling performance requirements could be viewed as a form of pro-investor protection that should appeal to developed, typically capital-exporting states.

While investment incentives may be suitable to correct market failures, or to address non-market concerns of importance to society, if they are inappropriate in terms of their design or size they have the potential to distort international trade and investment flows. This suggests that there is a need for international rules on incentives in order to ensure an appropriate balance between these instruments' legitimate aims and any damaging economic consequences.[22] Multilateral rules on investment incentives would create a degree of general agreement regarding the permissible limits of state aid policies in the investment field, which is currently lacking. It would also provide a benchmark of rules regarding the type of incentives that can be used based on whether they are efficient or not, or if inefficient, if they can be justified on some other non-economic policy ground. This should help limit the detrimental effects associated with incentive competitions[23] and foster developmentally beneficial FDI incentives.[24] As noted in Chapter 1, competition among countries to attract FDI through tax incentives has been likened to a prisoner's dilemma requiring coordinated regulation at the multilateral level.[25] Indeed, collective action failures among states, such as this one, is seen as one of the problems that lends international law much of its

---

[22] Daly (n 20) 7.

[23] J. Kurtz, 'A General Investment Agreement in the WTO? Lessons from Chapter 11 of NAFTA and the OECD Multilateral Agreement on Investment' (2002) 23 University of Pennsylvania *Journal of International Economic Law* 713, 730–31.

[24] Muchlinksi (n 1) 34.

[25] A. Nov, 'The 'Bidding War' to Attract Foreign Direct Investment: The Need for a Global Solution' (2005) 25 *Virginia Tax Review* 835.

legitimacy as a source of norm-creating behaviour.[26] A global treaty should work towards preventing the excessive use of incentives such as certain stabilization clauses that create inappropriately inflexible legal and fiscal regimes ultimately causing turmoil between governments, firms, as well as citizens.[27] Given the inefficiencies observed in many FDI incentive programs, it can be concluded that if all countries were to adopt such economically harmful policies, then there would be a misallocation of resources, not just nationally, but also at a global level, potentially damaging the interrelated world economy.[28] As such, a multilateral incentive regime could achieve at the global level what the EU framework has done for its member states. Economists agree that global coordination on the regulation of investment incentives is desirable.[29] A global regime regulating competition for FDI (effectively regulating investment incentives) would operate as a restraint on the discretionary element in decision-making by national governments who would otherwise be beholden to special-interest pressure groups or mobile international investors. Politicians would be able to "save face" by pointing to their international commitments as justifications for their failure to be responsive to the needs of various lobby groups. Faced with essentially identical rules in all jurisdictions, firms would not be able to pressure host states into adopting excessively generous incentive packages because these would constitute a breach of international law. In the words of one commentator, a multilateral regime for controlling investment incentives "serves as a political tool to resist undemocratic demands for subsidies by a limited number of powerful beneficiaries at the expense of the public".[30]

It is difficult to envision a global regime covering investment incentives where there is no global regime covering investment, and is unlikely to be one at any time soon, given outstanding debates on the content of IIAs and the jurisdiction of investor–state arbitration, as well as ongoing failures in WTO negotiations. It is perhaps ironic that one of the early attempts to justify a multilateral investment treaty was precisely to prevent the harm that investment incentives were inflicting on poor

---

[26] E.g. T. Franck, *Fairness in International Law and Institutions* (Clarendon Press, Oxford 1995) ch 1.

[27] Vale Columbia Center, 'Background Paper for the Eighth Columbia International Investment Conference on Investment Incentives: The Good, the Bad and the Ugly', Columbia University, Draft 8 November 2013.

[28] Nov (n 25) 844.

[29] Subrahmanyam (n 15) 301.

[30] Nov (n 25) 866.

countries that were ill-equipped to pay for such policies in light of their dubious benefits.[31] In particular, the involvement of developing countries in the crafting of multilateral rules on investment incentives has been recommended by critics.[32]

Given that a multilateral regime on performance requirements and investment incentives would achieve some level of standardization, the global business community might oppose such an instrument as a restraint on regulatory competition, even were it to restrict the use of performance requirements beyond current levels under TRIMs and various IIAs. For their part, states might perceive a global regime controlling the essentially unfettered use of investment incentives as a threat to sovereignty, possibly undermining their potential to become attractive to investors where natural endowments on their own are sufficient to draw MNEs. Likewise, greater restrictions on performance requirements may be viewed as an unacceptable encroachment on economic sovereignty.

With respect to the content of a multilateral agreement on performance requirements and investment incentives, some of the recommendations noted above under subsections (i) and (ii) may be advisable. In particular, categories of acceptable measures of either variety could be listed for the purposes of clarity. The imposition of acceptable performance requirements should not therefore constitute violations of standard IIA protections such as indirect expropriation and FET, just as the removal of incentives should not constitute breaches of these obligations. States must not be permitted to lower their existing regulatory standards to attract FDI and there must be provision for the application of conditions to FDI that serve designated social policy goals, so long as these are not used as a disguised attempt to favour local firms over foreign ones. In keeping with conventional IIAs, a multilateral instrument must preserve the right of investors to bring claims directly against states for the violation of its rules. Given the wide disparity in economic standing among the world's many nations as well as the special needs of lesser developed countries, there must be some room for developing countries to apply the treaty's obligations in a more flexible manner, possibly through transitional periods. Special rules for developing countries with respect to investment

---

[31] Z. Drabek, 'A Multilateral Agreement on Investment: Convincing the Skeptics' (WTO Economic Research and Analysis Division, Staff Working Paper No. ERAD-98-05, 1998).

[32] Subrahmanyam (n 15) 345.

incentives in particular have been advocated by some commentators.[33] Most importantly, there needs to be some mechanism, informed by economic logic, for distinguishing between good investment incentives and bad ones. Goods ones, meaning ones that achieve worthwhile domestic policy objectives, even where this may hamper competition, should be permissible. In the trade context, this is partially resolved by creating a distinction between export subsidies and domestic subsidies. Developing rules which establish the appropriate role for governments as they interact with markets will always be highly contextualized. A greater role for governments might be envisioned, for example, during times of economic crisis than times of prosperity. A pragmatic approach to this kind of assessment involving greater transparency and public participation will be considered in the next section below.

Applying national treatment (as well as most-favoured-nation) to all investment-oriented measures imposed by host states in a multilateral treaty would preclude the need to establish categories of prohibited and permissible performance requirements or investment incentives. It would also obviate the need for an assessment of legitimacy these measures' aims in terms of their economic benefits or public policy goals, nor would there need to be an evaluation of their adverse effects on trade flows. Mandatory national treatment would not resolve the problem of "positive" discrimination, unless wording were used that required the equivalent treatment of domestic and foreign investors, rather than simply no less favourable treatment for foreign investors.

A multilateral agreement on performance requirements and investment incentives should include provisions on transparency of such measures, including regular reporting. This could help contribute to greater public scrutiny of these types of policy tools, both domestically and internationally, allowing for a more complete assessment of their impacts on various stakeholders. Reporting of all performance requirements and incentives should be done ex ante rather than ex post, possibly preventing damaging consequences that cannot be fully compensated either through damages (were investor–state arbitration to operate as an enforcing mechanism) or through their removal without compensation (were WTO dispute settlement to operate if the treaty were to be applied).

In order to make a global regime for the regulation of performance requirements and investment incentives more feasible could be to restrict

---

[33] E.g. Y. Margalioth, 'Tax Competition, Foreign Direct Investments and Growth: Using the Tax System to Promote Developing Countries' (2003) 23 *Virginia Tax Review* 161.

its coverage to goods alone without extension to services. The failure to achieve greater liberalization of services through GATS negotiations might indicate an unwillingness of the global community to regulate this sphere of economic activity more tightly. If the control of performance requirements is to be done on an industry-by-industry basis, it would be sensible to avoid the use of an open-ended positive list approach when constructing the list of excluded performance requirements. An exhaustive positive approach of acceptable performance requirements would be the most effective.[34] Likewise, as suggested above, the agreement could be restricted by restricting the definition of investment, possibly excluding the application of rules to greenfield investment projects.

The need for multilateral rules on investment incentives has been criticized by a number of commentators. It has further been suggested that absent international or domestic spillovers, effectively capturing market failure, there is no compelling reason to subsidize FDI. Moreover, without positive international externalities or spillovers, there is no reason that there should be any international coordination on investment incentives at all. These claims rest on a few key assertions. First, to the extent that FDI subsidies counter oligopolitistic behaviour by firms (where there are few sellers raising the price for many buyers), trade liberalization allows foreign firms to compete via exports, often more advantageously than through FDI alone. In other words, as long as trade in goods is relatively open, global markets will discipline the use of market power by mobile investors. Second, despite the literature on races to the bottom discussed in Chapters 5 and 6, studies have shown that investment incentives tend not to be effective in attracting FDI. This is because most FDI is horizontal or market-seeking and is therefore motivated by the host state's inherent characteristics. Investment subsidies are therefore simply transfers from host-country governments to investors who did not truly care about them.[35] Lastly, there is very little evidence to suggest that MNEs actively seek harmonized investment provisions as a means of dealing with the confusing situation of many thousands of IIAs as well as domestic regulations. This last point is linked to the assertion that a multilateral agreement on investment, which has been proposed by a number of authors, would itself not lead to greater FDI flows.[36]

[34] U. Ofodile, 'Africa–China Bilateral Investment Treaties: A Critique' (2013) 35:1 *Michigan Journal of International Law* 131, 187.

[35] B. Hoekman and K. Saggi, 'Assessing the Case for WTO Disciplines on Investment-Related Policies' (2000) 14:4 *Journal of Economic Integration* 629.

[36] ibid.

While the above claims may have held true prior to the advent of global production sharing, some economists now hold that the current structure of complex global supply chains, coupled with the proliferation of regional trade agreements, has strengthened the need for a multilateral response to the control of investment subsidies. This is because vertical FDI (meaning FDI that takes place among affiliate firms linked through production chains or through corporate structure under a parent organization) is more freely mobile than conventional horizontal FDI (with multi-plant firms essentially duplicating the same work in several jurisdictions), which had dominated the previous era. Enlarged fragmentation of production associated with the shift to the global supply chain model of FDI intensifies regulatory complexity, because the laws of more jurisdictions are engaged in the production of goods, raising the transaction costs of compliance, leading to welfare losses.[37] Regulatory complexities associated with a multitude of bilateral trade arrangements is well documented in academic criticism.[38] Furthermore, it has been argued that the spread of preferential trade agreements may cause potential host states to offer greater investment incentives than they otherwise would as a consequence of the increased market access available for trade and FDI in states with which treaties have been signed: essentially, countries will feel coerced into offering incentives to firms from party states rather than to firms who will be most responsive to them. Competition for preferential trade agreements may lead to negative externalities, with weaker countries conceding more than they wish, a scenario which calls for global cooperation in order to contain a race to the bottom.[39]

Despite the difficulties associated with bilateralism on a large scale, harmonization of national laws may be a more feasible option than a binding multilateral agreement on performance requirements and investment incentives for the simple reason that it will be difficult to achieve global consensus on highly contentious matters of economic policy. As an alternative, the need for synchronization of national laws on performance requirements has been identified by some observers.[40] A number of commentators have called for a coordinated approach to the use of

---

[37] Blanchard (n 7) 22–7.

[38] E.g. J. Bhagwati, *Termites in the Trading System* (OUP, Oxford 2008) noting the "spaghetti bowl" effect of thousands of bilateral treaties, 61.

[39] Blanchard (n 7) 22–7.

[40] E.g. T. Shenkin, 'Trade-Related Investment Measures in Bilateral Investment Treaties and the GATT: Moving Towards a Multilateral Investment Treaty' (1999) 55 *University of Pittsburgh Law Review* 541.

investment incentives as a consequence of the adverse impacts that may result from competitive pressures in this sphere for lower-income countries.[41] Less ambitious than a multilateral regime, the possibility for coordinated national or regional measures to serve as an efficient mechanism to limit inefficient FDI incentives and constrain the negative impacts of FDI competition could be explored. The IMF has advocated harmonizing investment incentive policies,[42] possibly at the regional level.[43] Commentators have suggested that there is need for cooperation among governments to ensure that governmental revenue in the form of incentives is not used simply to move an existing investment from one state to another one. They urge that there is a need to develop strategies to prevent disadvantaged regions with limited resources from having to compete with wealthier regions that can easily outbid them in the pursuit of investment.[44]

The uneven usage of various incentive schemes around the world suggests that the negotiation of future rules on the restriction of investment incentives along the line of performance requirements should adopt a gradual, sequential approach, starting with the less widely-used incentives. Disciplines could be gradually enlarged to address the more widely-used ones.[45] Incorporating subsidies rules into regional agreements could be a useful way of controlling bidding wars among host states. Regional rules would be geographically comprehensive enough to counteract competitive incentive escalation in some industries, such as automobile assembly where corporate location decisions still tend to focus on a single region. So-called "no-raiding zones" have been proposed as a first step for countries to negotiate controls over investment subsidies. A no-raiding agreement commits a state to not give a subsidy to relocate an existing facility from another state. As such, it would not

---

41 S. Picciotto, *Regulating Global Corporate Capitalism* (CUP, Cambridge 2011) 164.

42 Independent Evaluation Office, International Monetary Fund, 'IMF Involvement in International Trade Policy Issues' (International Monetary Fund, 2009) 105 <www.ieo-imf.org/ieo/files/completedevaluations/Trade_Main_Report.pdf> accessed 1 August 2015.

43 ibid. 122 (referring to the example of the Caribbean and its generous tax incentives).

44 Vale Columbia report (n 27).

45 Subrahmanyam (n 15) 322.

apply to new investments. This is the basis of the sub-national agreements found in Canada and Australia.[46] Despite the mixed results of these regional initiatives, it is easier to demonstrate to policymakers the wastefulness of relocation subsidies, since they create no new jobs (at least from a national perspective), than it is to do for incentives for new investment, which are arguably justified in some contexts because of insufficient private gains in the short term. Accordingly, this type of arrangement could be regarded as a more feasible first step. Such a regime would help keep the value of location incentives to more reasonable levels, with a lower likelihood of distorting competition and international investment flows.[47]

(iv) Improving the Domestic FDI Climate

Instead of controlling the use of performance requirements and investment incentives under international law directly, it may be more advantageous to implement other types of domestic regulatory reforms in order to shape the nature of inward FDI. Such improvements could substitute both restrictions placed on foreign firms as well as artificial advantages offered to them. The rationale of this recommendation rests in part on the reality that the benefits of both varieties of measures that formed the subject of this book are by no means self-evident. It is not clear that performance requirements achieve their desired objectives: indeed, they can act as a deterrent to FDI. Evaluating alternative strategies for inward FDI and appreciating the costs and benefits of each requires a full assessment of the investment climate in each country. The subsidization of local employment and local development through the imposition of performance requirements may be achieved in equal measure by shifting the cost onto governments in order to promote efficiency. Likewise, traditional incentives may be a sub-optimal method by which to promote the particular domestic economic objectives, such as compensating for competitive weakness. Instead of relying on costly incentives, host states could make themselves more attractive to FDI through an improved regulatory environment. This logic is in keeping with studies which have revealed that investor protections, such as those enshrined in IIAs, are

[46] K. Thomas, 'Regulating investment attraction: Canada's Code of Conduct on Incentives in a comparative context' (2011) 37:3 *Canadian Public Policy* 343–57, and K. Thomas, 'EU control of state aid to mobile investment in comparative perspective' (2012) 34:6 *Journal of European Integration* 567–84.

[47] K. Thomas, 'How To Deal with Growing Incentives Competition?' Columbia FDI Perspectives No. 131 (29 September 2014).

less effective in terms of increasing FDI than local government policies towards investors.[48] It is widely held that traditional investment incentives do not work to attract FDI in the absence of well-developed institutions because foreign investors do not trust unstable governments to ensure that incentives that have been offered will be maintained.[49] While investment incentives clearly play a role in attracting foreign investors to particular countries and not others, stable domestic institutions have a stronger effect. Such was observed, for example, when a number of Eastern European countries joined the European Union and their FDI inflows remained strong (in some cases improving), despite EU state-aid rules.[50]

Domestic regulatory improvements would involve robust enforcement of legal entitlements, especially private property and contractual rights, along with neutral, efficient and effective dispute settlement at the host state level. These aspects of what might be termed "good governance" are captured by indicia such as the World Bank's annual *Doing Business* Rankings, which rank countries' approach to business activities using various regulatory indicia such as property and contract rights enforcement, ease of setting up a business and complexity of tax laws.[51] Improvements in the regulatory oversight of financial services in particular are a vital means of delivering an enabling environment for exporters and investors which need reliable access to capital.[52] All other factors being equal, a country with a pro-business regulatory regime will require far fewer incentives than one that is less open. Indeed, it is often thought that incentives which might otherwise appear to offer benefits to foreign firms might in reality merely neutralize existing regulatory disadvantages.[53] The advantage of an improved regulatory environment as an alternative to performance requirements is somewhat less clear, although

---

48 See e.g. J. Salacuase and N. Sullivan, 'Do BITs Really Work' in K. Sauvant and L. Sachs (eds), *The Effect of Treaties on Foreign Direct Investment* (OUP, New York, NY 2009).

49 Y. Zheng, 'Credibility and Flexibility: Political Institutions, Governance and Foreign Direct Investment' (2011) 37:3 *International Interactions: Empirical and Theoretical Research in International Relations* 293–5.

50 J. Witkowska, 'Foreign Direct Investment in the Changing Business Environment of the European Union's New Member States' (2007) 7:4 *Global Economy Journal* 1, 18–19.

51 <www.doingbusiness.org/rankings> accessed March 2015.

52 M. Bateman and C. Ha-Joon, 'Microfinance and the Illusion of Development: From Hubris to Nemesis in Thirty Years' (2012) 1 *World Economic Review* 13.

53 Subrahmanyam (n 15) 309.

it may be expected that firms which may have chosen not to invest in a particular country because of its performance requirements may be motivated to do so anyway because of the business-friendly regulatory environment, particularly where other states do not offer this. In other words, a country that is otherwise highly pro-investor in terms of its institutional integrity can afford to place conditions on firms seeking to operate within its territory.

Perhaps the most vital of all regulatory improvements that host states can make which could obviate the need for economically inefficient performance requirements or investment incentives are those relating to transparency. The lack of transparency is among the greatest barriers in constructing desirable investment regimes that can maximize the economic and social benefits of FDI. Greater transparency of host state laws could make the adaptation to performance requirements less painful for foreign firms, just as it could facilitate tailoring of specific incentive packages to the most appropriate firms.

Transparency is considered by some to be an emerging norm in international law which features in the text of many international instruments, including IIAs[54] and the agreements of the WTO.[55] There are transparency-specific provisions in many IIAs, requiring parties to provide full and accurate information regarding any laws which may impact upon foreign investors. Some of the benefits associated with these provisions, including mitigating some of the harm associated with regulatory changes, may be achieved through the FET standard. Transparency is often linked to an investor's legitimate expectations: investors expect that there will be reasonably complete disclosure of all information needed to conduct their business affairs in conformity with the law and that any changes thereto will be promptly notified. The need for greater transparency in this regime is tied to the wider search for legitimacy in international investment law generally, which contemplates as a component of transparency both accountability as well as

[54] J. Maupin, 'Transparency in International Investment Law: The Good, the Bad and the Murky' in A. Peters and A. Bianchi (eds), *Transparency in International Law* (CUP, Cambridge 2013).

[55] See e.g. P. Delimatsis, 'Institutional Transparency in the WTO' in A. Peters and A. Bianchi (eds), *Transparency in International Law* (CUP, Cambridge 2013).

participatory rights.[56] In this regard, investor–state arbitration, traditionally a confidential forum for dispute settlement, has begun to see more decisions being made publicly available and even some hearings taking place in public. The three signatory parties of NAFTA issued an interpretive statement establishing transparency as the default norm of investor–state arbitration under NAFTA.[57] All arbitration proceedings under NAFTA will therefore be made public unless there are compelling reasons against it. Although the revised ICSID Arbitration Rules prohibit ICSID from publishing a tribunal's award in its entirety without the written consent of both parties,[58] many parties now appear to be willing to agree to this. UNCITRAL recognized the importance of ensuring transparency in investor–state dispute resolution brought under its rules,[59] and again many parties operating under UNCITRAL rules choose to make their decisions public. Such changes to investor–state dispute settlement can mitigate some of the harms engendered by the unexpected implementation performance requirements and investment incentives both on the foreign firms which are subjected to them (in the case of performance requirements) and on the local firms which do not benefit from them (in the case of incentives). In the context of the WTO, Article 6 of the TRIMs requires members to notify the WTO of any trade-related investment measures and to make best efforts to respond to requests for information from other members regarding these measures. Article 25 of the SCM obliges all WTO members to notify the WTO of all of their existing subsidies, as defined under Article 1, whether or not they are classified as prohibited, actionable or non-actionable. In accordance with Article 25, the notification provided must be sufficient to enable other WTO members to understand how the subsidy operates and also to assess its impact on international trade in goods. Moreover, Article XV of the GATS contemplates information exchange between members for the purposes of establishing future multilateral disciplines on the subsidization of services. While WTO dispute settlement tends to be confidential, all panel and Appellate Body decisions are made public and there has

---

[56] See e.g. S. Schill, 'Enhancing the Legitimacy of International Investment Law: Conceptual and Methodological Foundations of a New Public Law Approach' (2011) 52 *Virginia Journal of International Law* 57.

[57] NAFTA Free Trade Commission, 'Notes of Interpretation of Certain NAFTA Chapter 11 Provisions' 31 July 2001.

[58] Rule 48(4).

[59] Report of United Nations Commission on International Trade Law, 41 Session, 16 June–3 July 2002 [314].

been some experimentation with public hearings as well as non-party participation.[60]

Despite these features of international economic law, the need for greater transparency at the national level especially in relation to investment incentives has been urged by commentators in response to the acute lack of information associated with many of these policy tools that has ensued as a consequence of intensifying global competition for inward FDI.[61] In order to combat incentive competition there must be continuing efforts to improve the transparency of location subsidies. This is especially so in regions where there are many competing governments at the national and sub-national level, where coordination of incentive promotion policy is difficult. Transparency also facilitates international policy discussion. The high regard foreign firms place on transparent rules relating to available incentives should not be underestimated.[62] EU rules on state aid rules have been successful in encouraging the disclosure of information relative to investment incentive packages. While EU state aid data does not capture all of the incentives offered by EU member states, nor the EU's institutions itself, the reporting requirements of this regime, along with their enforcement and the comprehensive public disclosure of the information, can be seen as an inspiration for an international response to this sphere. The importance of the EU state-aid disclosure initiative is illustrated by the fact that, outside of the EU regime, there is an unfortunate lack of publicly available comprehensive information on investment incentives, a situation which has undermined fruitful research and analysis into this topic.[63]

In addition to these domestic regulatory reforms, states should embark upon comprehensive improvements in infrastructure, human capital, as well as information services. So-called "cluster" development includes the provision of enabling infrastructure to MNEs. Host states could concentrate their efforts on providing a clearer picture of available investment opportunities in order to facilitate linkages with domestic firms and gain spillovers from FDI. Many existing FDI promotion programs in developing countries are targeted at large companies and are

---

[60] P. van den Bossche and W. Zdouc, *The Law and Policy of The World Trade Organization* (3rd edn, CUP, Cambridge 2013) 177–8.

[61] L. Oxelheim, 'EU–China and the Non-Transparent Race for Inward FDI' (2008) 19:4 *Asian Journal of Economics* 358.

[62] J. Witkowska, 'Foreign Direct Investment in the Changing Business Environment of the European Union's New Member States' (2007) 7:4 *Global Economy Journal* 1, 13, noting the transparency of the EU state aid rules.

[63] Vale Columbia report (n 27) 26.

therefore unhelpful to small and medium sized enterprises. These could be re-designed in order to stimulate FDI from these firms. Such alternatives to traditional investment incentives may be as or more effective in attracting FDI while imposing fewer costs on governments. These initiatives could be particularly beneficial in situations where the foreign investor is attracted to the country without the incentive, a situation which may not always be clear to host states lacking sufficient information about the nature of potential interest from foreign investors.

3. BEYOND TRANSPARENCY – PERFORMANCE REQUIREMENTS, INVESTMENT INCENTIVES AND NETWORK GOVERNANCE

Some commentators have questioned the wisdom of attempting to devise disciplines on subsidies given the complexity of governmental assistance to the private sector. In particular, the crafting of artificial tests and therein rigid rules based on economic impact do not reflect the economic reality that some forms of subsidization can be helpful in some contexts.[64] The assessment of these policy tools has been frustrated further because data on the use of performance requirements and investment incentives has been notoriously difficult to collect. Defining and identifying these measures is complicated and highly individualized.[65] The lack of coordination, information sharing and collective analysis between investment-promotion agencies may have resulted in greater economic distortions than would have otherwise ensued. Many governments use short-sighted, costly and potentially unnecessary incentives and disincentives to tailor FDI without fully evaluating the long-term impacts domestically or regionally. In many respects the problems associated with the instruments that have been the focus of this book is one of incomplete information.

The lack of comprehensive information on incentives in particular has been noted by a number of commentators. This is seen as one of the greatest barriers to their effective regulation under international law.[66] The need for more complete information from a wide range of sources in assessing the long term impacts of policies that affect FDI was identified in a study by the Commonwealth Secretariat on the use of investment

64 Sykes (n 8) 504.
65 Edwards and Lester (n 2) 177.
66 Daly (n 20) 7.

incentives by several commonwealth countries. Their study disclosed a multiplicity of investment-incentive schemes with little effort by the granting states to adapt existing programmes to new circumstances or to terminate them when they are no longer working, or never worked. This problem is tied to the fact that many states have not attempted to categorize or analyse their own incentive schemes, many of which appear to have multiple objectives that may or may not have been realized. Some investment-incentive packages that were studied appeared to be ill-fitted to their stated goals: programmes that were aimed at raising the living standards among economically disadvantaged minority groups where the structure of the incentive was actually better suited to encouraging SMEs. Politicians who were also eager to seize upon incentives as a tool for enlarging their own esteem may have been unwilling to let them go when they were not functioning in fear of reprisal among voters.[67] Similarly, a study of the European framework for state aid assessed the extent to which governmental authorities engaged in an ex ante evaluation of the costs and benefits associated with an incentive scheme.[68] The extent of aid that was granted varied significantly across all of the studied areas. Most critically, there were no instances of any prior evaluation conducted by governments in terms of the effect that the incentive would have on an investor's location decision.[69]

Critics of modern forms of government have observed the failure of market-based solutions to address issues of social costs, including externalities and informational deficiencies. Likewise, regulatory approaches often lack sufficient flexibility and are insensitive to the context in which they are applied, often premised upon an understanding of public interest that is too formalistic because it is dictated from the top-down, rather than being deliberative and bottom-up. This dilemma has resulted in the development of the theory of "reflexive governance", in which collaborative problem-solving is coordinated through benchmarking, comparison, mutual and self-evaluation in a process that is focused on learning; in other words, it empowers actors equipped with greater knowledge to re-frame a given situation and the adequacy of the regulatory responses to it. At the international regulatory level, the

---

[67] Commonwealth Secretariat (n 19) 13.

[68] 2007–13. 28 investment projects in seven member states were considered.

[69] Ramboll and Matrix, 'Ex-Post Evaluation of the Regional Aid Guidelines' 2007–13, Final Report (December 2012) <http://ec.europa.eu/competition/consultations/2013_regional_aid_guidelines/study_rag_evaluation_en.pdf> accessed 1 August 2015.

interdependency associated with globalisation is particularly well suited to this model of governance, because the broad range of actors and the relative lack of institutional hierarchy facilitates the capacity for collective participation, learning and ultimately adaptation.[70]

Linked to the theory of reflexive governance, new concepts of regulation adapted to multi-layered issues, such as those embraced by FDI policies, have been further identified as "network governance" because of their increased capacity to embrace non-hierarchical regimes through a highly-interconnected, negotiated interaction between public and private actors.[71] A key example of such a system of governance is that of the UN Global Compact, which orchestrates optimal results in the interaction of business and sustainability issues through a dialogue among multiple stakeholders including governments, firms and non-governmental organizations. One of the advantages of networked governance over traditional command-and-control regulation, such as that envisioned in the recommendations above, is its enabling of decision-making under conditions of intrinsic uncertainty and bounded rationality, meaning that there will always be limited information as well as limited time in which to evaluate and select from a range of options. In these circumstances, often associated with highly dynamic global issues like climate change or economic relations, networked governance can establish a synergy among different sources of knowledge, offering an important contribution to, for example, problems of collective action, asymmetrical information and imbalances of power.[72] As has been discussed throughout this book, these characteristics precisely articulate many of the central issues associated with the use of performance requirements and investment incentives as weakly controlled by international economic law.

Taking into account these highly conceptual regulatory models, recent studies in the nascent field of "social physics" may provide a compelling model for the construction of a framework to address the use of

---

[70] J. Lenoble and Marc Maesschalck, 'Renewing the Theory of Public Interest: The Quest for a Reflexive and Learning-Based Approach to Governance' in O. De Schutter and J. Lenoble (eds), *Reflexive Governance: Redefining Public Interest in a Pluralistic World* (Hart, Oxford 2010).

[71] D. Tapscott, *The Digital Economy: 20th Anniversary Edition* (McGraw Hill, New York, NY 2015) 198.

[72] T. Dedeurwaerdere, 'The Contribution of Network Governance in Overcoming Frame Conflicts: Enabling Social Learning and Building Reflexive Abilities in Biodiversity Governance' in O. de Schutter and J. Lenoble (eds), *Reflexive Governance: Redefining Public Interest in a Pluralistic World* (Hart, Oxford 2010).

performance requirements and investment incentives in order to achieve optimal results, which are taken to mean both wealth generation as well as the achievement of important social goals from FDI. A modern variant of behavioural science, social physics theorizes that the mass-interconnectedness that has arisen as a consequence of the unprecedented availability of data through the internet and social networks, can increase our understanding of how individuals behave in response to the influences of the groups to which they belong.[73] Low cost collaboration among global networks of individuals, governments and firms – including now in developing countries, thanks to the widespread availability of mobile telephones that has arisen in the past decade – has changed the way that goods and services are produced and traded. This has in turn dictated FDI strategies of MNEs. Theorists have suggested that the best way to harness the global trend of readily accessible information and heightened interconnectedness in order to overcome issues of information asymmetry is through greater transparency and peer sharing. This can be achieved through what has been described as "platforms of participation", which are large communities of individual actors who can innovate and create value through sharing of knowledge,[74] for example about available FDI opportunities and associated incentives or disincentives. Heightened interconnectedness of all affected actors allows for enlarged public participation in governmental decisions on how and when to impose a performance requirement or extend an investment incentive. Decision-making on the permissibility of certain incentives or performance requirements will be done from the bottom-up, with a limited role for governments at either the national or international level.

As alluded to above, the central tension associated with any attempts to control performance requirements and investment incentives under international economic law appears to be one of information deficiency: states do not know how or when to craft certain incentives or disincentives in order to attract FDI because they do not know what type of FDI they want or need. Wants or needs may also change over time just as the attainment of expected outcomes may be unrealistically optimistic. Governments, including supra-national systems of governance (for example, the WTO, the IMF) are further unsure about many of the side-effects of various policies, such as the long term impact of policies on domestic suppliers, labour markets, and the macroeconomic stability

---

[73] See generally A. Pentland, *Social Physics: How Good Ideas Spread – The Lessons from a New Science* (Penguin Press, New York, NY 2014).

[74] D. Tapscott and A. Williams, *Wikinomics* (Atlantic Books, London 2006) 192.

of global markets, including the reliability of each country's vital trading partners. These matters can never be fully knowable from a policy-crafting or foreign-investment-making perspective, as the permutations of national macroeconomics, let alone global macroeconomics, are highly complex and susceptible to randomness. Yet the identified problems of poor information, information asymmetry and imbalances of power can be minimized through a collaborative, dynamic and responsive regime such as envisioned by the theories of social physics, reflexive and networked governance as mobilized by twenty-first-century communication technology.

Largely as a consequence of the reporting and dissemination initiatives of international institutions like the WTO, the IMF, the World Bank as well as private firms, pervasive citizen stakeholder surveys and on-line participation platforms that transcend the ordinary democratic process, there is now an abundance of readily available information on the economic and non-economic costs and benefits associated with a wide range of policy instruments. With near complete information on the economic profile of virtual countries and regions, comprehensive data on the needs and aspiration of citizens and citizen groups, approaching full disclosure on the expertise and performance records of many commercial actors, the collective decision-makers associated with the phenomena of performance requirements and investment incentive should be able to reach near-optimal or at least progressively better outcomes.

Data made available as a consequence of these initiatives could help solve the two chief problems that are associated with governmental interventions in natural or marked-based FDI flows. These are Type I errors (or false negatives), meaning situations where allowing performance requirements unduly restricts beneficial FDI or distorts trade to the point that harm is suffered, which may take of global resource misallocations and so on. Regulatory solutions must also address Type II errors (or false positives), in which incentives are extended which encourage FDI that ultimately fails to yield revenue that compensates for the cost of the incentive. This latter scenario would include situations where the investor would have entered the host state irrespective of the incentive.

Moving now from the conceptual to the concrete, a feasible recommendation for a more efficient system of controlling performance requirements and investment incentives could take the form of neutral, flexible administrative screening, conducted by an international organization charged with evaluating the costs and benefits of a particular FDI incentive / disincentive package, based on economic data from a wide range of stakeholders across society in both home- and host states. This participatory forum would reach decisions regarding incentives and performance requirements on a case-by-case basis, based on their anticipated impact. As a highly responsive approach, this system would confront one of the central problems associated with the formal regulation of performance requirements as well as investment incentives: the excessive rigidity of standardized policies. Accordingly, the best method for implementing incentives and disincentives, in order to maximize their beneficial impacts while minimizing their harmful effects, is one that is highly flexible, meaning that the policies that are offered must be tailored to address specific policies goals (for example, regional advancement, technology, employment). It must also be receptive to externalities, such as market distortions and social unrest on the local or global scale. Measures assessed in this way can be more appropriately individualized, in that they can be strategically designed to suit the needs of specific sectors, industries and communities.[75]

Following from the principles of reflexive and network governance discussed above, this collaborative validation of performance requirements and incentives would encompass a wide range of data from many sources regarding the anticipated and actual results derived from a particular regime. Network governance theorists urge that the advent of the digital age means that information of this kind does exist and may be more readily accessible than many policy makers realize. A number of private firms, as well as NGOs such as the IMF and the World Bank, specialize in the consolidation of data on the global FDI market. Extensive databases are already in place which track the amount and variety of available incentives with information on the potential benefits of each investment project. This includes data about the estimated number of new jobs that will be created as well as how many existing jobs will be protected, in addition to basic data on the total amount of the investment itself.[76] Furthermore, a critical additional component of the networked governance approach to the oversight of performance requirements and investment incentives is what might be termed "soft data", which consists of meaningful public participation on the impact of these policies. Commentators have emphasized the important role of subjectivity in the assessment and management of risk, which necessitates

---

[75] S.J. Lim, 'Foreign Investment Impact and Incentive: A Strategic Approach to the Relationship Between the Objectives of Foreign Investment Policy and their Promotion' (2005) 14:1 *International Business Review* 61.

[76] <www.investmentmonitor.com>; <www.stateincentives.org> accessed March 2015.

stakeholder participation in the crafting of governmental policy.[77] This recognition has led to a number of international organizations incorporating mandatory public participation into the assessment and approval of large projects, such as those which receive funding by the World Bank, particularly where there is a potential for an adverse environmental impact.[78] Networked governance theory suggests that modern advances in communication technology have facilitated public input into the effects of performance requirements (for example, stimulating local industry and employment or raising prices for consumers) and investment incentives (spillovers such as employment and knowledge transfer or depleting government resources). Likewise, social physics in turn theorizes that this interconnectedness can lead to a form of participation that does not result simply in more information about government policies, but an enhanced capacity to cooperate and construct creative solutions, for example in relation to potential welfare losses that can result from inefficient policy approaches to FDI. Moreover, studies have shown that the increased use of site-location consultants has exacerbated bargaining-power imbalances between firms and governments. These professionals have specialized knowledge which they provide to investors, allowing them to coordinate their behaviour and attract greater returns from host states.[79] Closer collaboration between governments, citizens and firms could help eliminate this type of rent-seeking behaviour, allowing FDI schemes to be developed that are more closely aligned to actual needs and expectations, rather than those which are crafted according to free-riders. Incentive packages, with or without conditions attached, could be delivered through more direct engagement between governments and beneficiaries, precluding the need for expensive or corrupt go-betweens. Recent experimentation with the delivery of electronic cash transfers through mobile phones in Africa has shown the potential to eliminate much of the wastage

---

77 C.E. Foster, 'Public Opinion and the Interpretation of the World Trade Organization's Agreement on Sanitary and Phytosanitary Measures' (2008) 11 *Journal of International Economic Law* 427; T. Epps, 'Reconciling Public Opinion and WTO Rules Under the SPS Agreement' (2008) 7:2 *World Trade Review* 359.

78 See e.g. D. Collins, 'Environmental Impact Statements and Public Participation in International Investment Law' (2010) 7:2 *Manchester Journal of International Economic Law* 4.

79 'Investment Incentives: Growing Use, Uncertain Benefits, Uneven Controls' (Global Studies Initiative, Geneva, Switzerland, November 2007) 53–4 <www.iisd.org/gsi/sites/default/files/GSI_Investment_Incentives.pdf> accessed March 2015.

associated with traditional aid programmes.[80] Such person-to-person contactless payment initiatives could be appropriately structured to suit incentive regimes and may be particularly effective in stimulating tailored FDI by SMEs.

Rather than arbitrarily prohibiting them or creating artificial tests based on anticipated distortions on competitive conditions, it may be worthwhile for governments to consider randomized controlled trials (RCTs) of individual performance requirements and incentive schemes in conjunction with stakeholder input. In RCTs governments are able to assess the outcomes of a particular intervention by comparing it to the normal current practice, meaning without the application of a performance requirement or an investment incentive. Governmental departments in the United Kingdom have experimented with RCTs in a range of small programs, assisting in the identification of policies which have the potential to generate value on larger scales. RCTs are becoming increasingly regarded as powerful tools for establishing cost effectiveness. They capture emerging views that regulation must embrace de-centralized, trial and error policymaking that collaborates more closely with citizens, responding to feedback through enhanced transparency.[81] This kind of flexible, individualized assessment in which the harms associated with the interference with "normal" levels of FDI as represented by the absence of either performance requirements or investment incentives is already contemplated under EU state aid rules. EU Commission guidelines on regional aid indicate that the prohibition on state aid found in Article 87(1) can be lifted if the "equilibrium between the resulting distortions of competition and the advantages of the aid in terms of the development of a less favoured region could be guaranteed,"[82] evidently contemplating a degree of empirical testing. As a point of logic, it makes sense to investigate such outcomes in a controlled "experiment" before implementing them on a larger scale.

More fully informed by the views of experts and stakeholders, networked decision-making must consider ways in which FDI policies can be tailored to suit the needs of firms as well as the policy aims of governments and citizens. It is likely that this will involve stronger

---

80 E.g. C. O'Brien, 'A Guide to Calculating the Cost of Delivering Cash Transfers in Humanitarian Emergencies' Oxford Policy Management Working Paper, 1 June 2014.

81 L. Haynes, O. Service, B. Goldacre and D. Torgerson, *Developing Public Policy With Randomized Controlled Trials* (Cabinet Office Behavioural Insights Team, UK June 2012).

82 EU Commission Guidelines on National Regional Aid 98/C 74/06.

linkages between incentives to performance requirements as complimentary policies. Rather than being freely granted, incentives could be tied to requirements such as employment, training, research and development and the provision of infrastructure. Such arrangements would clarify that failure to fulfil these obligations could result in the revocation of existing incentives or the denial of future expected benefits. Investors could be further required to repay the value of the incentives already received, possibly with interest in the event of delay if anticipated benefits are not achieved. These arrangements could be made enforceable under the law of the host state, with provisions for dispute resolution either in the host state's courts or possibly under international arbitration through investor–state tribunals. Commentators have suggested that investment packages should be "back-loaded" rather than "front-loaded", meaning that incentives should be provided gradually over a period of time, subject to the achieving of certain benchmarks, rather than paid in their entirety from the outset. This strategy should help spread the risk that the FDI project will be unsuccessful between both the host state and the investor. It should also help establish more realistic, rather than unduly optimistic, cost–benefit analysis.[83] A similar approach could be taken with performance requirements, possibly by imposing them gradually in order to afford firms the opportunity to adapt to them over time. Alternatively, performance requirements could be removed incrementally, with firms able to establish themselves more readily from the outset so that they can offset additional costs at a later date.

The above discussion of a networked governance approach to performance requirements and investment incentives was not intended to provide a comprehensive solution to the treatment of these highly complex and contentious issues within international economic law. Rather, it was intended to draw attention to an innovative, bottom-up process that could be used to confront some of the major obstacles associated with traditional more direct forms of governance of these often poorly understood and misguided instruments under international and domestic law. With a collaborative, participatory and more fully informed system of shared decision-making, enhanced, responsive investment policies can be better tailored to suit the needs of a broader base of global constituents. In evaluating the effectiveness of various regimes, the policy-forming network of governments, citizens and firms would propose and ultimately select bespoke regulatory strategies to encourage and structure FDI in each circumstance. This method would incorporate not only

[83] Vale Columbia report (n 27) 70–1.

controls on the nature and extent of performance requirements and investment incentives in order to mitigate economic and social harms, but also instigate improvements to the domestic regulatory environment along with the illumination of future mutually beneficial investment opportunities.

Index